Conventional Wisdom and American Elections

Conventional Wisdom and American Elections

Exploding Myths, Exploring Misconceptions

Second Edition

Jody C Baumgartner
and
Peter L. Francia

ROWMAN & LITTLEFIELD PUBLISHERS, INC.
Lanham • Boulder • New York • Toronto • Plymouth, UK

Published by Rowman & Littlefield Publishers, Inc.
A wholly owned subsidiary of The Rowman & Littlefield Publishing Group, Inc.
4501 Forbes Boulevard, Suite 200, Lanham, Maryland 20706
http://www.rowmanlittlefield.com

Estover Road, Plymouth PL6 7PY, United Kingdom

British Library Cataloguing in Publication Information Available

Library of Congress Cataloging-in-Publication Data

Baumgartner, Jody C., 1958-
    Conventional wisdom and American elections : exploding myths, exploring misconceptions / Jody C. Baumgartner and Peter L. Francia.—2nd ed.
        p.   cm.
    Includes bibliographical references and index.
    ISBN 978-1-4422-0087-6 (cloth : alk. paper)—ISBN 978-1-4422-0088-3 (pbk. : alk. paper)—ISBN 978-1-4422-0089-0 (electronic)
        1. Elections—United States.   2. Politics, Practical—United States.
    3. United States—Politics and government.   I. Francia, Peter L.   II. Title.
JK1976.B34   2010
324.70973—dc22

                                                                            2010003914

Printed in the United States of America

For Anna Shen Baumgartner
and Victoria Rose Francia

Contents

Part III: Understanding Election Outcomes

Illustrations

TABLES

Preface

Elections, especially presidential elections, generate a seemingly limit-less supply of theories, opinions, and predictions from journalists, scholars, and political pundits. The ideas put forth by these political observers then make their way into popular accounts about elections. Unfortunately, many of these ideas and accounts oversimplify complex subjects or over hype the latest political fads, and with ever-increasing venues for people to exchange political ideas, it is inevitable that some exaggerated assertions and misinformation become part of the conventional wisdom about American elections.

During both the 2004 and 2008 elections, for example, many commentators emphasized the negative tactics and practices of the campaigns of the presidential candidates. One observer called the 2004 election "the ugliest" presidential election in American history, while another referred to the 2008 election as the "meanest." Such claims reflect a misunderstanding about the pervasive role that negative campaign tactics have always played in U.S. elections. For instance, critics of Thomas Jefferson stated that his election in 1800 would bring about legal prostitution and the burning of the Bible. Opponents of Andrew Jackson charged that he was a murderer and that his wife was a bigamist. Perhaps most scurrilous of all, Jackson's opponents even accused his dead mother of being a prostitute. Fundraising and the importance of money in elections is another subject that many do not fully understand. A Gallup poll, for example, reported that 59 percent of Americans believe that elections are "generally for sale to the candidate who can raise the most money." While fundraising is undoubtedly important, almost a quarter of candidates to the U.S. Senate in recent election cycles were victorious despite spending *less* money than their opponents.

These and many other falsehoods about American elections persist in the minds of citizens. Based on our experience as college educators, we have identified twelve widely believed myths and misconceptions about elections in America. The conclusions that we draw are based largely on the most current political science research.[1] In some instances, the literature is clear in debunking popular myths about American elections. On other issues, research findings are more mixed. In either case we clarify the issues such that readers can discern between those which scholars have largely resolved, and those in which honest debate remains.

PLAN OF THE BOOK

The basis of any election campaign is to understand who voters are and what they want. The first section of the book is devoted to exploring three misunderstandings that have arisen in recent years about the voting public. In chapter 1, we expose the myth that voter turnout in the United States is steadily declining, pointing to the fact that the way most people measure voter turnout is faulty. Although turnout has declined somewhat in recent decades, the decline is not nearly as precipitous as some would have us believe. The chapter also examines the various factors that influence voter turnout. Finally, we add our own perspective to that of many others on the subject of youth voter turnout.

Chapter 2 focuses on various divisions among the American electorate. Although the idea that Americans are engaged in a culture war on the political front is a question of some debate, there are significant divisions among the electorate that relate to the idea that we may be divided culturally. This chapter explores the nuances of these divisions, along the way suggesting that they may be widening. Chapter 3 examines two groups of voters who are often portrayed as being quite similar, namely, the so-called independent and swing voters. These two groups receive a disproportionate amount of attention from the media throughout the campaign. This is true in spite of the fact that there is little consensus as to how to define either group, there are far fewer of either than is widely believed, and relatively few of them actually vote. Further, as the chapter makes clear, most people who *do* vote cast their votes in a partisan fashion most of the time.

Section two of the books shifts attention from voters to various aspects of campaigns themselves. In chapter 4, we look at several misconceptions about campaign finance reform, and in particular, what campaign finance regulations have and have not accomplished, in spite of hyperbole to the contrary. For example, despite the best intentions of reformers, campaign finance laws have failed to limit the growth of money in politics or to slow the influence of special interests in American elections. Nevertheless, there have been several underappreciated successes of campaign finance reform, which we discuss as well.

Chapter 5 deals with the "veepstakes," a guessing game about who presidential candidates will choose as their running mates. The veepstakes pervades media coverage of the campaign, but unfortunately, much of this coverage is less than completely informed about what presidential candidates look for in a running mate. The chapter looks beyond issues of balancing the ticket at the factors that have emerged in the past several decades as being important in vice presidential selection. In chapter 6 we take on the belief that presidential campaigns have become nastier in modern times. In addition to discussing what negative campaigning really is, focusing mainly on the difference between personal attack ads and ads that attack the opposition's issue positions, we survey several of the truly vicious campaigns throughout our nation's history.

Many Americans also hold misconceptions about public opinion polls. While some think that polling data paint a precise and error-free representation of American political opinion during presidential campaigns, others see polls as a form of modern-day voodoo. Both views miss the reality. Chapter 7 reviews the basics of public polling methodology and discusses potential problems with, and misuses of, polls. In chapter 8 we turn the spotlight on the popular idea that news organizations present a biased view of political reality. In fact, while there is a bias in the news, it is not based in partisanship, but rather the product of commercial considerations, or the need to make a profit. The final chapter in this section takes on the notion that the major political parties are very similar in their outlook on the political world. We highlight prominent issue positions of the major parties in the past few elections, demonstrating that while presidents typically campaign and govern from the middle, they represent parties that have significantly different ideas about the role of government in society.

The third section of the book is devoted to understanding the course and outcomes of modern campaigns. In chapter 10, we focus on the idea that image is everything in presidential campaigns. The reality is that charismatic candidates who do not execute a well-organized on-the-ground campaign will go down to defeat. This was seen clearly in 2008, where Barack Obama's success was based both on his personal appeal and a well-run campaign.

Chapter 11 asks the provocative question of whether or not congressional elections, especially those to the House of Representatives, are meaningful contests. The chapter begins by establishing the fact that congressional elections are becoming increasingly less competitive and then provides insight into the various advantages incumbents have in congressional elections. In the final chapter we examine the myth that presidential campaigns are national contests. It is true that the president represents the entire country, and news about the campaign is certainly national in its scope and reach. But in reality, relatively few citizens are actually involved in the selection of the party candidates in any meaningful way. Moreover, the fall campaign is geared toward relatively few voters in a handful of battleground states.

Acknowledgments

In the course of writing and preparing this book we benefited from a great deal of assistance. Preparation of the first edition was helped greatly by the careful work of our graduate assistant, Michael Shaw. In addition, Nathan Bigelow of Austin College and Renan Levine of the University of Toronto both read the first edition and their suggestions helped improve the overall clarity and quality of this book.

Our colleagues in the political science department at East Carolina University (ECU) have also been quite helpful throughout our tenure here. Professor Jonathan Morris offered useful advice to us when we confronted difficulties during the project. Our department chair, Brad Lockerbie, offered many useful suggestions and was very generous with his support. Other colleagues at ECU have been exceptionally generous in encouraging our research efforts. In addition to the support we received from our colleagues at ECU, Thomas Crumblin and Michael Miller were kind enough to read the manuscript and offered many useful suggestions. Christopher Roper, Whitney Oliver, and Kristen Casper also helped with proofreading and research. We also owe a debt of gratitude to our editor at Rowman & Littlefield, Niels Aaboe, for his helpful suggestions and assistance with this project.

Finally, we would like to thank our wives, Lei Baumgartner and Kali Francia, for their support and patience.

I

VOTERS

1

✛

Vanishing Voters

*Misconceptions about Voter Turnout
and the Youth Vote*

V oting behavior is one of the most thoroughly studied subjects in
political science. One could literally fill entire rooms with the
amount of scholarship that has been devoted to understanding how and
why voters and potential voters exercise their most fundamental of democratic freedoms. Nevertheless, despite decades of voluminous research,
there are several commonly held assumptions about voting behavior that
are problematic.

For example, conventional wisdom, as well as several academic studies,
has long held that American voter turnout is in decline. While there is
some truth to this assertion, the overall picture is more complex. Recent
research suggests that the decline in American voter turnout might not
be as steep as many observers suggest it is.[1] Moreover, discussions about
declining voter turnout in the United States typically ignore the fact that
voter turnout has declined in most other established democracies as well.
A second myth that pervades discussion about voter turnout is the idea
that in any given election, young Americans (eighteen- to twenty-four-
year-olds) will turn out in record numbers to decide the election. But
while voter turnout within this age group increased in both 2004 and
2008, in neither year did it exceed the record set in 1972.

In the next section we will examine the factors that political science
research has suggested can affect voter turnout, either negatively or positively. Following this we will examine in some detail the source of the
myth of vanishing voters in the United States, namely, the way turnout
figures are usually calculated and reported. We then examine voter turn-

out in the United States and other established democracies in the past several decades. In the final section we turn our attention to the question of youth voter turnout.

FACTORS THAT AFFECT VOTER TURNOUT

Discussions about voting behavior in the United States often begin with the premise that Americans do not vote in numbers equal to the past or that they do not vote in numbers proportionate to citizens in other democracies. Most American government textbooks frame the discussion of voting in the United States in terms of low voter turnout, noting correctly that the United States ranks near the bottom of the world in voter turnout.[2] During the campaign of 2000, a number of stories covered subjects such as "why Americans don't vote," or predicted that "voter turnout may slip again."[3] The picture these accounts present, at least implicitly, is that our democracy is in decline.[4]

Many scholars echo similar sentiments. Works such as *The Disappearing American Voter*, *Why Americans Don't Vote*, *Why Americans* Still *Don't Vote* (emphasis added), *Why America Stopped Voting*, and *Where Have All the Voters Gone?* all suggest in their titles that American voter turnout is in decline.[5] One author, for example, explicitly refers to "the turnout problem."[6] Another summarizes, "In ever larger numbers over the past three decades, Americans have been tuning out campaigns and staying home on Election Day. Turnout has fallen in virtually every type of American election."[7]

There are a variety of explanations offered for the decline in voter turnout in this research. We can divide these explanations into two broad categories, institutional and non-institutional factors. Institutional factors focus, simply, on the rules governing the administration of elections. The act of voting in the United States is more difficult than it is in other democracies, and this, it is theorized, drives turnout down. Borrowing from economists, some political scientists hold that individuals are "rational actors" who weigh the costs of voting against its perceived benefits. For example, traveling long distances to reach a polling place might be too much of a cost when compared with the difference (benefit) one vote might make. A second set of explanations deals with characteristics of individuals themselves that might make them less inclined to participate or how the campaign itself might motivate or mobilize people to vote.

Institutional Factors: The Rules

The first and most important thing to understand about the rules governing the administration of elections in the United States is that states make most of these rules. Beyond complying with anti-discrimination provisions contained in the Voting Rights Act of 1965, states are free to set their own standards for voter registration, determine the location of polling places, how long these polling places will be open, set absentee ballot requirements, and more.[8] There is, for example, no universal answer to the question, "what do I have to do to register to vote?"

This said, several general aspects of election law in the United States are important to understand in a discussion of possible reasons why people do not vote. Many studies suggest that restrictive laws, such as registration laws, or in particular, deadlines that force citizens to register early in the election season, result in decreased levels of voter turnout.[9] For example, in most states, people are required to register to vote before Election Day. The length of time varies from state to state, but it is usually at least a few weeks prior to the election.

This is not the case in most established democracies, where voter registration is the responsibility of the government. North Dakota does not require citizens to register to vote, and in 2008, nine other states allowed for Election Day registration (EDR). A recent study shows that states using EDR saw up to nine percentage points higher turnout than in non-EDR states.[10] Some people, even the best intentioned, simply forget to register until it is too late or to re-register after moving.

In most other democracies in the world, voting takes place on weekends or special holidays dedicated to voting. In the United States, Election Day is on a Tuesday. This is significant because most people work on Tuesdays. In order to vote people have several inconvenient options. They can rise early and arrive at the polls before work, vote during a lunch break, ask the boss to vote during work, or vote after work. This additional inconvenience (or cost, in the language of rational choice theory) may reduce the likelihood of voting.

There are also more elections in the United States than in any other country. In most European democracies there are only a few elections (e.g., member of Parliament, representative to the European Union, and a scattering of local offices) held in any given four or five year period. By comparison, Americans are asked to vote in a bewildering array of elections almost every year. There are, for example, primary and general elections for the U.S. House of Representatives and other offices every two years (all even-numbered years). In addition, in some states and cities citizens vote in primary and general elections for governor, state legislature, mayor, city council, and so on, during odd-numbered years. Elections to decide on ballot propositions can occur in any year, as well, and at different times of the year. In some rare instances, citizens might even have to vote in a recall election. The point is that Americans are asked to vote with great frequency.

Voting in the United States is also a fairly complicated affair. In most democracies, citizens might be asked to cast a vote for a political party and maybe a single member of Parliament from their district, and perhaps a few other offices. The U.S. system of federalism and separated government means there are a multiplicity of offices that voters must decide on, from president down to county commissioner, local sheriff, circuit court judges, and more. In total, there are over one million elective offices in the United States, and ballots rarely simplify matters by giving voters the option of voting a straight-party ticket for all offices.[11] It is the rare individual who has taken the time to research each candidate running for each office. The array of choices citizens face at the voting booth can be intimidating, especially to first-time voters, who are inexperienced and more likely to be lacking in information about the process and the choices facing them. In fact it may be so intimidating that they decide to stay home.

Finally, with respect to the rules governing elections, all elections for federal office in the United States are decided by plurality-winner rules in single-member districts. This is unlike electoral systems in most other democracies, which employ proportional representation winning rules, either completely, or combined with plurality-winner/single-member districts. Some research has suggested that voter turnout is lower in plurality-winner/single-member district systems because they tend to produce two-party systems. Citizens who seek an alternative may be so disenchanted with their choices that they do not participate.[12]

While rules may depress voter turnout, there have been several efforts in recent years to ease the burden on citizens to vote. The first, and perhaps most prominent, was the National Voter Registration Act of 1993 (the Motor Voter Bill) that requires motor vehicle offices nationwide to accept voter registration applications and allows other government agencies and programs to do so as well. Mail-in voter registration also has become common in many states. Another recent change in voter registration requirements is the move, as noted earlier, toward Election Day registration.

In addition, many states seem to be doing more to reduce the burden of voting itself. All states have absentee ballots that allow individuals to vote from a location other than their designated polling place and at a time that is convenient to them. However, in 2008, thirty-two states allowed "no-excuse" absentee voting, allowing voters to request absentee ballots without justifying their request; of these, twenty-eight allowed absentee voting by mail. Thirty-two states now allow (no excuse) early voting. Finally, twenty-nine states require private businesses to give employees time off to vote (while thirty states mandate this for public employees).[13]

It should be noted that institutional reforms seem to have only marginally affected voter turnout.[14] For example, the 1996 presidential election saw record-low turnout, and this after the Motor Voter Bill was passed. Part of the reason these efforts (EDR, early voting, or absentee voting) may not have as much of an effect on turnout as proponents hope is that citizens must still make an effort to cast a ballot. While 2008 saw yet another increase in voter turnout, it remains to be seen whether this can be credited to various institutional reforms.

Non-Institutional Factors

Beyond institutional arrangements, there are several other factors that research has suggested have an effect, either positive or negative, on voter turnout. The first set of factors deals with individuals themselves. For example, one argument is that voting is a habit: the more a person does it, the more likely he or she is to keep doing it.[15] This helps explain why younger citizens are less likely to vote than their older counterparts.[16] People who feel connected to their communities are also more likely to vote, if only because they have something to protect or advocate (e.g., lower property taxes for homeowners).

Another reason why people do not vote is that many are either not interested in, or are cynical about, government, politics, and politicians. Many, for example, complain that campaigns are too long, too negative, and focus too much on personality rather than on the issues. This is significant because these negative perceptions lead to cynicism about campaign politics, the political system, and the belief that voting has the potential to effect change. These feelings are important because an individual's sense of political efficacy (the confidence an individual has in their own political understanding and abilities), trust in government, and sense of duty associated with citizenship are often significant predictors of voting.[17] Along these lines, people who identify with, or feel attached to a political party are more apt to vote than people who claim they are independents.[18]

Related to these general attitudes about politics and the individual's place in the political system is knowledge about politics. Those who are more knowledgeable about politics are more likely to vote. In fact, formal education itself has a similar effect on an individual's likelihood of voting. The more educated one is in terms of formal schooling, the more likely that individual is to vote.[19] This may be the result of the fact that our system of government, like the institutional arrangements governing elections, is fairly complex. Individuals can easily become confused about their choices and the implications of those choices. Moreover, in the midst of an election campaign, candidates and parties can often blur their differences in an attempt to capture the votes of the large numbers of citizens who see themselves as moderates. The point is that the choices facing citizens on Election Day may not seem as clear as they would like and they may become so intimidated that they decide not to vote.

A final set of factors that affect voter turnout has to do with the campaign itself. As it happens, competitive elections tend to experience higher voter turnout, quite likely because individuals are more likely to believe their vote will make a difference. This may be one reason why voter turnout was so low in 1996, a year few thought Bob Dole had a real chance to defeat the incumbent President Clinton. In addition, elections that generate more media coverage tend to stimulate greater interest, which in turn leads to greater turnout.[20] Similarly, candidates, parties, interest groups, and ordinary citizens can play a role in stimulating interest in the campaign as well, by talking to other citizens. One especially interesting recent research finding is that personalized campaign messages and appeals are a particularly effective method of generating increased turnout.[21] This is especially true with regard to person-to-person contact, which can be extremely effective in getting people to vote. In other words, one person can make a difference by simply talking to friends, family, co-workers, or associates.[22]

In sum, there are multiple factors that affect whether individuals will exercise their most fundamental of democratic freedoms. These are important to understand because, as it happens, voter turnout has declined somewhat in the past half century. In the next section we turn our attention to the myth of the "vanishing voter," focusing on how voter turnout is measured and reported.

VOTER TURNOUT: A STATISTIC IN SEARCH OF A STANDARD

Determining voter turnout would seem to be a fairly straightforward calculation: the number of votes cast (the numerator) divided by the number of potential voters (the denominator). It is relatively easy to tabulate the number of votes counted in any given election. Tabulating the number of potential voters, on the other hand, is not as simple to do as one might think. Voter turnout statistics typically utilize census data, counting all those living in the United States who are age eighteen or older. This is referred to as the voting age population, or VAP.

Until recently the VAP measure was the accepted standard in calculating voter turnout rates. However, political scientists Michael McDonald and Samuel Popkin have noted that the VAP measure is problematic because it fails to tabulate the number of eligible voters. Age, they note, is not the only criterion to be eligible to vote. Noncitizens are ineligible to vote, as are prisoners and convicted felons in many states. Several states even prohibit ex-felons from voting after completing their criminal sentence. Most accounts of voter turnout throughout American history fail to consider the actual eligible population.

McDonald and Popkin suggest that the decline in voter turnout in the past fifty to sixty years has been systematically overestimated because of the increase in the number of those eighteen years of age or older who are noncitizens or felons. In addition, some states do not allow the mentally incompetent to vote, although this is only a tiny fraction of the population (perhaps one-tenth of one percent). McDonald and Popkin also examine residency requirements in various states, which they estimate disenfranchise approximately one percent of the voting age population in any given election.[23] Finally, they note that the census has become more accurate over the past half century. In 1940, the Census Bureau estimated that their count missed approximately 5.8 percent of the population. Many of these "missed" citizens were likely to be poor and less educated, and therefore less likely to vote, resulting in potentially biased turnout statistics. This number shrank to 1.8 percent in 1990.

Their point is that the number of people incorrectly counted as potential voters—the voting age population—has grown relative to those who have reported voting. These discrepancies have collectively created a situation whereby the statistics have *overestimated* the number of people eligible to vote, thus *underestimating* voter turnout percentages.

To this point, we have discussed only one-half of the voter turnout equation—the number of eligible voters. A final aspect of our discussion centers on the calculation of the number of votes cast. Many experts believe that one of the reasons voter turnout was so high in the late 1800s is that there was a good deal of election fraud in various states and localities.[24] For example, some research suggests that in certain areas of the country corrupt election officials "stuffed" ballot boxes or deliberately reported false returns, often inflating the vote totals for the candidate of the party in power.[25] This would, of course, lead to inflated rates of voter turnout. Unfortunately, no complete data are available to estimate the effects of voting fraud on voter turnout.

McDonald and Popkin's research points to another fact worth considering. The numerator in the voter turnout equation relies on the number of votes cast for president (during presidential election years) or the number of votes cast for members of Congress (during midterm election years). However, this method systematically undercounts the number of votes cast because some citizens, albeit a small percentage (approximately two percent), show up to the polls to vote for ballot propositions or local offices but abstain from casting votes for higher offices.[26] This would not have been possible until the widespread adoption of the Australian ballot in the 1890s, a period that corresponds with yet another fairly sharp decline in turnout.[27]

Table 1.1 shows estimates of the turnout rate using the voting age population (VAP) as well as voting eligible population (VEP). Importantly, the VEP calculation only corrects for felons and noncitizens who are ineligible, not for the mentally incompetent, those disenfranchised by residency requirements, or census undercounting. In other words, the corrections are conservative. The final column shows a fairly significant increase in the difference using these two methods to calculate the turnout rate. The point is that while voter turnout is declining somewhat, VEP estimates of turnout suggest a less dramatic decline than do those based on VAP.

FRAMING THE ISSUE: REPORTING AND DISCUSSING TURNOUT RATES

Regardless of whether one calculates voter turnout using VAP or VEP, it is still true that turnout in the United States has declined over the past

Table 1.1   VAP vs. VEP: Voter turnout rates in U.S. elections, 1972–2000

Year	VAP Turnout Rate	VEP Turnout Rate	Difference
1972	55.2	56.2	1.0
1974	38.2	39.1	0.9
1976	53.5	54.8	1.3
1978	37.9	39.0	1.1
1980	52.8	54.7	1.9
1982	40.6	43.0	2.4
1984	53.3	57.2	3.9
1986	36.5	39.0	2.5
1988	50.3	54.2	3.9
1990	36.5	39.8	3.3
1992	55.0	60.6	5.6
1994	38.9	41.8	2.9
1996	48.9	52.6	3.7
1998	36.1	39.0	2.9
2000	51.2	55.6	4.4
2002	36.3	40.5	4.2
2004	55.4	60.7	5.3
2006	37.1	41.3	4.2
2008	56.9	62.3	5.4

Source: McDonald and Popkin, "The Myth of the Vanishing Voter," 966; Michael McDonald, "Voter Turnout" (1980-2008), at elections.gmu.edu/voter_turnout.htm.

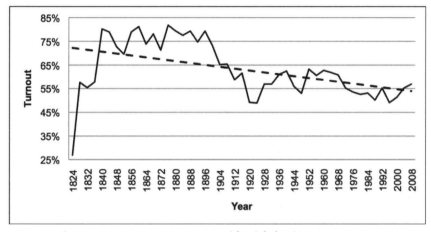

Figure 1.1   U.S. voter turnout, presidential elections, 1824–2008.

Source: John Woolley and Gerhard Peters, "Voter Turnout in Presidential Elections,"
American Presidency Project, www.presidency.ucsb.edu/data/turnout.php.

century and remains lower when compared with turnout in other established democracies. However, the way in which some political observers present this fact often makes the situation appear bleaker than it actually is. For example, figure 1.1 presents turnout rates (using VAP) in the United States from 1824 to 2008. Here, the decline in voter turnout appears to be dramatic.

However, figure 1.2 presents data measuring voter turnout from 1920 (when the size of the electorate effectively doubled) to 2008. Here a

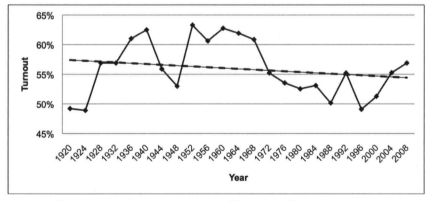
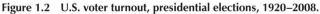

Figure 1.2   U.S. voter turnout, presidential elections, 1920–2008.

Source: John Woolley and Gerhard Peters, "Voter Turnout in Presidential Elections,"
American Presidency Project, www.presidency.ucsb.edu/data/turnout.php.

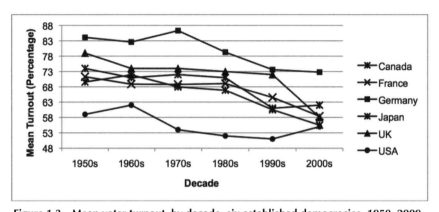

Figure 1.3   Mean voter turnout, by decade, six established democracies, 1950–2009.

Source: International Institute for Democracy and Electoral Assistance, www.idea.int/index.cfm.
All figures are calculated based on voting age population.

decline is apparent as well, but a comparison of the trend lines in each figure suggests that the recent decline might be less serious than some portray it to be. In fact, since 1976, when turnout was 55.2 percent (using VAP statistics), it has hovered consistently in the low-50s percentage range. This only reinforces the point that voters do not appear to be "vanishing."

While turnout has dropped modestly over the course of the past century or so, U.S. rates are consistently lower when measured against turnout in other established democracies. However, it is also true that voter turnout has been declining in other nations over the past fifty years.[28] As figure 1.3 indicates, average voter turnout from 1950 to 2009 has declined significantly in other established democracies as well. In fact, while U.S. voter turnout is lower than all of the others, the decline in the United States during this period is less than in any of these countries (see table 1.2).

To be clear, Americans are voting at lower rates than one hundred years

Table 1.2   Decline in voter turnout, six established democracies, 1950–2009

	Canada	France	Germany	Japan	U.K.	U.S.
Mean, 1950s	69.6%	71.3%	84.1%	73.7%	79.1%	59.3%
Mean, 2000s	55.5	58.4	72.8	61.6	58.0	55.4
Decline	14.1	12.9	11.3	12.1	21.1	3.9

Source: International Institute for Democracy and Electoral Assistance, www.idea.int/index.cfm.
All figures are calculated based on voting age population.

ago or when compared with citizens of other countries. However, to suggest that voters in the United States are vanishing overstates the case. Turnout has remained relatively constant over the past few decades, and any decline in voter turnout in the United States is quite consistent with developments in other countries. Whether or not this is a problem is certainly debatable, and one could make a good case that it is. But, at a minimum, it is difficult to argue that voter turnout in the United States is at crisis levels.

THE *REAL* STORY OF THE YOUTH VOTE

Heading into the 2008 election, predictions about how youth would turn out in record numbers abounded.[29] Some observers went so far as to suggest that the youth vote would be decisive. One claimed that "if politically active twenty-somethings have their way, 2008 is going to be their year."[30] Similarly, in 2004, several pre-election polls suggested that young Americans (eighteen- to twenty-four-year-olds) would vote in near-record numbers.[31] A May 2003 survey conducted by Harvard University's Institute of Politics reported that an estimated 59 percent of eighteen- to twenty-four-year-olds claimed that they would "definitely be voting" and that an additional 27 percent would "probably be voting" in the 2004 election.[32] Some 70 percent of Americans believed that youth voters potentially could be "very important" in defeating George W. Bush in 2004.[33] Several celebrities added to these high expectations by making special efforts to increase turnout among young voters. Sean "P. Diddy" Combs and his "Vote or Die!" campaign drew perhaps the most attention and led Combs to predict boldly that young voters were "gonna come out in numbers you've never seen before."[34]

This type of hyperbole is not new. In 1996, some speculated that the passage of the Motor Voter Bill, the rise of the Internet, and a growing number of youth organizations would lead to a larger-than-usual youth turnout.[35] Despite those developments, a dismal 39 percent of young voters turned out to the polls in 1996.[36] Even the 1992 election, which many consider a benchmark for youth participation, witnessed only a 51 percent turnout among eighteen- to twenty-four-year-olds.

To be fair, the youth vote did indeed increase in 2004 and again in 2008, and youth turnout in the 2008 primaries was at historically high levels.[37] This was certainly due, in part, to massive efforts to register young voters and get them to vote. Rock the Vote, for example, almost tripled the number of youth voters they registered from the 2000 to the 2004 election cycle.[38] Obama mobilized large numbers of youth with his efforts and presence on Facebook in 2008.

But in the end, the increase in the number of young voters accompanied

14   *Chapter 1*

an overall increase in turnout among voters from all age groups. Despite predictions that the eighteen- to twenty-four-year-old vote would play an especially significant role in the 2004 election, young voters comprised the same percentage of the electorate as they did in 2000.[39] The fact is that turnout rates were still lowest for those between the ages of eighteen to twenty-four.[40] The point is that the story line of high expectations for the youth vote followed by disappointing results seems to repeat itself in each election. This is puzzling, since research has long noted disparities in political participation, particularly in voter turnout, between younger citizens and their older counterparts.[41]

As seen in figure 1.4, youth voter turnout did indeed increase in 2004, and again in 2008. However, in neither case did it reach the high mark set in 1972 (54.6 percent), the first election in which eighteen- to twenty-four-year olds were eligible to vote.[42] However, a higher percentage of older Americans (those over the age of twenty-four) went to the polls than did younger Americans. To be fair, the difference between under-twenty-four- and over-twenty-four-year-old voter turnout rates dropped from 28.4 percent in 2000 to 19.6 percent in 2004, and 17.3 percent in 2008. This is an encouraging sign, but still greater than the 16.3 percent differential in 1972.[43]

But the picture is less encouraging when examining turnout rates for midterm elections (congressional elections held in nonpresidential election years). Although participation of all Americans is lower in these elections than in presidential elections, the difference between under-twenty-four- and over-twenty-four-year-old voter turnout rates here is greater,

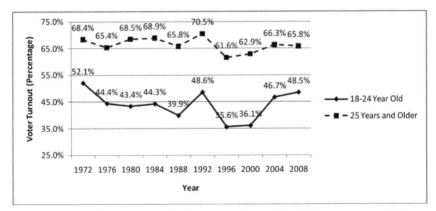

Figure 1.4   Youth and non-youth voter turnout in presidential elections, 1972–2008.

Source: The Center for Information and Research on Civic Learning and Engagement (CIRCLE), www.civicyouth.org/

averaging about 30 percent. Thus, in both presidential and midterm elections, turnout rates among young voters are consistently lower than they are among older Americans.

So, why is it that more youth do not vote? One factor that may explain low voter turnout among youth is the fact that registration requirements probably disproportionately affect young people, many of whom move frequently and know less about the process than do citizens who vote on a regular basis. Youth are also less likely to perceive differences between the two major parties and are more likely to be dissatisfied with the choices being offered.[44] Youth also report that parties and politicians do not address the issues they think are important and believe that they are being ignored; research confirms that they typically are.[45] As noted earlier, individuals who meet or are contacted by a candidate are far more likely to get involved than are those who have not.[46] In 1992, Bill Clinton made a concerted effort to address issues that matter to youth, and it resulted in one of the higher youth voter turnout rates in thirty years.

We saw a similar phenomenon in 2008 with the candidacy of Barack Obama. But in spite of his successful efforts to mobilize youth, and, despite claims to the contrary, the youth vote was not the decisive factor in Obama's victory in 2008. Analyses have shown that even without the youth vote he would have been victorious.[47]

CONCLUSION

Is nonvoting a cause for concern? Many maintain that it is not. Some argue that non-voting is an indication that people are content with their government and that most citizens desire to be less involved in political decision making.[48] Others make the case that only people who care enough to learn about the candidates and issues during the campaign and make the effort to vote should have their voices heard. This argument suggests that good government and good policy depends on informed choices.[49] Countering this argument is the idea that democratic citizenship is in many ways an acquired skill. People learn more and, importantly, appreciate the value of participation, by voting.[50] Another perspective suggests that voting is a choice and citizens thus have the right not to vote. Countering this is the argument that democracy requires participation by its citizens, and as a result, all citizens have a duty to vote.[51]

What can be done about low voter turnout? Institutional reforms may have a limited, but only a limited, effect in raising turnout. One recent finding dealing with attempts to increase voter turnout is the re-discovery that person-to-person mobilization matters. When an individual is contacted by party officials, campaign organizations, or fellow citizens, he or she is more likely to vote. In fact, the model of synthesizing online technologies to create neighborhood campaign teams to get out the vote used by the Bush campaign in 2004 was based on this premise. Obama improved the model in 2008, adding, among other things, social networking websites to the mix in order to bring even more people into the fold (see chapter 10). Even without the recent gains attributed to the Obama campaign, American voter turnout has declined only modestly, and even less so when one applies McDonald and Popkin's more precise measure that relies on the voting eligible population rather than voting age population in the denominator of the turnout statistic.

FOR MORE READING

Cultice, Wendell W. *Youth's Battle for the Ballot: A History of Voting Age in America.* New York: Greenwood Press, 1992.

Hill, David Lee. *American Voter Turnout: An Institutional Approach.* Boulder, Colo.: Westview, 2006.

Piven, Frances Fox, and Richard A. Cloward. *Why Americans Still Don't Vote: And Why Politicians Want It That Way.* Boston: Beacon Press, 2000.

Wolfinger, Raymond E., and Steven J. Rosenstone. *Who Votes?* New Haven, Conn.: Yale University Press, 1980.

2

✛

A Polarized Nation?

"The Culture War" and Divisions in American Politics

In April of 2008, then–presidential candidate Barack Obama, while attending a private fundraiser in San Francisco, told an audience, "You go into these small towns in Pennsylvania, and . . . small towns in the Midwest, the jobs have been gone now for twenty-five years and nothing's replaced them. . . . And it's not surprising, then, they get bitter, they cling to guns or religion or antipathy to people who aren't like them or anti-immigrant sentiment or anti-trade sentiment as a way to explain their frustrations."[1] Obama's comments triggered a rash of criticism from his political opponents who labeled his words "elitist" and "patronizing."[2] Yet the real controversy, according to one writer, was that it tapped into the cultural stereotype of the "liberal (who) looks down on average people, confident that he is a superior being."[3] "Bittergate," as the event came to be known, was less about Obama's gaffe and more about a larger "culture war" (i.e., divisions in American society based upon conflicting cultural values).

Well before Obama made headlines with his "bitter" comments, cultural divisions in American society had drawn the attention of scholars, journalists, and political leaders. Former speechwriter to President Richard Nixon and conservative commentator Pat Buchanan gave a speech at the Republican Party's 1992 national convention in which he told the audience that conservatives were engaged in a "cultural war" for "the soul of America."[4] In 1996, U.S. Supreme Court Justice Antonin Scalia, the author of the dissenting opinion in *Romer v. Evans* (a case concerning discrimination and sexual orientation) wrote, "I think it no business of the courts (as opposed to the political branches) to take sides in this *culture war* [italics added]."[5]

In addition to Buchanan and Scalia, several political observers have noted the significance of cultural divisions in American politics, with a few exaggerating these differences to the point of being humorous. One account described the stereotypes of red state voters who supported George W. Bush in the 2004 presidential election as "ignorant, racist, fascist, knuckle-dragging, NASCAR-obsessed, cousin-marrying, road-kill-eating, tobacco-juice-dribbling, gun-fondling, religious fanatic, red-necks."[6] Another summary described Democratic voters' perceptions of Republicans as "a collection of pampered rich people who selfishly seek to cut their own taxes, allied with religious fundamentalists who want to use government power to impose a narrow brand of Christianity on everyone else."[7]

Stereotypes of blue state voters who supported John Kerry in the 2004 presidential election were no more flattering. One account summarized them as "godless, unpatriotic, pierced-nose, Volvo-driving, France-loving, leftwing Communist, latte-sucking, tofu-chomping, holistic-wacko, neurotic vegan, weenie perverts."[8] Another added that Republicans view Democrats as little more than "godless, overeducated elitists who sip lattes as they look down their noses at the moral values of 'real Americans' in 'the heartland' and ally themselves with 'special interest groups' that benefit from 'big government.'"[9]

However, as the primacy of a culture war in American politics gained acceptance, several prominent scholars published books and articles that called this conventional wisdom into question.[10] Press accounts soon followed that echoed the skeptical view of a polarized and politically divided public. In 2005, for instance, one observer suggested that "American politics is polarized but the American public is not. In fact, what may be the most striking feature of the contemporary American landscape—a surprise, given today's bitterly adversarial politics—is not the culture war but the culture peace."[11] Another opined that polarization was at "the poles, not the center."[12] Still another declared that "The 'culture war' has become a pillar of the conventional wisdom. But is it real? . . . There is plenty of evidence that the very real disputes pushed by political activists and chair-throwing media yakkers—call this the Anger-Industrial Complex—are being carelessly extrapolated to include a far less vehement populace."[13]

Despite numerous proclamations about the nonexistence of the culture war, the issue re-emerged during the 2008 election with Obama's "bitter" comments, and later with Republican presidential nominee John McCain's selection of Alaska governor Sarah Palin as his running mate. Some speculated that Palin's small-town roots and reputation as a defender of socially conservative values would help the McCain campaign excite the base of the Republican Party by re-igniting the culture war. One pundit claimed that "Palin represents the reappearance of the one part of Bush that never died—the culture warrior. Democrats may have forgotten about the notorious red state–blue state divide, or hoped that the failures of the last eight years had made it go away. But it hasn't. It's been there all along."[14]

As these various conflicting accounts make clear, there remains considerable debate about the relevance of the culture war and the political polarization (or lack thereof) of the American public. We will not settle this debate. What we can do is make some sense of the controversies surrounding this subject. Although there is no uniform agreement among social scientists about the importance of cultural issues and the extent of polarization among the electorate, there is consensus on a few points that we attempt to highlight in this chapter.

There are, for instance, significant gaps among the electorate that are reflective of at least some degree of polarization in the electorate and that may relate to the culture war argument. First, there has been a clustering or "big sort" of Americans into like-minded communities that has contributed to growing regional gaps in voting behavior—what one author has referred to as the "politics of place."[15] Second, there is increased partisanship with respect to voting behavior. Third, a religious gap has widened in recent years, which has obvious implications for any discussions about cultural politics in the United States. However, to begin to understand the debate that surrounds the so-called culture war and polarization, some background and perspective is in order.

THE ORIGINS OF THE CULTURE WAR

The term "culture war" gained prominence in academic circles following the publication of sociologist James Davison Hunter's 1991 book, *Culture Wars: The Struggle to Define America*. Hunter argued that Americans are deeply split by two competing worldviews: progressivism and orthodoxy. Those adhering to progressivism believe in policies that will bring about social change. In contrast, those adhering to orthodoxy oppose social change and are deeply committed to maintaining existing traditions. According to Hunter, these values are the source of fundamental divisions among Americans on a range of social and cultural issues including women's rights, specifically abortion, school prayer, and homosexual rights.[16]

Many believe these divisions trace back to the social movements of the 1960s. Most, however, found their roots much earlier. For example, the debate over whether to teach evolution or creationism (known by some as "intelligent design") in public schools was a source of controversy in the nineteenth and early twentieth centuries. In 1844, for example, the city of Philadelphia experienced a series of violent protests and riots (the Philadelphia Nativist Riots) over which version of the Bible should be taught in public schools.[17] Perhaps the best-known example is the "Scopes" or "Great Monkey" trial in which the state of Tennessee brought charges against John Scopes for teaching evolution in his science class in 1925.

Similarly, the women's rights movement traces as far back as 1848 to the Seneca Falls Convention and the ensuing women's suffrage movement. The abortion movement finds its roots in the century-old battle to reform birth control laws. In 1916, Margaret Sanger opened the first birth control clinic in the United States and shortly after formed the National Committee for Federal Legislation for Birth Control. She led the effort to legalize various forms of contraceptives and organized Planned Parenthood in 1942.[18] Partly as the result of these efforts, the Supreme Court overturned a Connecticut law banning contraception in 1965 in the landmark case *Griswold v. Connecticut*. The Court's decision in the case of *Roe v. Wade*, which legalized most abortions, was based in large part on the right to privacy established in *Griswold*.

In short, there is a long history of social and cultural divisions in the United States. In fact, the counterculture movement of the 1960s itself traces its roots back to an earlier period, drawing inspiration from the "beat" movement of the 1950s. Referred to as "beatniks," members of the beat movement were sharply critical of traditional American values, especially what they perceived to be mainstream society's preoccupation with materialistic concerns and other elements of the dominant culture, such as Christianity. Politically, they supported desegregation and civil rights for African Americans during a time when many white Americans did not.[19] As one prominent political observer notes,

> There is a hidden assumption that we were once a happy, homogenous nation that came apart only when hippies preached free love, the religious right rose, secularists became more assertive, the Supreme Court began issuing liberal decisions, talk-show hosts began yelling, and intelligent designers began lobbying school boards. . . . we forget that the seeds of modern feminism were planted in Ozzie and Harriet's day. . . . We forget that the hippies of the 1960s were preceded by the Beats of the 1950s. . . . Before the battles in the 1960s and 1970s to legalize abortion, there were fights in the late 1940s to legalize birth control.[20]

This said, one reporter has described the 1960s as the "big bang" period in bringing about the social and cultural schisms of today.[21] The major political issues of that time involved protests over civil rights and the Vietnam War. However, the unrest of the 1960s transcended politics. The decade of the 1960s also saw a rebellion against mainstream culture. This "counterculture" encouraged people to "turn on, tune in, and drop out" and reject traditional sexual mores (such as monogamy), experiment with illicit drug use, and disengage from mainstream society.

Other social movements further challenged traditional social norms, such as the role of women in society. Betty Friedan's best-selling book, *The Feminine Mystique*, published in 1963, challenged the prevailing gender stereotypes that women could only discover true happiness in their role as a wife, mother, and homemaker. Feminists also pushed for reproductive freedom, campaigning to have state laws stricken that restricted access to birth control methods or that prohibited abortion.

In the 1970s, conservatives responded with counter-movements of their own. In Kanawha County, West Virginia, school board member Alice Moore (known as "Sweet" Alice), the wife of a fundamentalist preacher in rural St. Albans, West Virginia, helped spark a grassroots protest against sex education in the county public schools and books purchased by the school system's superintendent. Residents picketed school buildings with signs carrying slogans, such as "Even Hillbillies Have Constitutional Rights."[22] The events in Kanawha County were a microcosm of a growing conservative backlash to the progressive social movements of the 1960s.

The protests in West Virginia coincided with the founding of the Moral Majority by the Reverend Jerry Falwell and Paul Weyrich in 1979. This organization pledged to defend traditional values and mobilize social conservatives to participate in the political process. A year later, the Moral Majority claimed credit for Ronald Reagan's presidential victory and the defeat of six liberal U.S. senators. One study noted that more than one-fifth of Moral Majority's supporters who voted for Reagan had supported Jimmy Carter four years earlier in the 1976 presidential election.[23]

According to some experts these movements and counter-movements played a significant role in shaping contemporary cultural divisions. As one analyst summarizes, "Since the 1960s, the society and the culture have moved to the left, almost consistently, over the years, and as a result, Americans who have traditional views on social values have become increasingly alienated and even angry. That has now fully manifested itself in our politics."[24] (For a complete timeline of events related to the culture war since the 1960s, see box 2.1.). How these cultural divisions translate into politics is, as noted, a matter of some debate. We examine that debate next.

BOX 2.1

SIGNIFICANT EVENTS
IN THE "CULTURE WARS," 1965–2009

1965   *Griswold v. Connecticut* invalidates Connecticut law prohibiting use of
       contraception by married couples, establishing constitutionally
       protected "right to privacy."

1967   Colorado passes first law allowing abortion in cases involving rape,
       incest, severe defects, or threats to health of mother. Also, *Loving v.
       Virginia* overturns state laws banning interracial marriage.

1968   Pope Paul VI issues *Humanae Vitae*, condemning use of artificial birth
       control. The case of *Epperson v. Arkansas* declares any law forbidding
       teaching of evolution to be unconstitutional. Also, *Hair*, the first
       Broadway musical to depict nudity, premieres.

1969   Stonewall riots in New York City kick off the modern American gay-
       rights movement, the Woodstock music festival is held, and the X-rated
       Midnight Cowboy wins best picture award.

1970   New York passes law allowing abortion up to twenty-fourth week of
       pregnancy.

1972   The first issue of *Ms. Magazine*, cofounded by Gloria Steinem, appears
       on newsstands; *The Joy of Sex*, by Alex Comfort, is published; and *Deep
       Throat* premieres.

1973   The case of *Roe v. Wade* invalidates all state bans on abortion before
       third trimester, and *Miller v. California* holds that material can be banned
       for obscenity only if they "depict or describe patently offensive 'hard
       core' sexual conduct specifically defined." Also, George Carlin's "Seven
       Dirty Words" monologue airs.

1975   U.S. television networks establish a nightly "family hour" free of sex and
       violence.

1976   Episcopal Church permits female priests, and the New Jersey Supreme
       Court rules that parents of Karen Ann Quinlan, a woman in persistent
       vegetative state, may remove her respirator.

1978   Harvey Milk, first openly gay elected official in America, assassinated in
       San Francisco.

(continued)

BOX 2.1 *(continued)*

1979	Moral Majority founded under leadership of Jerry Falwell.
1980	Ronald Reagan elected on Republican platform that calls for *Roe v. Wade* to be overturned.
1981	The first test-tube baby born in the United States, and the debut of MTV.
1985	Debut of *Silent Scream*, controversial video of an abortion produced by abortion-provider turned pro-lifer Dr. Bernard Nathanson. Tipper Gore and other congressional wives found Parents Music Resource Center to combat "alarming trends" in popular music.
1986	*Bowers v. Hardwick* holds that sodomy is not protected under right to privacy.
1987	*Edwards v. Aguillard* holds that teaching creationism in public schools violates separation of church and state.
1988	Pat Robertson shocks the GOP by placing second in the Iowa caucuses.
1989	Pat Robertson founds the Christian Coalition.
1991	"Summer of Mercy" in Wichita, Kansas: pro-life activists launch an effort to shut down abortion clinics. Also, *LA Law* airs first lesbian kiss on network television.
1992	The case of *Planned Parenthood v. Casey* reaffirms right to abortion but accepts certain limitations. Dan Quayle attacks the television character Murphy Brown for glamorizing unwed motherhood. At the Republican National Convention, Pat Buchanan declares that the Cold War has given way to a "cultural war."
1993	Abortion doctor David Gunn shot to death by Michael Griffin in Pensacola, Florida. After failed attempt to allow homosexuals into the military, Bill Clinton announces the "Don't Ask, Don't Tell" compromise. Also, the Hawaii Supreme Court rules that prohibiting same-sex marriage might violate the state constitution.
1994	John Salvi shoots and kills workers at two abortion clinics in Brookline, Massachusetts.
1996	*Romer v. Evans* bars states from excluding gays from antidiscrimination laws, and Bill Clinton signs the Defense of Marriage Act, defining marriage as a "legal union between one man and one woman."

(continued)

BOX 2.1 *(continued)*

1997   The case of *Washington et al. v. Harold Glucksberg et al.* finds no right
        to assisted suicide in Constitution. The "Death with Dignity" law,
        allowing physician-assisted suicide, goes into effect in Oregon. Ellen
        DeGeneres "comes out" on her sitcom, *Ellen*, and *South Park*
        premieres.

1998   The Monica Lewinsky scandal erupts, and Matthew Shepard, a gay
        college student, is murdered in Laramie, Wyoming.

1999   Vermont passes a law permitting civil unions between homosexual
        couples, and the Kansas Board of Education votes to delete any
        reference to evolution from state's science curriculum.

2001   George W. Bush restricts federal funding for stem-cell research.

2003   The Episcopal Church consecrates its first openly gay bishop, in New
        Hampshire. George W. Bush signs a national partial-birth-abortion ban
        into law. The case of *Lawrence v. Texas* rules that bans on homosexual
        sodomy are unconstitutional, and the Massachusetts Supreme Court
        rules gays have right to marry under state constitution. Finally, Alabama
        chief justice Roy Moore is relieved of office for refusing to remove Ten
        Commandments monument from state Supreme Court building.

2004   George W. Bush calls for constitutional ban on gay marriage, and gay-
        marriage bans pass by referendum in eleven states. *The Passion of the
        Christ* is released, and Janet Jackson suffers "wardrobe malfunction" at
        Super Bowl.

2005   The Supreme Court allows Ten Commandments exhibit in Texas court-
        house but bans two such displays in Kentucky.

2006   President Bush vetoes legislation to lift funding restrictions on human
        embryonic stem cell research.

2007   New Jersey recognizes same-sex marriages performed in Massachusetts
        as civil unions; New Hampshire lawmakers approve civil unions.

2008   The Connecticut Supreme Court rules that same-sex couples in the state
        have the right to marry. Voters in California pass a constitutional
        amendment to ban same-sex marriage, following a ruling from the Cali-
        fornia Supreme Court, which had overturned a ban on same-sex
        marriage six months earlier.

(continued)

BOX 2.1 *(continued)*

2009   Miss America runner-up, Carrie Prejean, speaks out against same-sex marriage. The Iowa Supreme Court rules unanimously that the state's same-sex marriage ban violates the state constitution. The U.S. Congress passes a law to allow people to carry loaded guns in national parks and wildlife refuges. Congress debates public funding of abortion in health-care bill. Vermont legislature overrides the veto of Governor Jim Douglas to allow same-sex marriage in the state.

Source: Information for 1965–2005 adapted from E. J. Dionne Jr., "Why the Culture War Is the Wrong War," *Atlantic Monthly* (January/February 2006): 132–35. Information for 2006–2009 compiled by the authors.

THE DEBATE OVER THE IMPORTANCE OF CULTURAL POLITICS

While cultural battles in the United States have an extensive history, they have only recently been simplified and overlaid onto the colored-coded, red state/blue state maps used in presidential elections. Following the closely contested 2000 and 2004 presidential elections, one analyst summarized, "There is . . . a political and cultural divide that has turned America into a 50-50 nation . . . a seething cauldron of 'red' and 'blue' states, in the color-coded maps of network television analysts."[25] Yet, this geographic divide of red and blue states as a representation of the culture war has drawn criticism from scholars.[26]

One notable study concluded that residents in red states and blue states are only minimally divided on social and cultural issues. The results from the research demonstrated that most Americans are not polarized, but rather share moderate positions on most issues and are generally ambivalent in their political attitudes. According to the authors, the misunderstanding about polarization in red states and blue states derives from selective media coverage that tends to exaggerate differences between red and blue state voters. The study adds that the "myth" of a culture war also derives from confusion between politicians and political elites and average Americans. Political candidates, the authors contend, have become increasingly partisan in an attempt to "rally the base" with extremist language and overheated rhetoric.[27]

Although the red state–blue state divide does not reveal major differences between residents on social and cultural issues, there is research that finds cultural divisions have been significant in American politics. A

recent study finds that one's position on the abortion issue was a significant predictor of people who switched their party affiliation.[28] Similarly,
other research has shown that positions on abortion are a major determinant of vote choice.[29] Several political scientists have concluded that evangelical Christians have emerged as the "base of the Republican vote" and
that the "values divide" had widened in recent years.[30]

Some research further indicates that social and cultural issues have
been important in helping the Republican Party capture the votes of the
white working class. In the 1969 book *The Emerging Republican Majority*,
Kevin Phillips argued that the Republican Party would build a successful
coalition by winning over culturally disaffected working-class whites,
many of whom were strongly opposed to civil rights and affirmative
action programs.[31] Later research reinforced Phillips' predictions that the
close relationship that developed between the working class and the
Democratic Party during the New Deal era had disintegrated by the 1970s
due to social and cultural issues.[32] Indeed, a recent publication describes
the Republican coalition as comprising "managers, executives, and business and farm owners with *white middle-class and working-class Democrats*
[italics added], many of them Protestant evangelicals, who were alienated
by their party's support for civil rights and for the sixties counterculture."[33] Another account added that states with large white working-class
populations have "become less Democratic in presidential voting," as
Americans have begun "placing more value on social and cultural issues
and less on economic ones."[34]

One of the more prominent recent works to highlight the importance
of cultural politics is Thomas Frank's *What's the Matter with Kansas?* Frank
writes of a "Great Backlash" in which the white working class, once a pillar of the New Deal coalition, left the Democratic Party and joined the
Republican Party. According to Frank, the backlash against liberal policies and the Democratic Party occurred as a result of conservatism shifting its early emphasis on "fiscal sobriety" to its more recent emphasis on
"explosive social issues" such as abortion and gun control.[35] From Frank's
perspective, however, the conservative movement's shift in emphasis to
the "culture war" is little more than a front to pursue economic policies
that are harmful to the working class. As he writes, "Cultural anger is
marshaled to achieve economic ends. . . . Old-fashioned values may count
when conservatives appear on the stump, but once conservatives are in
office the only old-fashioned situation they care to revive is an economic
regimen of low wages and lax regulations."[36] The end result of this development, according to Frank, has been a dominant political coalition of
business and blue-collar workers.

Several scholars, however, challenge the premise that white working-
class voters are preoccupied with social and cultural issues and have

shifted their allegiance to the Republican Party.[37] One study finds that "in the white working class, as in the electorate as a whole, net Republican gains since the 1950s have come entirely among middle- and upper-income voters, producing a substantial gap in partisanship and voting between predominantly Democratic lower income groups and predominantly Republican upper income groups."[38] It adds that any significant losses by the Democratic Party of white working-class voters in presidential elections have come primarily from the South, and that in general, cultural wedge issues are not very important to most white working-class voters.[39]

These different perspectives make it clear that there is debate surrounding the significance of cultural issues in American politics. However, there is greater agreement that there are growing gaps among the American electorate with respect to voting behavior. In particular, sharper and more consistent geographic, partisan, and religious differences have increased in recent years.

POLITICAL DIVISIONS AND AMERICAN POLITICS

In spite of the fact that there does not seem to be a consensus about whether a culture war truly exists in American politics, there are several divisions among the electorate that exist, and may shed some light on the culture war argument. These include a growing tendency of Americans to settle in communities of politically like-minded individuals, and perhaps relatedly, a growing partisanship among, and increased role of religion for, many Americans. We investigate each of these trends briefly below.

Geographic "Sorting" and Polarization

Several works have noted that geographic divisions in the United States capture significant political differences within the electorate.[40] Perhaps the most extensive work on the politics of geography (or the "politics of place") comes from Bill Bishop's *The Big Sort*. Bishop's work shows that most counties in the United States have become increasingly partisan (see figure 2.1). In the nationally competitive presidential election of 1976, for instance, 26.8 percent of the public resided in a county where either Republican Gerald Ford or Democrat Jimmy Carter won by a landslide (more than 20 percentage points). However, in 2000 and 2004 the percentage of people living in a landslide county increased to 45.3 percent and 48.3 percent respectively (see table 2.1); in 2008, the percentage was 48.1 percent.

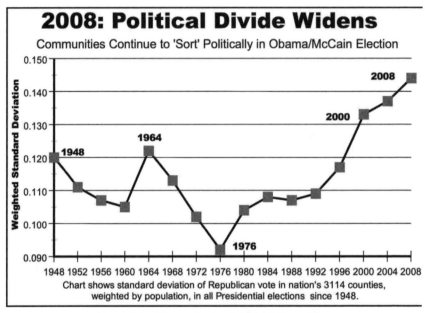

**Figure 2.1   Change in standard deviation of the
presidential vote at the county level, 1948–2008.**

Source: Bill Bishop, personal communication, September 26, 2009.

**Table 2.1   Percentage of landslide presidential elections at the county level for years
with a nationally competitive presidential election (popular vote margin within 10
percentage points)**

Year	Percentage of landslide counties
1948	35.8%
1960	32.9%
1968	37.2%
1976	26.8%
1988	41.7%
1992	37.7%
1996	42.1%
2000	45.3%
2004	48.3%
2008	48.1%

Source: For 1948–2004, Bill Bishop, *The Big Sort* (New York: Houghton Mifflin, 2008), 10. For 2008, Bill
Bishop, "The Big Sort," *Slate*, www.slate.com/blogs/bigsort. Presidential election years in which the popular
vote margin exceeded 10 percentage points are excluded.

According to Bishop, as Americans have clustered into like-minded communities that share the same political and cultural values, divisions across different communities have grown.[41] He notes, for example, that in Republican landslide counties in 2008, "there were five Anglos of voting age for every black or Hispanic" whereas in "Obama-landslide counties, there are 1.3 whites for every black or Hispanic. Obama counties and McCain counties are very different places."[42]

Even at the state level, landslide results have become more common. In 1976, there was an average winning margin of ten percentage points in the fifty states and the District of Columbia. This increased to fifteen percentage points in 2000, sixteen percentage points in 2004, and then to seventeen percentage points in 2008. Likewise, there were only fourteen states where the presidential contest was decided by ten points or less in 2008 compared to thirty-one states in 1976. Political scientist Alan Abramowitz has concluded that, "the divide between the red states and blue states is deeper than at any time in the past sixty years."[43]

A clear example of this is the fact that divisions between rural and urban America have grown. In 2008, Barack Obama's urban Chicago background contrasted sharply with the rural Alaska background of Sarah Palin. Perhaps not surprisingly, the Democratic ticket performed best in urban communities and the Republican ticket best in rural communities. One possible explanation for the differences in the voting behavior of residents of rural and urban areas is that different value orientations develop in these regions based on lifestyle differences. For example, rural residents are more likely to be married than urban residents. This has political implications because those who are married exhibit different political attitudes and behavior than those who are single.[44] In addition, rural residents are more likely to be homeowners than urban residents, which can direct their political interests toward issues such as property taxes, an issue that is less important to most urban residents who are more likely to rent property.[45] Rural residents are also more likely to be gun owners and, as a consequence, are less likely than others to support gun-control policies.[46] Table 2.2 illustrates some of the differences in lifestyle characteristics of urban and rural Americans.

While it is little surprise that rural communities leaned Republican in 2008 (see figure 2.2), what is more interesting is that rural and urban divisions are increasing. The voting patterns of rural and urban residents differed only slightly in 1976. However, by 2004, George W. Bush dominated in rural America, winning roughly three of every five votes there. Obama performed slightly better than Kerry in rural counties in 2008, but he also increased the Democrats' winning margin in urban counties. As Bishop's latest research demonstrates, "Republican and Democratic counties were entirely different kinds of places. The average population of an Obama

Table 2.2   Lifestyle characteristics of urban and rural America

	Rural (%)	Urban (%)
Religion		
Church attendance (every week)	39.4	33.5
Religion provides a great deal of guidance in everyday living	47.9	31.8
Prayer several times a day	37.3	29.8
Bible is the actual word of God	48.9	34.9
Home Life		
Never married	8.4	24.9
Own a gun	68.5	30.5
Own a home	84.9	66.5
Lived in community fifteen years or less	29.6	43.6

Source: Peter L. Francia and Jody C Baumgartner, "Victim or Victor of the 'Culture War'? How Cultural Issues Affect Support for George W. Bush in Rural America," *American Review of Politics* 26 (Fall/Winter 2005–2006): 356, table 3.

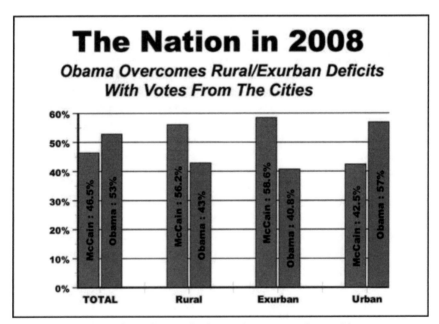

Figure 2.2   Rural, exurban, and urban voting patterns for president, 2008.

Source: Bill Bishop and Tim Murphy, "Obama Closes Gap in Rural Vote, Wins Bigger in Cities," *Daily Yonder*, www.dailyyonder.com/obama-closes-gap-rural-vote-wins-bigger-cities.

landslide county was 278,601. The average McCain landslide county had 37,475 people."[47] These aggregate patterns suggest that communities are growing more politically polarized. It would come as little surprise, then, to see some evidence of a culture war between urban and rural communities.

The Partisan Gap

Several studies note that partisan polarization has increased over the past several decades. Democrats and Republicans hold significantly different opinions on numerous political issues (see chapter 9). This partisan polarization even extends to evaluations of the president. According to one account, "Evaluations of presidential performance have become much more divided along party lines since the 1970s and evaluations of George W. Bush in 2004 were sharply divided along party lines. Ninety-two percent of Republican voters approved of Bush's performance and 70 percent strongly approved; in contrast, 86 percent of Democratic voters disapproved of Bush's performance and 69 percent strongly disapproved. Evaluations of George W. Bush were more divided along party lines than those of any president since the University of Michigan's National Election Studies survey project began asking the presidential approval question in 1972."[48]

Preferences of Democrats and Republicans also differ significantly on a number of issues, with Democratic voters expressing quite liberal views and Republican voters quite conservative views. Perhaps, most important, evidence indicates that these differences are not driven by a small group of party activists. As one study reports, "Active participants are not a small group of left-wing and right-wing extremists. They are a large minority of both parties' primary voters."[49] Perhaps not surprisingly, Democrats and Republicans are also sharply divided on cultural issues. Democrats are significantly more likely than Republicans to support the legalization of abortion, gay rights, and an equal role for women in society.

The dominant explanation for the growing gap between Democrats and Republicans is the partisan realignment of the South. Conservative southerners, once a dominant bloc in the Democratic Party, began to drift to the Republican Party in the 1960s. Issues related to race (notably the passage of the 1964 Civil Rights Act, the 1965 Voting Rights Act, and the 1967 Open Housing Act) contributed to realignment, although some recent evidence also attributes the change to rising incomes in the region.[50] As the South transformed, there began a steady decline in conservative southern Democrats. As southern conservatives moved into their more natural home in the Republican Party, another significant change also occurred in the South. Democrats gained African American voters in the South, who gained the vote following reforms, such as the Voting Rights Act of 1965. These changes fundamentally altered the base of the two parties. The Republican base became more conservative, and the Democratic base became more liberal.

Indeed, there is evidence that indicates the Democratic electoral coalition is more liberal and includes a greater percentage of minorities than in earlier decades (see table 2.3). The Republican coalition, in contrast, has become less moderate and more conservative. In the words of one scholar, "moderate-to-conservative whites made up 59 percent of Jimmy Carter's electoral coalition, but they made up only 33 percent of Barack Obama's electoral coalition. And conservative whites made up only 48 percent of Gerald Ford's electoral coalition but they made up 61 percent of John McCain's electoral coalition."[51]

The Religion Gap

There are also significant religious differences across party lines. Since the 1980 presidential election, the Republican Party has become increasingly associated with religious conservatism and "moral traditionalism."[52] White Americans who attend church regularly or identify themselves as a born-again or evangelical Christian are far more likely to identify with the Republican Party and vote for that party's presidential candidate. In fact, religious factors are more strongly correlated with party identification and voting behavior than income, education, gender, marital status, and union membership.[53] As two prominent religious scholars declare, "The fact of the matter is that there is a religious gap in American voting behavior."[54]

Table 2.3   The changing party coalitions

	1976	1992	2008
Democrats			
Liberal whites	21%	28%	28%
Mod/con whites	59	42	33
Nonwhites	20	31	39
Republicans			
Con whites	48%	54%	61%
Mod/liberal whites	47	36	33
Nonwhites	4	10	6

Source: Alan Abramowitz, "Diverging Coalitions: The Transformation of the American Electorate," *Center for Politics,* www.centerforpolitics.org/crystalball/article.php?id=AIA2009040901.

prevailed in 2000 with Dick Cheney, who registered in Wyoming (three votes). As it happens, the number of Electoral College votes in the candidate's home state is less important than how competitive the state is.

As one expert notes:

> Although presidential tickets have carried the home state of the vice presidential candidate 17 of 24 times (71%) since 1960, coming from either a safe state or a state the ticket has no chance of winning would seem to offer no electoral advantage. On the other hand, selecting a running mate from a competitive state might boost the ticket's chances of winning that state.[26]

While there are different ways of determining which states are competitive, we can safely conclude that they are *not* states that the candidate is sure of winning or losing.

Having said this, not all vice presidential candidates come from competitive states. For example, the Obama campaign was probably not concerned about winning Biden's Delaware, a state that had gone Democratic since 1992. Similarly, the last time Palin's Alaska voted for a Democratic candidate was in 1964. Recent examples notwithstanding, statistical analysis confirms the idea that since 1960, the competitiveness of the vice presidential candidate's home state matters.[27] In 2004 John Kerry's selection of John Edwards was in part made in an attempt to win North Carolina, although the last time the state had voted for a Democratic candidate was 1976 (for Jimmy Carter). In 1992, Clinton's selection of Gore may have been a reflection of the fact that his home state of Tennessee was perceived to be competitive. In fact, the Democratic ticket carried Tennessee in both 1992 and 1996, reversing Republican wins in 1980, 1984, and 1988.

One of the more common misconceptions in the modern era is that the presidential candidate might select their main rival from the primary season for the nomination. This is simply not the case. In fact, the modern vice presidency is built around the premise that the vice president is the president's loyal lieutenant. Because of this, a bitter primary struggle that leaves hard feelings all but precludes the nominee from selecting his main opponent. This, perhaps more than anything, was why Hillary Clinton was reportedly not even considered among the finalists for Obama's eventual selection, or why George W. Bush's main rival, John McCain, was never considered in 2000.[28]

On the other hand, if the nominee's main opponent either withdraws from the race soon after it becomes obvious they will not win the nomination, or, stays in the race but does not campaign too aggressively, there is some chance of being selected. In 2004, for example, after it became clear that John Kerry would win the Democratic primary, John Edwards withdrew and began campaigning for him. Similarly, although Ronald Reagan's main rival, George H.W. Bush, had earlier criticized Reagan, he withdrew from the race at an early stage and backed away from earlier criticism of him. Although Joe Biden was not Obama's main opponent in 2008, he withdrew after the first contest without making any harsh public comments about Obama. The point is that doing well in the presidential primaries is no guarantee that one can eventually secure the vice presidential nomination.[29]

Having served in some capacity in the military seems to have been a significant factor in vice presidential selection since 1960, although this may be changing. Since 1960, only seven vice presidential candidates (of a total of twenty) have not served in the military, but only two of these ran prior to 2000 (Hubert Humphrey in 1964 and Geraldine Ferraro in 1984). Since 2000, all five vice presidential candidates (Dick Cheney and Joe Lieberman, 2000; John Edwards, 2004; Sarah Palin and Joe Biden, 2008) had no military experience.[30]

In addition to military experience, youth seems to be a desirable factor in selecting a vice presidential candidate in the modern age. The average age of a vice presidential candidate since 1960 is fifty-four years. Joe Biden was older than this average at the time of his run in 2008 (sixty-six), but only nine years older than the average age of those who were being considered by Obama. Biden is the second-oldest vice presidential candidate in the modern era, behind Lloyd Bentsen, who ran with Democrat Michael Dukakis in 1988. At sixty-seven, Bentsen was twelve years older than the average age of those being considered by Dukakis. Sarah Palin, on the other hand, was forty-four years old, twelve years younger than McCain's possible choices. The youngest candidate during this time period was Dan Quayle (Republican, 1988), who at the age of forty-one was eleven years younger than the average of all the candidates George H. W. Bush was considering. Al Gore was forty-three at the time he ran with Bill Clinton in 1992, also eleven years younger than the group average. In all, nine of the candidates from this period were younger than the average of the group that was being considered.[31]

There are two other important factors in the vice presidential selection process that have emerged in the modern era. The first is political experience. Despite the recent example of McCain selecting the relatively inexperienced Palin, the trend in this regard is to draw from a more experienced pool of individuals. For example, of the twenty vice presidential candidates since 1960, twelve have come from the U.S. Senate. Only two have come from the House of Representatives: William Miller, who ran with Republican Barry Goldwater in 1964, and Geraldine Ferraro, Democrat Walter Mondale's running mate in 1984. Others have brought other high-level experience to the ticket (e.g., Dick Cheney was Secretary of Defense under George H. W. Bush).[32] Only two candidates had *only* sub-national government experience (Spiro Agnew and Sarah Palin) before their run for vice president.

Unlike vice presidential selection in the historical era, political experience has become an important factor in the selection process. The good news here is that political experience may translate into competence or fitness to assume the presidency in the event of a presidential vacancy. In other words, modern vice presidential candidates are probably more qualified than their pre-modern counterparts. This is ironic. The original, pre–Twelfth Amendment system for selecting a vice president was to take the second-place winner in presidential balloting. This almost guaranteed that the vice president was of presidential caliber. The Twelfth Amendment relegated one candidate on the ticket to the second spot, all but ensuring that great leaders would not seek the position.[33]

The average candidate for vice presidential office in the modern era brought nineteen years of governmental experience to the ticket, of which only five were spent in sub-national (local and/or state government) office. Some few were exceedingly qualified. In 1960, Democrat Lyndon Johnson had twenty-five years of experience in national government, with twenty-three of those in Congress; his opponent, Henry Cabot Lodge brought twenty-three years of experience to the Republican ticket. Similarly, in 1964 the Democrat Hubert Humphrey boasted of twenty-one years' experience, his opponent William Miller, eighteen years. In 2000, Dick Cheney could claim twenty-one years of public service, while his Democratic opponent Joe Lieberman had twenty-five years. The candidate with the most experience in the modern era was Joe Biden, who had thirty-eight years of experience in government, thirty-six of which were in the U.S. Senate.

Of course there are exceptions to this trend toward selecting more competent running mates. In 1968, for example, Richard Nixon selected the moderately well-known governor of Maryland, Spiro Agnew, as his running mate. Agnew had a total of nine years of government experience. Like the campaign against Sarah Palin in 2008, his inexperience was blatantly exploited throughout the campaign by the Democrats. After Thomas Eagleton withdrew from the Democratic ticket in 1972, George McGovern selected Sargent Shriver, who had seven years' appointive experience in various national government agencies. In 1980 Ronald Reagan selected George H. W. Bush, who only had nine years of experience in government. In 1984, Walter Mondale selected little-known, three-term House member Geraldine Ferraro, who had a total of ten years of government experience. George H. W. Bush's choice in 1988 was Dan Quayle, who had served two relatively undistinguished terms in the U.S. Senate. John Kerry's choice in 2004 was John Edwards, a first-term U.S. Senator with no other political experience. And in 2008, John McCain selected Sarah Palin, who, in spite of having served for twelve years in local and state politics, was widely perceived to have been under-qualified.[34]

The point is that there is now a great deal of pressure to select a running mate capable of assuming the presidency. Presidential tickets that ignore this pay a heavy political price, as was the case with Nixon-Agnew in 1968, Bush-Quayle in 1988, or McCain-Palin in 2008. While it is true that Agnew and Quayle became vice president, the campaign worked overtime to counter claims they were not qualified.

A final factor that has emerged as significant in the selection process is attention from, or exposure in, the national media. This has become especially important in the Carter model of vice presidential selection, since presidential candidates must do extensive vetting of their possible choices. Allowing the media to do this, wittingly or otherwise, makes good sense.

> No presidential candidate has the resources to fully research every aspect of a potential vice president's background . . . [presidential] nominees have increasingly in recent years turned to . . . people who not only have been fully investigated but also have extensive experience dealing with the national media.[35]

Few candidates want a surprise similar to the one McGovern received in 1972 about Thomas Eagleton's psychiatric history. It has been argued that one of the reasons Dan Quayle had the reputation for being less intelligent than some is the fact that the Bush campaign surprised the media by selecting a relative unknown and Quayle mishandled some early appearances.[36] Regardless of how qualified and competent Sarah Palin may actually be, the McCain campaign's biggest mistake was selecting someone unknown to most of the media elite. Conversely, Joe Biden (2008), John Edwards (2004), Dick Cheney and Joe Lieberman (2000), Jack Kemp (1996), and Al Gore (1992) were all fairly well known by media elite, and had extensive experience with and exposure in the national media. This has become the norm.[37]

Table 5.2 summarizes the characteristics of the twenty non-incumbent vice presidential candidates since 1960. In the next section we summarize our discussion, rating several of the most recent choices according to the analysis presented here.

CONCLUSION: RATING RECENT VICE PRESIDENTIAL CANDIDATES

Analyses of vice presidential selections since 1960, comparing the ones who were chosen to those who were not, demonstrate that the old model

Table 5.2 Characteristics of vice presidential candidates, 1960–2008

Year	Candidate	State (E.C. Votes)	Regional Balance?	Ideological Balance?	Competitive State?*	Age	Military Service	Years Gov't. Experience (Subnational, National)	Media Exposure**
1960	Lyndon Johnson (D)	TX (24) ‡	Yes	Yes	Yes	52	Yes	25 (0, 25)	High
	Henry Cabot Lodge (R)	MA (16)	Yes	Yes	No	58	Yes	23 (3, 20)	High
1964	Hubert Humphrey (D)	MN (10) ‡	Yes	Yes	Yes	53	No	21 (3, 18)	High
	William Miller (R)	NY (43)	Yes	No	Yes	50	Yes	18 (4, 14)	Low
1968	Spiro Agnew (R)	MD (10)	Yes	No	Yes	50	Yes	9 (9, 0)	Low
	Edmund Muskie (D)	ME (4) ‡	Yes	Yes	Yes	54	Yes	25 (15, 10)	Low
1972	Sargent Shriver (D)	MD (10)	Yes	Yes	No	57	Yes	7 (0, 7)	High
1976	Walter Mondale (D)	MN (10) ‡	Yes	Yes	No	48	Yes	20 (4, 16)	Low
	Bob Dole (R)	KS (7) ‡	No	Yes	No	53	Yes	25 (10, 15)	High
1980	George H. W. Bush (R)	TX (26) ‡	Yes	No	Yes	56	Yes	9 (0, 9)	High
1984	Geraldine Ferraro (D)	NY (36)	Yes	No	Yes	49	No	10 (4, 6)	Low
1988	Dan Quayle (R)	IN (12) ‡	Yes	Yes	No	41	Yes	12 (0, 12)	Average
	Lloyd Bentsen (D)	TX (29)	Yes	No	No	67	Yes	26 (2, 24)	High
1992	Al Gore (D)	TN (11) ‡	No	No	No	43	Yes	16 (0, 16)	Average
1996	Jack Kemp (R)	NY (33)	Yes	Yes	Yes	61	Yes	23 (1, 22)	High
2000	Dick Cheney (R)	WY (3) ‡	Yes	No	No	59	No	21 (0, 21)	High
	Joe Lieberman (D)	CT (8) ‡	Yes	No	Yes	58	No	25 (13, 12)	Average
2004	John Edwards (D)	NC (15)	Yes	No	Yes	51	No	5 (0, 5)	High
2008	Joe Biden (D)	DE (3) ‡	Yes	No	No	66	No	38 (2, 36)	High
	Sarah Palin (R)	AK (3) ‡	Yes	No	No	44	No	12 (12, 0)	Low

Note: Incumbent candidates are not listed. In 1972 Sargent Shriver is listed as the choice, having run on the Democratic ticket after McGovern's first selection, Thomas Eagleton, withdrew.

* "Competitive" is when the average margin of victory from the previous three presidential elections was less than 10 percent.

** Based primarily on author calculations of number of stories that named candidates in *Time* magazine and the *New York Times* in the eighteen months prior to the selection of the vice presidential candidate.

‡ Ticket won the VP candidate's home state.

of understanding the process no longer suffices. While regional balance is still important, ideological balance is not. Moreover, state size is less important than whether the vice president's home state is perceived as being competitive. Youth, military service, political experience, and exposure in the national media are also important in the modern age. As a side note, various demographic factors like gender, race and ethnicity, and religion, while often discussed in terms of balancing the ticket, are not statistically significant factors in the selection process. This is likely because the eventual selections are no more or no less diverse than the ones who are not chosen.

So what of recent selections? How well do they fit this model? Bill Clinton's selection of Al Gore in 1992 flew in the face of both geographic considerations in that both were southerners, and Gore's Tennessee was not an extremely competitive state for the Democrats (in spite of this, the Democrats did carry the state). Gore was younger, had military experience, only slightly less than average political experience, and enjoyed an average amount of exposure in the national media. Bob Dole's selection of Jack Kemp in 1996 brought regional balance to the ticket, and Kemp came from New York, at the time a fairly competitive state. While slightly older, he also had military experience, a higher than average number of years in government, and exposure in the national media.

In 2000, both Dick Cheney and Joe Lieberman brought regional balance to their respective tickets, but Cheney's Wyoming was not a competitive state whereas Lieberman's Connecticut was. Both men were slightly older, neither had military experience but both had an above average number of years of political experience. Of the two, Cheney had a great deal of exposure in the national media, while Lieberman had an average amount. John Edwards in 2004 provided the Democratic ticket with regional balance, and, North Carolina was somewhat competitive, although the ticket did not carry the state. He was young, but boasted no military service and little political experience. He did, however, have a higher than average level of exposure in the national media.

Finally, in 2008, Barack Obama selected Joe Biden, which balanced the ticket regionally, but with a non-competitive state that the ticket would surely have won otherwise. Biden is older, and he too lacks military experience. However, he brought a wealth of experience to the Democratic ticket, as well as a relatively high profile in the media. The selection of Sarah Palin by John McCain also added regional balance to the ticket, but with a state that was similarly non-competitive. She is young, but like Biden lacks military experience. However, unlike Biden, she had a relative lack of political experience, and virtually no exposure in the national media.

So why did McCain select Palin, especially given the controversy that the choice generated? One of the reasons why the veepstakes will never be a perfect science is that presidential candidates select their running mate in part to emphasize or de-emphasize a particular aspect of their own candidacy. These decisions are, almost by definition, idiosyncratic, and cannot be captured effectively in a statistical model.

For example, one of the reasons Bob Dole selected the energetic Jack Kemp was to offset the impression that Dole was dour. Al Gore's selection of Joe Lieberman was made in part because Gore wanted to distance himself from the Clinton-Lewinsky scandal, and Lieberman was the first Democratic senator to denounce Clinton publicly. John Kerry selected John Edwards in part to bring a charismatic personality to the ticket. McCain's selection of Palin can be understood in this light. First, it was unconventional (to state it mildly), emphasizing his reputation as a "maverick." Beyond this, it helped mobilize support from the previously lukewarm Republican base of evangelical Christians.

Whether this was a strategically sound move by McCain is open to debate. However, it does, along with the analysis presented here, highlight the idea that predicting vice presidential selection is rather complex, dependent on a number of factors. The notion of regional and ideological ticket balancing with a selection from a large state is a good way to understand vice presidential selection in a previous era, but no longer suffices.

FOR MORE READING

Baumgartner, Jody C. "The Veepstakes: Forecasting Vice Presidential Selection in 2008," *PS: Politics and Political Science* 41 (October 2000): 765–72.

Baumgartner, Jody C *The American Vice Presidency Reconsidered*. Westport, Conn.: Praeger, 2006.

Goldstein, Joel. *The Modern American Vice Presidency*. Princeton, N.J.: Princeton University Press, 1982.

Light, Paul C. *Vice-Presidential Power: Advice and Influence in the White House*. Baltimore: Johns Hopkins University, 1984.

Mayer, William G. "A Brief History of Vice Presidential Selection," in William G. Mayer, ed. *In Pursuit of the White House 2000: How We Choose Our Presidential Nominees*, 313–74. Chatham, N.J.: Chatham House, 2000.

6

✛

Myth or Reality?

Presidential Campaigns Have Become Nastier

I n almost every election, political observers comment on the declining quality of political campaigns. One of the most frequently made charges is that negative campaigning has grown worse over the years. In 2008, for instance, a political observer characterized the presidential election as history's "longest, meanest and most expensive."[1] Opinion pieces flashed headlines with titles such as, "McCain Campaign is the Ugliest Ever."[2] Others involved in the campaign made accusations about the shrill content of their opponents' campaign attacks. Cindy McCain, the wife of John McCain, commented to a newspaper in Tennessee that the Obama campaign had "waged the dirtiest campaign in American history."[3] Obama's running mate, Joe Biden, countered that the McCain team was "running the most scurrilous campaign in modern history."[4]

This reaction was due, at least in part, to some controversial attacks that surrounded the 2008 presidential election. Some charged that the McCain campaign was attempting to scare voters about Barack Obama using attacks akin to the "Swift Boat accusations of 2004" and the "racist Willie Horton ads of 1988."[5] Specifically, critics of the McCain campaign cited its efforts to label Obama as a socialist, a traitor, and as someone who "pals around with terrorists," a desperate and even dangerous attempt that was "sowing the seeds of hatred and division."[6] Obama supporters noted that the McCain advertisements, such as those connecting Obama with 1960s radical Bill Ayers, had contributed to a hostile environment best illustrated by a McCain supporter who screamed "Kill him!" (in reference to Obama) at a rally led by McCain's running mate, Sarah Palin.[7]

Republicans noted that the Obama campaign used "coded language" about McCain's age and health (McCain was seventy-two years old as the campaign reached the general election phase and would have been the second oldest president to be inaugurated).[8] Conservatives were especially upset with some of the harsh attacks by Obama supporters against Sarah Palin. A McCain campaign spokesman explained that the Obama campaign had "compared Palin to a Nazi sympathizer and called her a secessionist. . . . They've unfairly dug into her past . . . and attacked Palin's family."[9] When asked to comment about Cindy McCain's contention that the Obama campaign had "waged the dirtiest campaign in American history," the same spokesman replied, "Mrs. McCain made an observation that is based on irrefutable truth. She's entitled to it, and we stand behind it."[10]

While few can dispute the fact that the McCain-Obama contest was replete with egregious examples of political attacks, it is highly debatable that the 2008 election was the dirtiest presidential election ever. Negative campaign tactics have always played a pervasive role in American presidential elections. Opponents of Thomas Jefferson suggested that his victory would lead to the rise of atheism and the burning of the Bible.[11] Andrew Jackson had to endure attacks by his political opponents that his deceased mother was a prostitute.[12] These and other examples illustrate that the mean-spirited, personal attacks of American campaigns are hardly new to the political landscape.

Of course, there is a subjective nature to evaluating just how negative a campaign is. Indeed, there are slightly different definitions in the literature about what exactly constitutes negativity in a campaign, although there is some agreement that it typically involves discrediting, criticizing, or publicizing the deficiencies of the opponent.[13] Some political scientists suggest that negative campaigning has had a deleterious effect on American democracy. Their research finds that negative advertisements heighten political cynicism, depress voter turnout, and reduce political efficacy.[14]

Others argue that negative advertisements provide important information to voters, help draw clearer distinctions between candidates, and improve voters' recall of information and memory of the ad.[15] Moreover, there is good justification for the notion that in a political campaign some mention of the opponent's background, experience, and public record should be part of the campaign discourse. Political ads that focus on these aspects are not negative but more properly thought of as comparative. These comparative ads bring or highlight some aspect of the opposition candidate's record or background that the voting public should know before they make their decision about who will best serve their interests if elected.[16]

Nevertheless, our intent in this chapter is not to quantify whether one campaign was more negative than another. Instead, the point of the chapter is more basic: We wish to demonstrate to the reader that the personal attacks of modern elections have long been a part of American politics. We focus on presidential elections. Although state and local elections certainly can be very negative at times, presidential races are the "Super Bowl" of campaigns, and perceptions of American elections are most heavily shaped by these contests.

In the next section we briefly review three presidential elections from the nineteenth century that stand out as particularly negative. These historical examples cast some reasonable doubt on the repeated claims that "today's campaigns are the most negative ever." Following this, we examine some recent campaigns, illustrating that even the worst of these have been no more negative than campaigns in earlier times.

NEGATIVE CAMPAIGNS IN THE NINETEENTH CENTURY

Scholar Kerwin Swint in his book, *Mudslingers*, examines the twenty-five dirtiest political campaigns in history. According to Swint, four of the five dirtiest campaigns occurred in the nineteenth century. We review three of the examples from his list: the presidential elections of 1800, 1828, and 1864.

The Election of 1800

The election of 1800 pitted the Federalist President John Adams against his Democratic-Republican Vice President Thomas Jefferson. Besides the election precipitating the passage of the Twelfth Amendment, the election was significant in that it set a standard for negativity and viciousness that would generate notice, even by today's standards.[17] While there were legitimate differences separating the two on many issues, supporters often focused their efforts on negative personal attacks.

Adams' supporters spread stories that Jefferson had "cheated his British creditors, obtained property by fraud, robbed a widow of an estate worth ten thousand pounds, and behaved in a cowardly fashion as Governor of Virginia during the Revolution."[18] Another attack claimed Jefferson was "mean-spirited" and the "son of a half-breed Indian squaw, sired by a Virginia mulatto father."[19] One newspaper opined that a victory for Jefferson in 1800 would result in the teaching and practice of "murder, robbery, rape, adultery, and incest" and added that the "air will be rent with cries of the distressed, the soil will be soaked with blood, and the nation black with crimes."[20] The president of Yale University believed that Jefferson's election would result in "the Bible [being] cast into a bonfire . . . our wives and daughters [becoming] the victims of legal prostitution."[21] Others attacked him as a dangerous rebel "who writes against the truths of God's word" and "without so much as a decent external respect for the faith and worship of Christians."[22]

Jefferson's supporters attacked Adams as a "fool, hypocrite, criminal, and tyrant."[23] Jeffersonians also planted a rumor that Adams had intended to arrange a marriage between one of his sons and one of the daughters of King George III in a plot to reunite the United States and Great Britain. Another rumor suggested that Adams had sent his running mate, General Charles Pinckney, to England on a trip to secure four mistresses, two for each of them. To these charges, Adams famously retorted, "If this be true, [then] General Pinckney has kept them all for himself and cheated me out of two."[24]

While negativity swirled in both directions, the political environment favored Jefferson in 1800. Adams would garner just 39 percent of the popular vote compared to 61 percent for Jefferson. In the Electoral College vote, however, Jefferson received seventy-three of the necessary seventy Electoral College votes to win the presidency, while Adams received sixty-five. However, because the Electoral College at the time did not distinguish between votes for president and vice president, Jefferson's running mate, Aaron Burr, also received seventy-three Electoral College votes, creating a tie and moving the election to the House of Representatives. There, Jefferson was finally elected president on the thirty-sixth ballot.[25]

The Twelfth Amendment eventually altered the chaotic process that ensued following the tie between Jefferson and Burr, giving the election of 1800 special historical significance. The election of 1800 was also significant in that many credit it as the first seriously contested campaign for the presidency. This first campaign set a standard for negativity and viciousness that would generate notice even by today's standards.[26]

The Election of 1828

The election of 1828 matched incumbent President John Quincy Adams (the son of former President John Adams) of the Whig Party against challenger Andrew Jackson, a Democrat and former army general who led American troops to a decisive victory over the British in the Battle of New Orleans during the War of 1812. The election was a rematch of sorts of the previous election, which had ended in bitter controversy.

In 1824 Jackson faced Adams, as well as William Crawford and Henry

Clay. Jackson garnered 41 percent of the popular vote, ten percentage points more than Adams. However, all four received votes in the Electoral College: Jackson (99), Adams (84), Crawford (41), and Clay (37). Because no candidate received a majority of Electoral College votes, the election was thrust into the House of Representatives.[27] In the House, Clay was disqualified for finishing fourth (the Twelfth Amendment stipulates that the House may consider only the top three finishers). However, as the Speaker of the House, Clay wielded considerable influence, and because he deeply disliked Jackson[28] threw his support to Adams. The Adams win infuriated Jackson supporters because their candidate received the most popular and the most Electoral College votes. To add to the outrage, Adams named Clay his secretary of state, prompting critics to suggest that the two had struck a "corrupt bargain."[29] This set the stage for the bitter 1828 rematch.

Jackson supporters attacked Adams for his excesses, suggesting "King John the Second" lived in "kingly pomp and splendor."[30] The charge centered on Adams' purchase of a billiards table, which Jacksonians falsely claimed was purchased at taxpayer expense. Jacksonians also questioned Adams' religious sincerity, claiming he sometimes traveled on Sundays and had had "premarital relations" with his wife. These attacks came despite the fact that Adams was a Puritan and, by all reasonable accounts, a devout Christian. Most outrageous was the Jacksonian claim that, while serving as the minister to Russia, Adams handed over a young American girl to Czar Alexander I.[31]

The Adams campaign played equally dirty in attacking Jackson. A pro-Adams political handbook claimed Jackson was "wholly unqualified by education, habit and temper for the station of President,"[32] but this was tame compared to other accusations. Adams' supporters attacked Jackson with an endless barrage of scurrilous charges that included adultery, bigamy, gambling, drunkenness, theft, and even murder. The murder charge involved Jackson's approval to execute six militiamen for desertion during the Creek War in 1813. A pro-Adams editor described the event as "the Bloody Deeds of General Jackson," cold-blooded murder in which Jackson sanctioned killing innocent soldiers.[33]

Attacks against Jackson even extended to his family. One newspaper story was particularly vicious, attacking Jackson's mother as a prostitute. According to the account, "General Jackson's mother was a COMMON PROSTITUTE, brought to this country by the British soldiers. She afterward married a MULATO [sic] MAN, with whom she had several children, of which GENERAL JACKSON IS ONE!!!"[34] Jackson also had to endure attacks against his wife. Adams supporters spread misleading stories that Jackson's wife, Rachel, was an adulterer and a bigamist. The story underlying the charge, however, was more complicated. Jackson's wife had been married previously and believed she had rightfully divorced her first husband when she began her relationship with Jackson. This, however, was not the case. By the time Jackson and Rachel became aware of this, the two had already married.[35]

In the end, Jackson defeated Adams in the 1828 election, winning 56 percent of the popular vote and 178 of the 261 Electoral College votes. However, the victory came at deep personal cost to Jackson. His wife, Rachel, died a month after the election in December 1828. Jackson blamed Adams's supporters for their relentless attacks against his wife, referring to them as "murderers" and vowing never to forgive them. At her funeral, Jackson declared, "May God Almighty forgive her murderers, as I know she forgave them. I never can."[36]

The 1828 election certainly rises to the highest levels of viciousness in American campaigns. In fact, many scholars consider the election of 1828 to be one of the dirtiest presidential contests in American history.[37] As negative as modern campaigns can sometimes become, it seems difficult to argue that the 2008 election contained anything that surpassed the attacks of the 1828 election.

The Election of 1864

The two principal candidates in the 1864 presidential election were President Abraham Lincoln (Republican) and challenger General George McClellan (Democrat) of New Jersey. While Lincoln is revered today as one of the greatest presidents in American history, he was not nearly as popular in 1864. The Civil War was responsible for rising death tolls and mounting financial costs, which critics suggested was Lincoln's fault. His opponents in the Democratic Party believed that this presented them with an opportunity to win the White House.

During the campaign, Lincoln's opponents labeled him ignorant, incompetent, and corrupt. Others went further, referring to him as "Ignoramus Abe." Additional pejorative descriptions of Lincoln included ape, gorilla, Old Scoundrel, despot, liar, perjurer, thief, swindler, robber, buffoon, monster, fiend, and butcher.[38] One critic claimed the "idea that such a man as he should be president of such a country is a very ridiculous joke."[39] Another attack involved a false story that Lincoln demanded one of his officers sing him a song while passing the bodies of dead Union solders after the Battle of Antietam.[40]

Other anti-Lincoln groups relied on overtly racist appeals in their attempts to discredit Lincoln. One pamphlet labeled Lincoln as "Abraham Africanus the First" for his opposition to slavery (see figure 6.1). Another was titled "Miscegenation: The Theory of the Blending of the Races, Applied to the American White Man and Negro," and claimed that

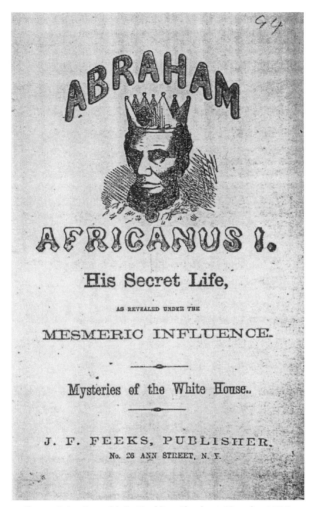

Figure 6.1   Pamphlet attacking Abraham Lincoln, 1864.

Source: www.answers.com/topic/united-states-presidential-election-1864.

Lincoln favored "race mixing" and actively encouraged and supported the "intermarriage" between whites and blacks. Many anti-Lincoln newspapers aggressively publicized the pamphlet.[41]

Lincoln supporters attacked McClellan personally as well, labeling him a "coward" and criticizing his "defeatism" and "lack of patriotism."[42] Some even suggested that Democratic opposition to the war constituted treason. Republicans ridiculed McClellan as "Little Mac," and attacked his military credentials as a general, noting that he had "nothing to offer but a tradition of defeat."[43] In Pennsylvania, Republicans warned in one poster that a McClellan victory would lead to anarchy, despotism, and the end of civilization (see figure 6.2).

The election concluded with a clear victory for Lincoln and had significant implications for American history. Lincoln's presidency would also be remembered for its high ideals. However, even "Honest Abe" could not avoid negative campaigning in the election of 1864.

MODERN "NEGATIVE" CAMPAIGNS

Extreme examples of negative campaigning exist in the modern era as well. Similar to the nineteenth century, modern campaigns have contin-

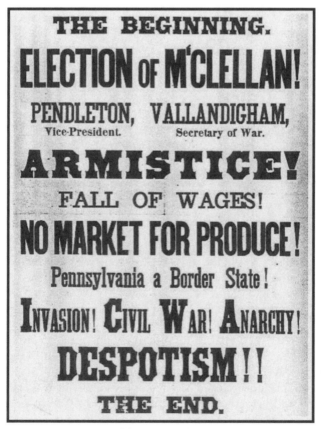

Figure 6.2.   Republican Party election poster, 1864.

Source: www.answers.com/topic/united-states-presidential-election-1864.

ued the practice of ruthlessly attacking the opposition. However, unlike the nineteenth century, modern campaigns could package negative messages into thirty-second television advertisements capable of reaching millions of citizens. Television also provides a "perfect medium" for tapping into voters' "surface feelings."[44] The emotional appeals of television can have the effect of mobilizing citizens to vote and participate in the political process.[45] In the television era, two campaigns stand out as particularly negative: the presidential elections of 1964 and 1988.[46]

The Election of 1964

The presidential election of 1964 was a contest between two candidates with sharply different views about the proper role of government. The political ideologies of the incumbent president, Democrat Lyndon Johnson of Texas, and his Republican challenger, Senator Barry Goldwater of Arizona, could not have been more different. Johnson believed in an active role for government to combat poverty, racism, and other social ills, whereas Goldwater campaigned on a conservative platform that smaller government was essential to expanding individual freedom and liberty. Indeed, Goldwater himself promised voters a "choice rather than an echo."[47]

As the incumbent president, Johnson faced little serious opposition for the Democratic nomination. However, Goldwater's nomination divided the Republican Party. Moderates, led by governors Nelson Rockefeller of New York and George Romney of Michigan, refused to support Goldwater or campaign on his behalf. Goldwater alienated Dwight Eisenhower as well, referring to his presidential administration as a "dime store New Deal."[48] When asked about the presidential prospects of Eisenhower's brother, Milton Eisenhower, Goldwater told *Time Magazine*, "One Eisenhower in a generation is enough."[49] Goldwater also exacerbated tensions with moderate Republicans in his acceptance speech at the Republican convention in San Francisco, famously remarking that "extremism in the defense of liberty is no vice . . . [and] that moderation in the pursuit of justice is no virtue."[50] Reacting to the speech, Senator Kenneth Keating of New York and others from the New York delegation walked out of the convention in protest.

Goldwater faced not only divisions within his own party, but also was up against his own tendency to provide colorful, highly controversial public statements, which the Johnson campaign exploited. In particular, the Johnson campaign made use of several Goldwater statements in its advertisements to paint him as a dangerous, pro-war candidate. In a short twenty-second television ad, viewers saw a nuclear explosion as an announcer recites: "On October 24, 1963, Barry Goldwater said of the

nuclear bomb, 'Merely another weapon.' Merely another weapon? Vote
for President Johnson. The stakes are too high for you to stay home."[51]

The aforementioned advertisement, however, is less well-known than
the so-called "Daisy commercial," which one scholar dubbed "the Mother
of all televised attack ads."[52] In this ad, a young girl plucks the petals of
a daisy while the ad transitions into a nuclear countdown that ends in an
atomic explosion. Although the ad never mentions Goldwater by name,
it clearly makes a less than subtle suggestion that Republican challenger
Barry Goldwater would lead the nation into nuclear war (see figure 6.3).
Interestingly, while the "Daisy" ad would go on to become one of the
most controversial commercials in presidential election history, it was
only aired once (on CBS' *Monday Night at the Movies*, September 7, 1964).
However, because the ad generated near-instant controversy, all three
networks replayed it the following day. The Goldwater campaign reacted
in outrage at the ad and filed a complaint with the Fair Campaign Practices Committee. The attention that the ad generated helped more people
see the ad and likely increased its effects.

Perhaps equally vicious was a Johnson spot that attacked Goldwater's
opposition to a treaty banning atmospheric testing of nuclear weapons.
The so-called "Ice Cream" ad suggests that Goldwater's opposition to a
nuclear test ban treaty could lead to the poisoning—and even death—of
innocent children. The sixty-second advertisement features a young girl
licking an ice-cream cone, while a female announcer warns of Strontium
90 and Cesium 137 (present in nuclear fallout) and the potential dangers
of electing Goldwater (see box 6.1).

The Johnson campaign also went after Goldwater for his opposition to
the 1964 Civil Rights Act. One ad goes so far as to tie Goldwater to the
Ku Klux Klan. As a cross burns with Ku Klux Klan members in the background, a narrator quotes Robert Creel, the leader of the Alabama Ku
Klux Klan, who offers his support for Goldwater, stating: "I like Barry
Goldwater. He needs our help."[53] Other Johnson spots suggested that
Goldwater would destroy Social Security and that he harbored animosity
toward Americans living on the east coast (with one ad quoting Goldwater as saying, "sometimes I think this country would be better off if we
could just saw off the Eastern Seaboard and let it float out to sea").[54] The
Johnson campaign added to the assault by altering Goldwater's slogan of
"In your heart, you know he's right," to "In your guts, you know he's
nuts."[55]

The Goldwater campaign hit back at the Johnson campaign. Goldwater
ran advertisements suggesting that Johnson was corrupt and morally
deficient, noting his connections to disgraced figures such as Billy Sol
Estes who was involved in a scam to swindle the Department of Agricul-

"DAISY GIRL"
Lyndon Johnson, 1964

[Girl]: One...two...

three...four...five

seven...six...six

eight...nine...nine
[General (fade over)]: Ten...

nine...eight...seven...six...five

four...three...two...one

zero! **[sounds of explosion]**

[Lyndon Johnson]: These are the stakes, to make a world in which all of God's children

can live, or to go into the dark.

We must either love each other, or we must die.

[Narrator]: Vote for President Johnson on November Third

The stakes are too high for you to stay home.

Figure 6.3 The 1964 "Daisy Girl" ad.

Source: University of Wisconsin Advertising Project, wiscadproject.wisc.edu/historic-ads/daisygirl.php.

BOX 6.1

TRANSCRIPT OF "ICE CREAM" AD

Female Announcer: Do you know what people used to do? They used to explode atomic bombs in the air. Now children should have lots of Vitamin A and calcium, but they shouldn't have any Strontium 90 or Cesium 137. These things come from atomic bombs and they're radioactive. They can make you die. Do you know what people finally did? They got together and signed a nuclear test ban treaty, and then the radioactive poisons started to go away.

But now, there's a man who wants to be president of the United States and he doesn't like this treaty—he fought against it. He even voted against it. He wants to go on testing more bombs. His name is Barry Goldwater. And if he's elected, they might start testing all over again.

Male Announcer: Vote for President Johnson on November 3. The stakes are too high for you to stay home.

Source: The Living Room Candidate, http://www.livingroomcandidate.org/commercials/1964.

ture out of millions of dollars. In one ad, Goldwater accuses Johnson directly of "running a country" by "buying and bludgeoning votes."[56] Goldwater also used his advertisements to make dire predictions. In an ad entitled "Moral Responsibility," Goldwater himself tells the audience that the Johnson administration was "not far from the kind of moral decay that has brought on the fall of other nations and people. The philosophy of something for nothing . . . is an insidious cancer that will destroy us as a people unless we recognize it and root it out now."[57]

Like Johnson, Goldwater was also willing to use children in his ads. In one ad, a boy rides a bicycle as an announcer tells the audience, "Don't look now young man, but somebody has his hand in your pocket. It's the hand of big government. It's taking away about four months' pay from what your daddy earns every year—one dollar out of every three in his paycheck. And it's taking security out of your grandmother's Social Security."[58]

Despite Goldwater's counter-attacks, Johnson went on to win the election easily. Johnson won forty-four states, amassing 486 Electoral College votes to 52 for Goldwater. Johnson also won 61 percent of the popular vote, marking one of the largest landslide victories in presidential election history. However, Johnson's victory was only part of the story. Ultimately, the presidential election of 1964 marked what one scholar claimed was the "moment when the negative TV ad was born."[59] This pioneering election certainly set a negative tone that few campaigns have since reached.

The Election of 1988

Vice President George H.W. Bush faced Massachusetts Governor Michael Dukakis in the presidential election of 1988. The election followed the two-term presidency of Republican Ronald Reagan. Bush assumed the role as Reagan's heir apparent and pledged to continue the "Reagan Revolution" of lower taxes, famously proclaiming at the Republican convention, "Read my lips, no new taxes." In contrast, Dukakis campaigned on a platform to balance the federal budget, which increased significantly under Reagan, and to cut military spending for increased spending on education, health care, and other social programs.

In the early stages of the election, Dukakis led in most polls.[60] However, with the assistance of political consultant Lee Atwater, the Bush campaign went on the attack, calling into question Dukakis's patriotism, ability to lead the military, environmental record, and his commitment to fighting crime. The Bush attacks effectively cut into the Dukakis lead and ultimately propelled Bush to frontrunner status in the late stages of the election.

Perhaps the most memorable negative advertisements against Dukakis was the infamous "Willie Horton" spot, which suggested that Dukakis was ineffective in fighting violent crime during his time as governor of Massachusetts. The ad featured the picture of a convicted murderer, Willie Horton, who raped a Maryland woman during a weekend furlough from a Massachusetts prison, as an announcer tells viewers, "Dukakis not only opposes the death penalty, he allowed first-degree murderers to have weekend passes from prison."[61] Significant controversy followed, with critics making charges of racism because the ad featured an African American, which some claimed was an attempt to exploit "racist fears" about crime.[62] A similarly themed ad, "Revolving Door," also attacked Dukakis's record on crime, although without the image of Willie Horton. The ad, nevertheless, suggests that a Dukakis victory was a "risk" for the nation (see box 6.2).

The Bush campaign attempted to paint Dukakis as not only weak on crime, but also on military and defense issues. Dukakis had attempted to address this perceived problem by visiting the General Dynamics plant in Michigan and then riding in an M1 Abrams tank for a campaign photo op. While riding in the tank, Dukakis wore a large helmet and grinned awkwardly. Instead of failing to dispel the attack against him as unfit to be commander-in-chief, the so-called "Dukakis in the tank" footage

BOX 6.2

TRANSCRIPT OF "REVOLVING DOOR" AD

Male Announcer: As Governor Michael Dukakis vetoed mandatory sentences for drug dealers he vetoed the death penalty. His revolving-door prison policy gave weekend furloughs to first-degree murders not eligible for parole.

[Text appears on screen: "268 Escaped"]

Male Announcer: While out, many committed other crimes like kidnapping and rape and many are still at large.

[Text appears on screen: "Many are still at large"]

Male Announcer: Now Michael Dukakis says he wants to do for America what he's done for Massachusetts. America can't afford that risk.

Source: The Living Room Candidate, http://www.livingroomcandidate.org/commercials/1988/.

became synonymous with public relations disasters. The Bush campaign used this footage to reinforce its attacks that Dukakis was not a credible military leader (see box 6.3).

The attacks against Dukakis extended in other areas as well. The Bush campaign skewered Dukakis for his record on environmental pollution, citing problems with Boston Harbor (see box 6.4). There were also false rumors spread during the campaign that Dukakis received treatment for mental illness and that his wife, Kitty, burned an American flag in protest of the Vietnam War.

The Dukakis campaign was slow in responding to the attacks, which some believe contributed to his sharp declines in the polls as the election progressed. Dukakis ultimately fought back by questioning Bush's honesty and claiming in one ad that Bush had taken a "furlough from the truth."[63] Other ads attacked Bush for his record in the war on drugs, blamed the Republicans for increasing the federal deficit, and poked fun at the selection of Bush's running mate, Senator Dan Quayle of Indiana, who was perceived by some as too young and inexperienced to be president. There were also rumors spread by a member of the Dukakis staff that Bush had an affair with his secretary, Jennifer Fitzgerald. Dukakis, however, failed to regain his early lead and won just 111 Electoral College votes compared to 426 for Bush.

BOX 6.3

TRANSCRIPT OF "TANK RIDE" AD

Male Announcer: Michael Dukakis has opposed virtually every defense system we developed.

Male Announcer and text: He opposed new aircraft carriers. He opposed anti-satellite weapons. He opposed four missile systems, including the Pershing II missile deployment. Dukakis opposed the stealth bomber, a ground emergency warning system against nuclear testing. He even criticized our rescue mission to Grenada and our strike on Libya. And now he wants to be our commander-in-chief. America can't afford that risk.

Source: The Living Room Candidate, http://www.livingroomcandidate.org/commercials/1988/.

CONCLUSION

As noted at the outset of this chapter, the 2008 presidential election had its fair share of negative attacks. Yet, while the 2008 election contained numerous examples of nasty personal attacks, it was probably not "the dirtiest" presidential election in American history. As the examples pre-

---

BOX 6.4

TRANSCRIPT OF "HARBOR" AD

[Text appears on screen: "Harbor"]

Male Announcer: As a candidate, Michael Dukakis called Boston Harbor an open sewer. As governor, he had the opportunity to do something about it but chose not to. The Environmental Protection Agency called his lack of action the most expensive public policy mistake in the history of New England. Now Boston Harbor is the dirtiest harbor in America. It cost residents six billion dollars to clean. And Michael Dukakis promises to do for America what he's done for Massachusetts.

Source: The Living Room Candidate, http://www.livingroomcandidate.org/commercials/1988/.

sented in this chapter make clear, vicious personal attacks and negative campaigning are virtually as old as the republic.

There are certainly additional examples that one could note. One could even argue that the previous presidential election in 2004 was more negative than the presidential election was in 2008. Few Democrats have forgotten a series of advertisements sponsored by the Swift Boat Veterans for Truth that attacked Democratic presidential nominee John Kerry. In one of the ads, the organization claimed that Kerry had "not been honest about what happened in Vietnam"; that he "lied about his first Purple Heart"; that he "lied to get his bronze star"; that he "lacks the capacity to lead"; that he is "no war hero"; and that he "betrayed the men and women he served with."[64] On the other side of the political aisle, filmmaker Michael Moore released an anti-Bush documentary film entitled *Fahrenheit 9/11* during the summer of 2004. The two-hour film makes the case that President Bush failed to address the threat of Islamic terrorism in the months leading up to the 9/11 attacks (one scene shows Bush casually playing golf as he answers a reporter's question about the threat of terrorism). The film then takes sharp aim at Bush's handling of the situation in the aftermath of the 9/11 attack. The documentary generated enormous publicity in the summer months preceding the November election, and was one of the most memorable anti-Bush pieces of the 2004 campaign.

As the 2004 contest and the other elections profiled in this chapter illustrate, negative campaigning has been and continues to be a part of presidential elections. Future elections will undoubtedly bring about the familiar calls that the current election is the "most negative ever." Such lines certainly make for flashy headlines and provocative quotations; however, as the historical record rather plainly suggests, these claims come much closer to hyperbole than they do to reality.

FOR MORE READING

Boller, Paul F., Jr. *Presidential Campaigns: From George Washington to George W. Bush.* New York: Oxford University Press, 2004.

Buell, Emmett H., Jr., and Lee Sigelman. *Attack Politics: Negativity in Presidential Campaigns since 1960.* Lawrence, Kans.: University Press of Kansas, 2008.

Geer, John G. *In Defense of Negativity: Attack Ads in Presidential Campaigns.* Chicago: University of Chicago Press, 2006.

Mark, David. *Going Dirty: The Art of Negative Campaigning.* Lanham, Md.: Rowman & Littlefield, 2006.

On the Web: "The Living Room Candidate: Presidential Campaign Commercials, 1952–2008." Available at: http://www.livingroomcandidate.org/.

7

✛

Science or Voodoo?

Misconceptions about
National Election Polls

I re-word Winston Churchill's famous remarks about democracy and say, "Polls are the worst way of measuring public opinion . . . or of predicting elections—except for all of the others."

—Humphrey Taylor, chairman of the Harris Poll.[1]

Public opinion polls are ubiquitous. Rarely does a day pass without a major newspaper, such as *USA Today*, featuring the results of some poll. The frequency of polls only increases during an election season, and this is especially true during a presidential election. However, many people do not understand enough about polling to be able to interpret polls accurately. To make matters worse, media outlets occasionally misrepresent the results of polls. Pollsters themselves also miss the mark from time to time, providing forecasts and predictions that fail to materialize. This raises a few questions: Can national election polls be trusted? Are pollsters really able to gauge what Americans believe? One poll conducted in 2000 suggested that only 2 percent of Americans believe that national polls are "always right," while almost 60 percent believe they are right "only some of the time" and 7 percent "hardly ever."[2]

We offer a mixed answer to the question of whether people can trust polls throughout the election cycle. Our objective is less to dispel a particular myth than to give the reader a better understanding of the enterprise of public polling during an election. This understanding is crucial to following news stories throughout the campaign. Our goal is to give readers a set of guidelines on how to use—read, analyze, and interpret—polling results during an election.³ In the end, whether or not to trust a particular national opinion poll depends on a variety of factors.

THE BASICS OF PUBLIC POLLING

Election polls have a long history in the United States. Since 1824, newspapers have conducted and reported the results of so-called straws, or straw polls, during presidential elections.⁴ Straw polls are informal polls taken to gauge public opinion (which way the wind is blowing the straw). During the nineteenth century, most newspapers were partisan publications. While newspapers purportedly used polls to give readers a sense of which candidate might be more likely to prevail, in actuality they were intended to advance the paper's partisan agenda by giving the public the impression that the paper's favored candidate was in the lead.

The methodology of nineteenth-century polls was hardly scientific. To conduct a poll, a journalist might ask questions of the passengers aboard a particular train or citizens attending a public gathering.⁵ For example, in 1876, the following story ran in the *Chicago Tribune*: "An excursion train containing some 200 people from Dayton, [Ohio], and neighboring towns, arrived last evening via the Pan Handle Road. . . . A vote was taken, resulting as follows: Hayes 65, Tilden 13, neutral 3, Cooper 2."⁶

Straw polls grew in popularity throughout the nineteenth century and, by the early part of the twentieth century, had become a regular feature in newspaper coverage of presidential elections. However, as popular as they were, they were not very useful in predicting the outcome of presidential elections. This was in part because people who did not sympathize with a given paper's partisan leanings would often refuse to return their questionnaires, leading to wildly biased estimates of the vote totals.

Among the many publications that conducted presidential polls was *Literary Digest*, which at the time was the most widely circulated general readership magazine in the nation. Starting in 1916, *Literary Digest* conducted polls predicting the presidential vote. While the magazine's predicted vote totals were often inaccurate, it correctly predicted the winner in five consecutive elections (1916–1932). However, in 1936 it predicted that the Republican candidate for president, Alf Landon, would receive 57 percent of the vote to Franklin Roosevelt's 43 percent. Of course, Roosevelt won, garnering 62.5 percent.⁷

The ushering in of the modern era of scientific polling began with the *Digest*'s failure in 1936. In addition to the fact that the magazine had incorrectly predicted Landon's victory, three enterprising individuals with backgrounds in market research correctly predicted the outcome.

George Gallup, Elmo Roper, and Archibald Crossley were able to do so by employing more systematic methods of sampling.[8] To understand how Gallup, Roper, and Crossley correctly predicted the winner, and how the *Digest* did not, it is important to examine what pollsters do and how they do it.

A poll is a device used to measure what a group of people thinks about a particular subject or question. Because it is almost impossible to ask all of the people in a particular group (e.g., registered voters) what they think about a particular topic and because such an effort would be too time consuming or costly to be practical, a pollster asks a smaller group of people, or a sample. From this sample, pollsters then estimate what the larger group thinks.

To understand this process better, imagine trying to predict how a large lecture hall with five hundred students will vote in a presidential election. One approach would be to ask all five hundred students: by the time one handed out, collected, and counted all of the ballots, however, the class would be over. Is it reasonable to believe that one could estimate the likely vote outcome by polling only fifty people? Under the right circumstances, the answer is yes.

The reason for this is that polling is based in part on a branch of mathematics known as probability theory, which attempts to quantify how likely it is that a certain event will occur.[9] Probability theory (in particular, the central limit theorem) suggests that if one flips a coin one hundred times, it is likely that heads will land face up about fifty times. However, to make a sound prediction, one would first need to flip the coin a certain number of times. In other words, a certain number of actual observations are required. Probability theory allows pollsters to infer what Americans think based on the actual answers given by approximately 1,500 people, sometimes less.[10]

Before applying the theories of probability to predicting vote outcomes, at least one condition needs to be specified. Based on previous research, we know that women are more likely to vote Democratic, and men are more likely to vote Republican. Using the example of the class of five hundred, we would want to make sure that the poll sampled women and men in roughly similar proportions to their numbers in the whole class. If our class was evenly divided by gender (250 women, 250 men), we would want to poll approximately twenty-five women and twenty-five men. Furthermore, we know that people who frequently attend church vote differently than those who do not, that the more affluent cast their ballots differently than those who are less economically fortunate, and so on. Thus, to have any confidence that the results from our fifty-person sample would correctly predict the vote of all five hundred students, we would want to ensure that the fifty students polled were broadly representative of the entire class.

How is a representative sample identified by a pollster? There are four main strategies for doing this, all of which rely—in some way—on randomly selecting the individuals who take the poll. In the language of survey research these are known as "probability samples," a reference to the fact that randomness—or random selection of the cases used to make the prediction—plays a central role in theories of probability.

The first strategy is random sampling. In a simple random sample, each person in the larger group, or population, has an equal chance of being selected. For example, if everyone in our hypothetical class of five hundred had a seat number, we could put slips of paper numbered one to five hundred in a basket, shuffle them around, and pick fifty. If conducted fairly (e.g., all sheets of paper are of equal size, folded in half to hide the number, sufficiently shuffled or mixed), the process would provide an equal chance for each student to be selected.

A second strategy, a variant of the first, is systematic sampling. Instead of selecting individuals strictly at random, systematic sampling involves moving through a list and selecting names according to a preset strategy. The list itself is assumed to be randomly distributed. For example, in systematic sampling, we could go through our alphabetical class roster and select every tenth name in order to create a fifty-person sample.

Another technique is stratified sampling. Here, the pollster divides the sampling frame, or the entire group, into strata, or smaller groups. Within each stratum (group), the pollster selects a sample using simple random or systematic sampling. This helps to ensure that the sample sufficiently represents all relevant subgroups. If our class has three hundred men and two hundred women, we would select a sample of thirty men and twenty women.

Multistage cluster sampling follows a similar principle, although here, rather than use subgroup characteristics as the initial basis for sampling, geography is used instead. A pollster could first select a geographic unit (say, a state), and within that unit, select a smaller unit (a county), and within that unit, choose an even smaller one (a neighborhood) and then select potential respondents—at random—from the smallest unit. This process reduces costs for the polling firm by concentrating efforts in several small areas. In our class example, we might think about selecting every fifth row of students, then randomly selecting respondents from each.

The important point with respect to sampling, regardless of the technique used, is that the respondents must be representative of the population that the pollster or researcher examines. Probability sampling rests on an assumption that if selected randomly, a sample will be representative of the population. Box 7.1 summarizes these four techniques.

This admittedly simplistic explanation of sampling allows us to understand why the *Literary Digest* poll failed to predict Roosevelt's victory correctly in 1936. The magazine sent out over ten million questionnaires, and over 2.3 million people filled out and returned these surveys. This was more than a sufficient number upon which to base a prediction of how the American public would vote. However, the list of people the magazine used in mailing the questionnaire was produced from automobile registration and telephone number lists. The problem with this was that in 1936, people who owned automobiles or had telephones in their home were more likely to have been Republicans (thus, Landon voters) rather than Democrats (Roosevelt supporters). In addition, subsequent research has shown that Landon voters were more likely to return their questionnaires. Coupled together, this produced a sample that was biased, or not representative of the general population.[11]

In sum, assuming that researchers administer a survey to a sufficiently large and representative sample, and assuming that the questions they ask are fairly worded, most polls can be trusted. However, not all polls are created equal. In particular, presidential campaign polls have some common pitfalls worth noting.

BOX 7.1

TECHNIQUES FOR SELECTING A PROBABILITY SAMPLE

Random: Individuals are selected from the entire sampling frame by chance.

Systematic: Individuals are selected from the entire sampling frame according to a set strategy.

Stratified: The sampling frame is divided into subgroups, and within each, a certain number of individuals are selected either randomly or systematically.

Multistage Cluster: A number of geographic areas are identified, and within each, individuals are selected either randomly or systematically.

THE PROBLEM OF PSEUDO POLLS

There are many reputable polling firms, as well as countless research institutions and university professors around the country that conduct scientifically grounded polls. In general, the results of these polls are trustworthy, if one uses a certain amount of discretion in interpreting the results. However, anyone can write and administer a poll. As noted earlier, a variety of different sources present us with various poll results every day. Which polls should we trust, or more to the point, which should we *not* trust?

"Pseudo polls" are one general category of polls to disregard, especially in understanding the dynamics of a presidential campaign. Web sites (including blogs), local news organizations, talk radio, college newspapers, and others often administer these types of polls. The major problem with pseudo polls is that they typically rely on what are referred to as "convenience," or non-probability samples. Here, poll administrators simply invite people to participate in the poll and then tabulate the results. The individuals who take the survey are, in other words, self-selected—not randomly selected. CNN's "QuickVote" was a good example of these types of polls, and while they included a disclaimer stating that the poll results were not representative of the general public, it is unclear whether the average viewer understands what this means.[12]

The problems with polls that rely on self-selected samples are twofold. First, not everyone has a chance to participate. For example, in the case of Internet polls, the sample includes only those who visit the poll's web site. Moreover, many of these organizations cater to a specific type of person (e.g., most talk radio listeners tend to be conservative).[13] Another problem with this sampling technique is that people who are motivated to respond to the poll usually have more extreme views than the general population. The end result is that the samples in pseudo polls are not representative of the population at large, nor are the views expressed in these polls representative of the views of the population at large.[14]

HOW TO DETERMINE LIKELY VOTERS?

A reliable poll of presidential preference should probably sample only those people who will actually vote. To understand the scope of this problem, consider that in 2004 there were approximately 197 million citizens over the age of eighteen in the United States. Of these, roughly 142 million (72.1 percent) were registered to vote, and only 125 million (63.8 percent of citizens over the age of eighteen) actually voted.[15]

How should a polling organization construct a sample of people who will vote, or who will be likely to vote? Unfortunately, there is no reliable or accepted way to determine whether an individual will exercise this most basic of political freedoms. Simply asking a person if they are likely to vote will not help identify likely voters. Most people, based on ideas about good citizenship, are reluctant to admit they might not vote. Thus, voter turnout is typically substantially lower than the percentage of people who say they are likely to vote. For example, the Pew Research Center conducted a survey prior to the 1996 election asking respondents about their intention to vote. Of those responding, 69 percent said they were "absolutely certain" they would vote, and another 18 percent replied they were "fairly certain." In actuality, voter turnout in 1996 was 49 percent.[16]

Most polling firms will use at least one, and typically several, screening questions in their attempt to narrow their sample down so it only includes likely voters. The first stage of this screening is almost always to ask whether the respondent is a registered voter. From those who respond in the affirmative, the polling firm will ask additional questions in an attempt to gauge how likely the individual is to vote. For example, the Gallup Organization has asked whether respondents are likely to vote, how often they have voted in the past, whether they know where their polling place is, their level of interest in politics, their interest in a particular campaign, and their level of commitment to a particular candidate. Most of the reputable national polling organizations use some combination of questions similar to Gallup's to gauge whether an individual is likely to vote.[17]

In a presidential preference poll, especially one conducted close to the election, the sample should consist of only those who are registered and likely to vote. How well the polling firm constructs the sample in this regard can have a direct effect on the results. For example, a Harris Poll from October of 2004 suggested that President Bush was leading Senator John Kerry by two percentage points according to one measure of likely voters. A second method had Bush ahead by eight points (51 percent to 43 percent).[18]

Therefore, it seems prudent to take note of whether the poll bases its results on responses from registered or likely voters. Most major news organizations will include this information somewhere in the story. A *Washington Post* story from early August 2004 reported that John Kerry had "the support of 50 percent of all registered voters." Another story from late October 2004 suggested that Bush led Kerry "by 51% to 46% among *likely* voters" (emphasis added).[19]

WHAT ABOUT UNDECIDED VOTERS?

As complicated as it is to ensure that a poll sample includes only those voters most likely to vote, another issue is how to count the people who say they are undecided. In most presidential campaigns, the number of "undecideds" is as high as 15 percent, and although this percentage drops as the campaign nears its end, it can still be as high as 5 percent in the days prior to Election Day. While it would be a simple matter for a news organization to report the percentage of undecideds in addition to the percentage that favor each candidate, most do not, because it makes for less interesting reading if the poll numbers present an uncertain picture. One strategy to deal with undecided voters is to have a follow-up question asking the respondent if he or she "leans" toward, or favors, either candidate.[20] While this reduces the number of undecideds, it paints an inaccurate portrait of voter preferences, given that many of these people might change their minds.[21] This was one of the factors responsible for the Gallup Organization mistakenly calling the 1948 election for Thomas Dewey (morning newspapers proclaimed that Dewey won, when in fact, Harry Truman was the victor).[22] Another way to reduce the number of undecideds is to present respondents with a secret ballot, but this requires face-to-face interviewing, a rather costly method.

A more common strategy is to allocate the undecideds to one candidate or the other, based on some formula. For example, one way to allocate them would be to assign them in proportion to each candidate's strength. If 46 percent of those who responded have expressed a preference for Candidate A, the pollster might allocate 46 percent of the undecided vote to Candidate A. This strategy, however, poses considerable risks given that the closer Election Day looms, the more likely it is that momentum can shift, disproportionately favoring one candidate over the other. There are other formulas for allocating undecideds as well, including using the respondent's past voting record or partisan identification (if any) as a clue for future voting intentions, whether there is an incumbent in the race (undecideds are generally thought to be anti-incumbent), as well as other, more complex solutions.

Additional ways to address this issue are to continue polling as close to Election Day as is feasible. This reduces the number of undecided voters in the poll. However, this strategy too can result in less than perfect results. In fact, there is a fair degree of error in many of the pre-election polls conducted by major polling firms when compared to the actual vote totals. Table 7.1 lists the actual vote margin between the two candidates and the margin taken from the least accurate major poll, and the difference between these two figures, from each election cycle from 1980 to 2008.

To be fair, the track record also shows that with the exception of one year, at least one of the major polling firms projected the outcome either exactly or correctly to within one percentage point, and in only one case (the election of 2000) did any firm project the winner incorrectly. In 1980,

Table 7.1 Actual and projected margins from select election polls, 1980–2008

Year	Winner, actual vote margin	Margin from least accurate projection	Difference
1980	Reagan +10	Reagan +1 (CBS/*New York Times*)	9
1984	Reagan +18	Reagan +10 (Roper)/ +25 (*USA Today*)	8/7
1988	Bush +8	Bush +12 (Gallup)	4
1992	Clinton +8	Clinton +12 (Gallup/CNN/*USA Today*)	4
1996	Clinton +8	Clinton +18 (CBS/*New York Times*)	10
2000	Bush and Gore (even)	Bush +7 (Hotline)	7
2004	Bush +2.4	Bush +6 (*Newsweek*)	3.6
2008	Obama +7.3	Obama +13 (CBS News)	5.7

Sources: Data from 1980 through 2000 adapted from Robert S. Erikson and Kent L. Tedin, *American Public Opinion: Its Origins, Content, and Impact*, 7th ed. (New York: Longman, 2005), 44. 2004 data from Robert S. Erikson and Kent L. Tedin, *American Public Opinion: Its Origins, Content, and Impact*, Updated 7th ed. (New York: Longman, 2007), 51. Data from 2008 from "White House 2008: General Election Trial Heats, Presidential Trial Heat Summary," *PollingReport.com*, www.pollingreport.com/wh08gen.htm, accessed June 1, 2009.

all of the major firms underestimated Ronald Reagan's margin of victory over Jimmy Carter (NBC/AP came within three percentage points of the correct margin). Seven organizations called the election for George W. Bush and two for Al Gore in 2000, while the actual vote was virtually even (Gore actually polled one-half of a percentage point more than Bush). Table 7.1 illustrates the reality that many voters make their decision in the final days of the campaign, after the completion of the last polls. It also highlights the difficulties polling organizations have in dealing with late-deciding voters.

THE PROBLEM OF TIMING: PHASES OF THE CAMPAIGN

Polls taken and released during certain periods of time during the campaign can be misleading, giving a false impression of a candidate's strength or weakness. Readers of these polls need to interpret them cautiously. This is especially true with respect to polls taken during the preprimary phase of the campaign, immediately after each party convention, and after the debates.

Preprimary polls, or those taken before the Iowa caucuses and New Hampshire primary, have in the past been a fairly good predictor of who will win the party nomination. From 1980 to 2000, all but one candidate (Gary Hart, in 1988) who was leading in the Gallup poll of party identifiers immediately prior to the Iowa caucuses has won their party's nomination.[23] This said, there is considerable fluctuation in these poll numbers before January of the election year. In 2003, several candidates, including

Joe Lieberman, Dick Gephardt, Wesley Clark, and the eventual presumed front-runner, Howard Dean, led in these preprimary polls.[24] John Kerry was the eventual winner of the Democratic nomination. In fact, in 2008, neither of the two candidates who led in the final poll before Iowa (Hillary Clinton and Rudy Giuliani) went on to secure their party's nomination.

These "trial heat" polls are not measuring actual preferences as much as they track name recognition or simple familiarity with the name of the individual.[25] In addition, these polls are sensitive to the news cycle. Before Wesley Clark's formal entrance into the race on September 17, 2003, most polls showed other Democratic candidates leading the field. However, in the month following his announcement to enter the race, Clark consistently ranked among the top tier of candidates. One can only assume this was at least partly the result of the media coverage generated by his announcement, because he won only one Democratic primary.[26] Republican Senator Fred Thompson, who also starred in the television series *Law and Order* for five seasons, announced his candidacy in early September of 2007 and polled between 15 and 20 percent throughout the remainder of the year. He did not, however, win a single primary. While polls taken immediately prior to the Iowa caucuses and the New Hampshire primary are a good indicator of who will be the eventual nominee, polls taken much earlier than November or December of the year prior to the election year are not very reliable.

In a similar way, polls taken immediately after each candidate's party convention typically do not measure actual candidate strength. While there are exceptions (e.g., 1984, 1996), it is very common for each party candidate's numbers to go up 5 to 10 percent after the convention. Many political observers commonly refer to this as the post-convention bump or bounce. Typically, challengers benefit more than incumbents from the post-convention bounce because they are less well known to the general public. However, convention bounces for either candidate can dissipate quickly, as was the case with Al Gore in 2000 or John McCain in 2008, but they can also be a prelude to a strong fall campaign, as happened for Bill Clinton in 1992.[27] In short, one should treat polls taken immediately after the conventions with caution.

Polls following presidential debates are similarly volatile. This is partly a function of the fact that firms must hastily conduct post-debate polls, using smaller than normal samples (about six hundred people). In addition, post-debate polls are sensitive to media coverage of the debate.[28] Often different organizations report somewhat contradictory—or at least differing—results. For example, after the first presidential debate in 2004 (on September 30), one poll had Kerry winning the debate by a margin of forty-two percentage points (sixty-one to nineteen), another by thirty-two, (fifty-eight to twenty-six), and yet another by only sixteen (fifty-three to thirty-seven).[29] All clearly suggested that Kerry won but by varying margins. And, all reported that Bush's slim lead going into the debate remained largely intact.[30] In other words, post-debate polls might suggest something about how voters viewed the candidates' performances in the debates, but they are a poor indicator of how well a particular candidate is doing in the campaign.[31]

Taken in isolation, few of these polls (preprimary, post-convention, post-debate) are good indicators of candidate strength. Moreover, as suggested above, there is often considerable variation in candidate strength as Election Day approaches. The closer to Election Day that one conducts a poll, the more likely it is to be accurate.

SAMPLES, DATA, AND REPORTING

As we have stressed throughout this chapter, most polls that major news organizations report are well designed and administered. However, sometimes they do not fully explain the results. For example, as previously mentioned, some stories might not indicate whether their sample consisted of registered or likely voters. It is more common to misrepresent what a poll actually means, especially with respect to the margin separating the candidates. This leads to a discussion of the margin of error of polls.

In discussing sampling, it is possible to infer what a population thinks by relying on the responses of a properly constructed probability sample. It is important to remember, however, that the theory driving this inference is one of probability, not certainty. If we flip a coin one hundred times, it is probable that heads will land face up about fifty times. However, common sense suggests that it might be as many as fifty-three times, or as few as forty-seven. Probability theory suggests that if one repeated the coin flip twenty times, heads would come up approximately 50 percent of the time in nineteen cases.[32] The difference between the expected outcome (heads fifty times, or 50 percent) and what repeated tests would actually yield is known as the margin of error.[33]

Most news organizations report the sampling error of a given poll by telling consumers that a poll is accurate to within a certain percentage. This number is given in plus or minus terms ($+/-$) and is variously referred to as the margin of error, sampling error, or the poll's error margin. One story from 2004 reported that 42 percent of the people who watched the last presidential debate believed Kerry was the winner and that the poll "results have a 4.5 percent error margin."[34] Translated, this means that as few as 37.5 (42 minus 4.5) percent, and as many as 46.5 (42 plus 4.5) percent thought Kerry performed better than Bush in the debate.

This is important to understand because headlines and news stories sometimes misrepresent what is actually happening in election polls with respect to sampling error.[35] Although the story qualified the claims, one Harris Poll report from October 2000 claimed that "Bush Leads Gore by Five Points," 48 to 43 percent. However, with the survey's margin of error (3 percent) factored in, Bush could have had as little as 45 percent, and Gore as much as 46 percent.[36] CBS News reported in 2000 that Gore won the last presidential debate by five percentage points over Bush (45 to 40 percent), but the margin of error for this poll was 4 percent—almost as much as the difference between the two.[37] Margin of error matters, especially if the two candidates are in a competitive race, which is usually the case in presidential elections.

Another point is that the media often report the poll numbers of various subgroups in pre-election presidential polls as well. In these polls, a reliable sample size is sometimes a problem. A national poll based on responses from one thousand individuals would have a 3 percent margin of error associated with it. If there was a split in the sample according to gender, there would be a subsample of approximately 490 men. The margin of error would be greater for this subsample. If there was a split in the sample for men according to their party identification, the sample would split further into three more categories: one each for Republicans, Democrats, and independents. The sample would continue to grow smaller with further divisions along race, income, or other socioeconomic characteristics. With each division, the sample becomes smaller and therefore associated with a greater margin of error. As such, group analyses of presidential polling data need to be treated with caution given that subgroups have higher margins of error associated with them.[38]

APPLYING NATIONAL POLLING RESULTS
TO A STATE-BY-STATE CONTEST

This particular problem with pre-election presidential polls is centered on the fact that most of the pre-election polls the national news organizations report are national polls. If done well, the results mirror the outcome one would expect to find in a national vote for the president. However, the United States does not have a national vote for president. Electoral College votes are allocated on a state-by-state basis, dependent (in all but two states) on the winner of the popular vote in that state. Only once in the past one hundred years has the loser of the popular vote been selected president, in the election of 2000. Interestingly, most pre-election polls during that campaign season had George W. Bush—the eventual loser of the popular vote and winner of the Electoral College vote—ahead.[39]

For those who are only passively interested in following presidential campaigns, tracking national polls will probably suffice. However, if one is truly interested in the dynamics of the campaign, watching state polling results is a better answer. Fortunately, in the age of the World Wide Web, this has become fairly convenient. Several web sites collate such information into easily accessible pages.[40] This approach is especially important in close races (as it was in 2000 and 2004) when it is known in advance that the outcome might hinge on the results from a few key "battleground" states (states with a fairly large number of Electoral College votes that could realistically swing to either candidate). Watching state polls allows one a more nuanced—and accurate—view of how each candidate is doing and, more importantly, where each candidate is doing well or poorly.

CONCLUSION

So, is polling an art, a science, or some form of modern voodoo? As we hope our discussion has made clear, polling is a science but hardly an exact science. Table 7.1 is a good example of this point. One objective of this chapter was to provide the tools to become better consumers of pre-election presidential polls. Box 7.2 summarizes the various points made throughout the chapter in short question form. While it is not necessary to study every poll intensively, moving mentally through this checklist is a helpful way to understand what the polls are really telling us.

FOR MORE READING

Asher, Herbert. *Polling and the Public: What Every Citizen Should Know*, 6th ed. Washington, D.C.: CQ Press, 2004.

Erikson, Robert S., and Kent L. Tedin. *American Public Opinion: Its Origins, Content, and Impact*, 7th ed. New York: Longman, 2005.

Traugott, Michael W., and Paul J. Lavrakas. *The Voter's Guide to Election Polls*, 3rd ed. Lanham, Md.: Rowman & Littlefield, 2004.

INTERPRETING PRE-ELECTION POLLS: A CHECKLIST

- Who conducted the poll? A reputable firm or university research team?

- Is the poll based on a representative sample of the population?

- Is the poll based on responses from registered or likely voters?

- How has the poll dealt with undecided voters?

- Is the poll focused on too narrow a phase of the campaign, and if so, does the accompanying story account for that?

- Is the sample or subsample large enough to base inferences on?

- Does the accompanying story or headline properly account for the poll's margin of error?

- In a close presidential race, does the story accompanying the poll account for the fact that certain state races will be more important in determining the Electoral College winner?

8

✛

"It's the Ratings, Stupid"
Misconceptions about Media Bias

M any Americans believe there is a bias, either liberal or conservative, in the mass media's coverage of politics. According to a recent survey, a majority (53 percent) of people "believe that news organizations are politically biased, while just 29 percent say they are careful to remove bias from their reports."[1] In another poll, 67 percent agreed with the following statement: "In dealing with political and social issues, news organizations tend to favor one side."[2] Yet another report found that "78 percent of adults agree with the assessment that there is bias in the news media,"[3] and one showed that almost two-thirds (64 percent) disagreed with the idea that "the news media try to report the news without bias."[4] Most Americans (51 percent) describe news organizations as "liberal," while a smaller segment of the public perceives the press as "conservative" (26 percent), and an even smaller group believes the press is neither liberal nor conservative (14 percent).[5] Still, in one poll, 46 percent of respondents viewed their newspaper as more liberal than they are, while 36 percent perceived their newspaper to be more conservative than they are.[6] In short, healthy percentages of Americans see ideological bias in the news.

Does the perception that news is biased match reality? More interesting for our purposes, does news coverage of campaigns favor one candidate or the other? How objective has reporting been in recent elections? In this chapter, we explore these questions. First, we briefly review the legal environment in which the press operates in the United States and the emergence of objective journalism as a professional norm, highlighting the idea that for the first one hundred years or so of the republic it was accepted that news carried with it a partisan slant. Next we examine the forms, or possible sources of bias in news coverage of campaigns, as well

113

as what researchers have found with respect to charges of partisan bias in the media. In the end we suggest that bias in the media is primarily commercial in nature, reflecting the fact that news organizations are for-profit enterprises that are forced to consider the bottom line in their campaign coverage. We then explore the forms this commercial bias takes during coverage of a presidential campaign.

FREEDOM OF THE PRESS AND ITS IMPLICATIONS FOR NEWS

The U.S. Constitution does not prohibit the press from presenting the news in a biased fashion. Quite the contrary; the First Amendment of the U.S. Constitution clearly states that "Congress shall make no law . . . abridging the freedom of speech, or of the press." Many people associate this constitutional provision with the ability to say or write whatever they wish (with the exceptions of libel and slander). However, this provision also has powerful implications for the organization of the media. In particular, if the law specifies that Congress cannot abridge press freedom, it is also saying that government cannot control the media. This obviously applies to issues of censorship, but, by extension, to ownership of media outlets as well. As the old adage goes, "He who pays the piper calls the tune." If government owned and operated the media, it could control the news we receive.

This is why the media environment in the United States is mainly characterized by private ownership. In most other constitutional democracies, there is both private and public (government) ownership of media outlets, especially broadcast (radio and television) media.[7] There are very few government-owned or government-sponsored media outlets in this country. Partial exceptions exist, but these are restricted mainly to foreign broadcast services (e.g., the Voice of America), which cannot air in the United States. So-called public broadcasting (National Public Radio and the Public Broadcasting System) are actually joint ventures funded by federal, state, and local governments, universities, private sponsors and foundations, and individual citizens.[8]

Publicly owned media outlets are, to some extent, free from the pressures of making money. Conversely, private media outlets are continually under pressure to make money. In the case of newspapers and magazines, this translates into selling copy; for television and radio, it means selling airtime to advertisers. The greater number of viewers or listeners a television or radio station or network has, the more it can charge for its advertising time. In the end, television and radio stations attempt to attract viewers, much in the same way that newspapers and magazines try to sell copy. All media outlets are thus under pressure to make money by orienting their product toward what consumers (viewers, listeners, readers) want. Commercial considerations, which are inevitable products of the First Amendment, are never far from the minds of those responsible for news production in the United States.

THE EMERGENCE OF OBJECTIVE JOURNALISM AS A PROFESSIONAL NORM

In colonial times the expectation of journalistic objectivity did not exist. The original newspapers were produced by printers, who were small businessmen. These individuals were interested in selling papers, and therefore attempted to maintain editorial neutrality in order to avoid controversy. The "news" they printed was mainly foreign news, which because of its distance from local affairs, was less controversial. This began to change as conflict with England intensified during the Revolutionary War period. Following independence from England, Federalist sympathizers controlled most newspapers, meaning that much of the news that was printed during this period was pro-government—hardly unbiased. Antigovernment opinion was further suppressed by anti-treason and sedition laws in several states, as well as the federal Sedition Act of 1789. The act expired in 1800, but most editors and printers still did not subscribe to the idea of press objectivity or neutrality.[9]

This became even more evident in the nineteenth century, when most newspapers had an identifiable partisan bias. For example, the *Albany Argus* was the newspaper of the nation's first political machine, the Albany Regency (the Democratic Party machine).[10] While the *Argus* prided itself in the accuracy of its reporting, coverage of political campaigns remained selective at best. This was true of many other newspapers during the golden age of political parties, a time when politics meant party politics, and the party machine was a powerfully influential political institution, at least at the local level.[11]

The demise of the partisan press began with improvements in printing technology, which made it possible to mass produce newspapers at a low price. New urban centers provided potential markets for these "penny papers," and as a business, many thrived, attracting major advertising dollars. By the late 1800s, owners and editors began to understand that partisan presentation of news effectively cut them off from half of their potential market. Republicans, for example, would not buy a Democrat-leaning newspaper, and vice versa. The notion of presenting the news impartially was therefore not a high-minded ideal but rather a response to commercial considerations.

As the century progressed, newspapers began to feature more local news stories in a further attempt to increase sales.[12] This helped usher in the era of yellow journalism. Somewhat similar to the contemporary era of news production, as one account explains, "stories of crime, sex, and violence captured the headlines and sold papers. . . . Joseph Pulitzer's *New York World* and William Hearst's *New York Journal* set the standards for this era of highly competitive 'yellow journalism.'"[13] Driven by sales, this focus on local stories meant that newspapers began to employ more reporters. One report suggests that by 1895 the *New York World* employed 1,200 people, scores of whom were reporters.

It was perhaps natural that as the number of reporters increased, so did the development of "journalism as an occupational culture." Reporters began frequenting the same clubs, restaurants, and taverns. The Missouri School of Journalism, the world's first, opened in 1908. Joseph Pulitzer endowed the Columbia University School of Journalism, where classes started in 1913, for the purpose of raising "journalism to the rank of a learned profession." Within a few decades other schools had begun programs as well. These schools began to inculcate in their students a "self-conscious ethic of objectivity."[14] By the 1920s, these journalists and others began to articulate this ethic as a professional norm. The American Society of Newspaper Editors, formed in 1922, adopted the "Canons of Journalism," one of which was impartiality. Other newly formed professional associations (e.g., the Newspaper Guild, formed in 1933) followed.[15]

The norm of objectivity thus emerged in part because of the commercial nature of news production. As newspaper production technology improved, supply increased and prices dropped, while at the same time demand and competition grew. Part of the increased demand included a desire on the part of readers for more local news, rather than stories about foreign affairs previously printed in London or elsewhere. The desire for local news created a need for more reporters, who, as they increased in numbers, began to see themselves as professionals with their own code of ethics. This code of ethics included the notion that journalists report their stories fully and accurately, devoid of value judgments.

Further driving a move toward impartiality was the emergence of, and reliance of newspapers on, the national wire services. Following the same commercial logic that drove local papers away from partisan presentation of the news, the Associated Press and United Press wire services understood that neutrality in reporting was necessary for them to sell stories.[16] In short, the development of news as an industry and as big business helped drive the emergence and acceptance of objectivity as a journalistic norm.

BIAS

Before proceeding any further in our discussion of bias in the news we should make two points in order to clarify the discussion. First, we should be clear about what we mean by the word *bias*. As it relates to news, bias refers to the idea that the selection and presentation of a particular story explicitly or implicitly reflects the political views of some person or persons involved in the news production process. In other words, bias in the news results in a presentation that does not adequately or completely reflect reality.

Second, when we talk about news bias, we are not talking about political commentary given by individuals on television or radio political talk shows, or essays that appear in the editorial and opinion pages of the newspapers. They are, by definition, biased, because they are the opinions (informed or otherwise) of individuals.

When we refer to bias in campaign news, we are typically referring to unequal coverage or treatment of one or the other candidate or party. The notion that election news should be impartial is based on the idea that voting should be an informed choice, and the only way for citizens to make an informed choice is to have facts, not value judgments or opinions, at their disposal. Therefore the standard that news organizations adhere to and that citizens use to evaluate them is one of objectivity.

It should be noted here that by 2008 the cable news market had segmented into distinct partisan camps, perhaps reminiscent of the nineteenth century era of the partisan press. Fox News Channel began in 1996 in response to a perceived need by conservative Americans for a counterbalance to the dominant liberal media establishment. Programming on Fox is generally acknowledged to be more conservative in nature, in spite of their claim to be "fair and balanced." MSNBC, also launched in 1996, took a sharp turn to the left in 2007, in order to capture more of a share of the cable news market. However, even these two exceptions demonstrate that profit motives drive news coverage in that both are supplying a product to a "niche" market.[17]

There are many possible sources of bias in the news. Many, for example, point to the political leanings of those responsible for news production, like editors, producers, reporters, and so on. Studies conducted in the past two decades show that newspaper reporters are more liberal than the average citizen. Similar studies (surveys of reporters) also show that reporters tend to vote Democratic.[18] Other research has demonstrated that the owners of media organizations tend to be more conservative and vote Republican.[19]

Do these tendencies manifest themselves into an ideological or partisan slant in the news? If there was bias in news coverage of presidential campaigns, what form would it take? The following list outlines several possibilities:

- One of the candidates might be the subject of more news stories than the other, resulting in a greater amount of coverage;
- Alternatively, stories about one of the candidate's campaign effort might consistently be longer or shorter than the others, also resulting in a greater amount of coverage;
- Regardless of the amount of coverage a candidate receives, one or the other candidate might consistently be cast in a more positive or negative light (for example, a focus on a scandal of some sort);
- Stories about one of the candidate's campaign effort might consistently be placed more prominently (for example, on the front page of the newspaper, or the lead story in a news broadcast) than those of the other;
- The focus of the story or stories of one of the candidates might be consistently accompanied by pictures or video casting the candidate in either a positive (cheering crowds in the background) or negative (worried or harried look on their face) light.

Can these, or any other patterns, be detected in news coverage of presidential campaigns? Is news coverage of presidential campaigns biased, or less than adequate or complete? Fortunately, there is an abundance of research informing us on this subject. Most scholars have concluded that there is no convincing evidence of media bias in either a liberal or a conservative direction. One recent and comprehensive study found no ideological or partisan bias in newspapers, and a slight, but statistically insignificant (meaning the authors question the findings) Republican bias in news magazines and Democratic bias on television.[20] In fact, some suggest that because reporters tend to be more liberal they overcompensate to some extent in their treatment of political candidates, slightly favoring Republicans.[21] Does the fact that there is no discernable ideological or partisan bias in the news mean that we always get the complete story? The answer is, decidedly not. In the next section we illustrate that the true bias in news coverage of campaigns is of a commercial nature.

COMMERCIAL BIAS IN CAMPAIGN COVERAGE

"News" is the product of a series of decisions made by owners, editors, producers, reporters, and journalists. While the masthead of the *New York Times* claims the paper presents "all the news that's fit to print," in actuality there are any number of newsworthy events that occur in a given day that go unreported or underreported. The individuals working in news organizations decide what stories are worthy of attention and how to present them. Commercial factors also balance these considerations. Editors, for instance, are more likely to choose stories that will capture the average news consumer's attention. This explains why there is so much celebrity news, or why scandal and sex are often prominently featured in the news.

The need to make a profit naturally puts pressure on news organizations to keep costs down and sales up. This manifests itself clearly in national coverage of political campaigns, which displays a distinct commercial bias.[22] Below, we discuss some of the ways that this commercial bias is evident in national news coverage of presidential campaigns.

Horse Race Coverage

Most campaign coverage falls into the category of what political scientist and media scholar Thomas Patterson labels "horse race" coverage.[23] Most stories focus on or are framed around the competitive or strategic aspect of the campaign: who is leading, who fell behind, and why. This type of coverage dominates news about the campaign from the preprimary season through Election Day.[24] According to authoritative sources, approximately two-thirds of all coverage throughout the 2008 campaign were stories focused on the horse race.[25] Conversely, substantive (issue-oriented) stories accounted for only 18 percent of the coverage on the three major television networks (ABC, CBS, and NBC) in 2004. This was down from 22 percent in 2000 and compares with an overall average of 26 percent from 1988 to 2004.[26]

The reason horse race coverage dominates campaign news is rather straightforward: it makes for a more exciting story, and all other things being equal, more exciting stories sell better. Of course, news organizations can only present a certain number of stories in any given day, and therefore, horse race coverage pushes out other types of stories, which include an examination of issues, policy positions of the candidates and parties, qualifications, and so on. This horse race coverage, as we will show, affects campaign coverage in other ways as well.

The Press as Kingmaker or Winnower

The decisions that news organizations make about the deployment of their resources and the stories that they run often have a profound impact on who will eventually win the party nomination. In part, this is because most people do not know much, if anything, about many of the aspirants for their party's nomination. This is especially true in years when there are many candidates vying for the nomination. In the year preceding the election, media organizations make decisions about which candidates they will and will not cover. These decisions translate directly into the amount of coverage a given candidate receives in print or on television. Here, the rule of thumb is that better-known candidates are more likely to be the subject of a story than their lesser-known opponents.

This is partly due to simple economics. In a crowded field of aspirants, media organizations must make decisions about how to deploy scant resources. News organizations simply cannot assign a reporter to cover every candidate and every campaign event. In 2004, the cable television network MSNBC assigned an "embedded" journalist to travel with and cover each of the nine Democratic hopefuls, but this was an exception to the rule.[27] Generally, news organizations focus primarily on candidates who are leading in early preprimary polls (those taken the year prior to the Iowa caucuses). This, of course, means that candidates who are not doing well in public opinion polls receive less attention in the news, thus making it more difficult for them to raise their public profile, attract campaign contributions, and ultimately, do well. To overstate the case somewhat, many of the hidden decisions made by news organizations about whom to cover, in effect, become self-fulfilling prophecies.[28]

The candidates leading in the polls as 2007 drew to a close included Democrats Barack Obama, Hillary Clinton, and John Edwards, and Republicans John McCain, Mitt Romney, Rudy Giuliani, and Mike Huckabee. Not surprisingly, these individuals captured most of the press attention in coverage throughout the primary season.[29] In 2003, Howard Dean, Wesley Clark, John Kerry, and Joseph Lieberman were the focus of most of the television news stories about the Democratic hopefuls. They were also, not coincidently, leading in the preprimary polls throughout the year.[30] After January 1st, the pattern of coverage shifted to account for John Edwards's increased popularity and Joseph Lieberman's decreased popularity (as well as the fact that he did not compete in Iowa).[31] Similarly, in 1999, Al Gore and George W. Bush had more than double the television news coverage than their main rivals for the nomination (Bill Bradley and John McCain, respectively) combined. Although coverage was much more even-handed as the Iowa caucuses and New Hampshire primary approached, it became even more lopsided afterward, with more than quadruple the number of stories about Gore and Bush than their opponents.[32]

Winnowing also occurs in the substance of the coverage. One analysis of articles by several leading political pundits in early 2004 suggests that Democratic candidates Carol Moseley Braun, Dennis Kucinich, and Al Sharpton were all but dismissed in analyses by these writers.[33] Few were as blunt as Ted Koppel, the host of ABC's *Nightline*, who hosted a Democratic debate in Durham, New Hampshire, on December 9, 2003. In preparation before the debate, Koppel asked staffers,

> How did Dennis Kucinich and Al Sharpton and Carol Moseley Braun get into this thing [the debate]? Nobody seems to know. Some candidates who are perceived as serious are gasping for air, and what little oxygen there is on the stage will be taken up by one-third of the people who do not have a snowball's chance in hell of winning the nomination.

During the debate Koppel asked provocative questions of each of these three candidates and, at one point, asked directly whether they would eventually "drop out" or continue their "vanity" candidacies.[34] Koppel's apparent resentment of the minor candidates and their dismissal by others is related to the fact that news organizations have limited resources with which to cover the campaign. Moreover, likely losers usually do not make for good stories.

The amount and substance of news coverage toward presumed front-runners has the effect of forcing lesser-known candidates to withdraw from the race earlier than they otherwise might. While it is highly unlikely that Democrats Joe Biden, Chris Dodd, Bill Richardson, Mike Gravel, Dennis Kucinich, or Tom Vilsak, or Republicans Sam Brownback, Duncan Hunter, Ron Paul, Tom Tancredo, Fred Thompson, or Tommy Thompson would have been able to secure their party's nomination in 2008, each was a recognized candidate whose inclusion in the race added something to the democratic process. Whether intentional or not, bias in the form of noncoverage or less than favorable coverage contributed, at least slightly, to their early withdrawal, and thus detracted from the campaign.

The Expectations Game

In addition to helping winnow the field of primary candidates early by way of devoting less coverage to those who are doing poorly in the polls, the press handicaps the primaries. The expectations game actually starts long before the primaries begin, escalating during the fall of the year prior to the Iowa caucuses. Pundits regularly report on who is leading in the polls, who is raising how much money, who is endorsing which candidate, and more. Based on this, they typically anoint a front-runner who is therefore expected to win either the Iowa caucuses, the New Hampshire primary, or both. If the presumed front-runner loses either, the resulting story line is typically framed in terms of the uphill battle faced by the candidate in upcoming contests. Interestingly, however, if the front-runner wins, but does worse than expected, the story is framed in terms of a loss or setback.

In 1992, for example, George H. W. Bush, who was expected to win in New Hampshire, was declared the loser after placing first, only sixteen percentage points ahead of Pat Buchanan. This was the result of Bush falling short of expectations and Buchanan exceeding them. A similar situation occurred in that year's Democratic primary in New Hampshire when Bill Clinton finished ahead of previous front-runner Paul Tsongas. In 1996, the Republican nominee Bob Dole lost a few early and unimportant primaries, and his candidacy was declared dead. In 2000 John McCain's victory in the New Hampshire primary over favored George W. Bush propelled him to front-page news, while Al Gore defeated his Democratic rival Bill Bradley in what one source called an "uncomfortably tight race."[35] While the victories of McCain and Bradley were indeed newsworthy, few observers believed that given their financial and organizational resources they could actually secure the nomination.

In addition, because the primary season begins early, the media often pay a disproportionate amount of positive attention to the underdog, or candidate trailing in the race. For example, long after it was apparent that John McCain would secure the Republican nomination in 2008, the press paid a great deal of attention, most of it positive, to the candidacy of rival Mike Huckabee.[36] During the latter part of 2003, when Howard Dean was the front-runner for the Democratic nomination, he was the recipient of much negative press. Shortly after his loss in Iowa, however, coverage became more favorable.[37] John McCain was the media favorite throughout the 2000 Republican primary season, in part because he was trailing Bush. The reason for this focus on the underdog is simply that it makes for a more exciting and compelling story.

Focus on the Negative

Similar to its ability to anoint a winner, the press can also help drive candidates from the field with a focus on mistakes, scandals, and gaffes. This is especially true during the primary season. In 1988, Democratic candidate Senator Joseph Biden was charged with plagiarizing parts of his speeches. He withdrew from the primary race after a flurry of negative media attention. That same year the Democrat Gary Hart dropped out of the race after a widely publicized sex scandal.

George H. W. Bush delivered a campaign speech in 1988 in which he mistakenly referred to September 7 as the anniversary of the attack on Pearl Harbor (the actual date is December 7). His audience caught the mistake, and based on their reaction, he quickly corrected himself. While the audience seemed to pay no further attention to the incident, all three television networks featured a story about it that evening. Their coverage was less than flattering. Dan Rather of *CBS News*, for example, told viewers that "Bush's talk to audiences in Louisville was overshadowed by a strange happening."[38]

In addition to simple gaffes, the media often focus on more salacious stories. An inordinate amount of coverage in 1992 centered on charges that Bill Clinton had been unfaithful to his wife, had experimented with marijuana, was a draft dodger, and had burned an American flag while a student in England.[39] Of course Clinton was able to overcome this focus on the negative and secure the Democratic nomination. This negative focus on simple mistakes, scandals, and so forth, is part of a pattern in American journalism referred to by Larry Sabato as "attack journalism." Sabato uses the metaphor of a "feeding frenzy" to describe how the press is drawn to, highlights, and repeats negative news from the campaign trail.[40]

Often the focus on the negative is not scandal-related, but simply mistakes made on the campaign trail. In 2000, for example, days of coverage were devoted to an alleged subliminal message ("rats") found in a George W. Bush campaign ad or the fact that Bush, thinking his microphone was off, referred to long-time reporter Adam Clymer as a "major league a**hole." In 2004, media organizations ran numerous stories about John Kerry's testimony to the Senate after his service in Vietnam, whether President Bush had lied about his National Guard service, the fact that Kerry mentioned Vice President Dick Cheney's gay daughter Lynn during the final presidential debate, and more. Similarly, in 2008, an inordinate amount of attention was paid to the fact that Obama stopped wearing his American flag lapel pin or to a comment Michelle Obama made about her husband's candidacy being the first time as an adult she was proud of her country.[41]

According to one study, in 1968 there was only one instance where a television network newscast took notice of a "minor incident unrelated to the content of the campaign."[42] The reason for the change is best summarized by the "orchestra pit" theory of politics coined by former Republican media consultant and now-president of Fox News Channel, Roger Ailes. As Ailes explained, "If you have two guys on stage and one says, 'I have a solution to the Middle East problem,' and the other guy falls into the orchestra pit, who do you think is going to be on the evening news?"[43]

Pack Journalism

Exacerbating the commercial patterns of campaign coverage noted above is a phenomenon known by many as "pack journalism." A term originally coined by Timothy Crouse in his 1973 account of the Nixon campaign,[44] it refers to the fact that much of what appears in the news media is remarkably homogenous. Crouse argued this was because reporters who spend a great deal of time together (on the campaign trail) end up with similar ideas, but the homogeneity of news coverage has other sources as well. For example, the competitive pressure of knowing another network or newspaper is running a particular story exerts pressure on producers and editors to do the same.[45]

The pressure to meet deadlines also contributes to uniformity in the news, as reporters have less time to explore a story. Smaller media organizations tend to take their cues from more prestigious outlets (*New York Times*, *Washington Post*) and, in many cases, subscribe to the same wire service stories (Associated Press, Reuters). The end result is uniformity in campaign coverage. If the aforementioned commercial biases were not operative, this might not be problematic. However, pack journalism only multiplies these biases as each story repeats itself.

Other Commercial Biases

There are several other patterns evident in the news coverage of presidential primaries that reflect a commercial bias in the media. One is a focus on attractive personalities. In particular, there is a tendency for the media to give attractive personalities more positive press, especially during the primary season. This particular bias was apparent in 2004. The highly telegenic and upbeat John Edwards received the best press of any major candidate since 1988. A full 96 percent of the coverage of Edwards by the three major television networks (ABC, CBS, and NBC) from January 1 through March 1, 2004, was positive.[46] Barack Obama probably benefited from this focus on attractive personalities in 2008 as well (more on this below).

Another pattern, evident during both the primary and general election season, is an anti-incumbency bias. This is because sitting presidents (or vice presidents, in the case of George H. W. Bush in 1988 or Al Gore in 2000) are not fresh "news." Challengers add something new to the race, thus making it more attractive to news consumers. While Bill Clinton received more favorable coverage than challenger Bob Dole in 1996, virtually all incumbents since Jimmy Carter in 1980 have been the recipients of negative press during their reelection campaign. This also holds true for the incumbent vice presidents George H. W. Bush in 1988 and Al Gore in 2000. In 2004, coverage of the incumbent George W. Bush on the three broadcast networks from September through November was only 37 percent positive, as compared with John Kerry's 59 percent. In addition, Bush was the target of almost twice as many jokes on late night television as was Kerry.[47]

CONCLUSION

Criticizing the media has become something of a national pastime. However, in a media environment dominated by private ownership, news organizations must attract viewers or readers. This makes commercial bias inevitable. Of course, this is a welcome trade-off to government ownership of the media, which is anathema to the First Amendment and to a free and independent press.

By way of a postscript, it should be mentioned that there is some consensus and considerable evidence to suggest that in 2008, Barack Obama was the clear favorite of news organizations and that this favoritism was reflected in biased reporting. Obama, for example, was the recipient of positive press in 75 percent of the stories about his candidacy throughout the primary season, while others saw their coverage evenly matched. During the fall campaign season, he received 68 percent more coverage than McCain, and the ratio of positive to negative coverage was 2:1, while McCain's was 2:1 negative.[48] While we will not seek to justify this, we will note again that research suggests this is the exception rather than the rule.

However, because of the need to attract viewers, attack journalism has become a norm in newsrooms. The sharp and sometimes unfair criticisms of political candidates frequently bring about charges of ideological bias in the media. Yet despite a good deal of research on the subject, there is no clear consensus to support those charges. Generally speaking, campaign coverage during a presidential election campaign is fairly objective in terms of its partisan or ideological orientation. Instead, the pressure for profit, rather than some broad left-wing or right-wing conspiracy, is what predominantly shapes media coverage of American elections and campaigns.

FOR MORE READING

Bennett, Stephen Earl, et. al. "Video Malaise Revisited: Public Trust in the Media and Government." *Harvard International Journal of Press/Politics* 4, no. 4 (1999): 8–23.

Bennett, W. Lance. *News: The Politics of Illusion*, 7th ed. New York: Longman, 2007.

Fallows, James. *Breaking the News*. New York: Vintage, 1996.

Graber, Doris. *Mass Media and American Politics*, 7th ed. Washington, D.C.: CQ Press, 2006.

Jamieson, Kathleen Hall, and Paul T. Waldman. *The Press Effect: Politicians, Journalists, and the Stories That Shape the Political World*. New York: Oxford University Press, 2002.

Patterson, Thomas E. *Out of Order*. New York: Vintage Books, 1994.

licans, who rely on volunteers, housewives, small business owners, and retirees,[46] mounted a sophisticated, and largely successful, effort to increase turnout in 1984, contributing to Reagan's victory.[47]

In 2000, both parties engaged in intensive turnout efforts in battleground states. The Democratic Party had an estimated forty thousand volunteers making personal contacts with voters, in addition to sending an estimated fifty million pieces of mail. Several key interest groups aided this effort. For example, the National Association for the Advancement of Colored People (NAACP) actively raised voter awareness among African Americans in Florida, whose turnout in 2000 was almost double what it was in 1996. Their campaign included recorded telephone messages from President Clinton and African American leaders urging people to vote, as well as reminders from the ministers of black churches of the importance of voting. Republicans were active as well. In the last week of the campaign they made approximately eighty-five million telephone calls and sent over 110 million pieces of mail. During the final two weeks, they distributed roughly sixteen million pieces of campaign literature to people's doors, 1.2 million yard signs, and over one million bumper stickers. The National Rifle Association, pro-life organizations, and other groups helped in this effort.[48]

Still, according to Bush's main strategist Karl Rove, some four million conservative voters stayed home in 2000. Rove subsequently built a GOTV operation designed to increase turnout in 2004. The effort focused on districts "where Republican candidates underperformed against the Democratic profile of the district."[49] The effort started with the purchase of commercial databases to pinpoint voters based on, among other things, shopping habits and magazine subscriptions. Gun owners, for example, were targets, as were subscribers to magazines like *Christianity Today*.[50] Republicans tested the operation in the 2002 congressional elections and increased turnout over 1998 by five million voters (as opposed to only two million for Democrats).[51] The commercial databases allowed the campaign to target appeals to members of thirty-two different subgroups in 2004.[52]

Rove also focused on increasing registration.[53] To mobilize young adults Republicans dispatched a fifty-six-foot, eighteen-wheeled mobile voter registration center named Reggie the Registration Rig to various youth-oriented events such as MTV's "Total Request Live."[54] The Bush team registered approximately 3.4 million voters who had recently moved, also focusing on roughly seven million identified Republicans who did not consistently vote and another ten million unaffiliated voters.[55] In all, the campaign allocated approximately 125 million dollars for voter mobilization, more than three times the amount spent in 2000, and other groups (e.g., Progress for America Voter Fund,[56] various churches[57]) assisted in the effort as well.

As important as the more traditional registration efforts was the aggressive and innovative use of new technologies the Bush campaign made in 2004, using the Internet to build networks of people who canvassed neighborhoods and built other networks.[58] This "one-on-one politics" effort was a throwback to an earlier era, with a modern twist. On the Bush web site individuals could type in their zip code and receive directions to their polling places, a list of five people in their immediate area, and directions to their homes. One person would volunteer to recruit a few people, each of whom in turn recruited several more, resulting in a network of volunteers connected by e-mail to the national campaign organization. This resulted in approximately 1.4 million volunteers in key battleground states.[59] Daily messages and communications from national team leaders encouraged these local leaders and kept them informed.[60] The web site also provided links to local talk radio, boilerplate letters to the editor, and other campaign materials.

Taken together, the Bush campaign reported they made as many as eighteen million attempts to contact voters in battleground states in the last four days of the campaign.[61] Democrats were active as well. The Kerry campaign reportedly spent sixty million dollars in voter mobilization efforts, more than twice the amount spent by Democrats in 2000. In addition, the American Federation of Labor and Congress of Industrial Organizations (AFL-CIO) spent forty-five million dollars in sixteen battleground states and America Coming Together employed 2,500 people to register and contact new voters. They claim to have alone made approximately sixteen million telephone calls in the last three weeks of the campaign, sent twenty-three million pieces of mail, and delivered eleven million flyers.

Although Barack Obama had an enormous amount of personal appeal he also understood that the presidency is not won by image, but on the ground. From the perspective of campaign mechanics the Obama effort was unprecedented in organization, execution, and scope. Although based on the model Rove employed in 2004, it went, according to one account, "well beyond even what Rove built. . . . [using] its record-breaking fundraising to open more than 700 offices in more than a dozen battleground states, pay several thousand organizers, and manage tens of thousands of volunteers."[62] In a summer 2008 editorial, Rove himself called Obama's ground game "brilliant."[63]

Like the Bush campaign, Obama also harnessed the Internet to recruit and organize an enormous army of volunteers. His advantage over McCain in this regard was due to the fact that he had four times as many supporters than McCain on social networking sites like MySpace and

Facebook.[64] In any case, Internet mobilization translated into a systematic effort on the ground. For example, Ohio was broken down into 1,231 "neighborhoods" which contained 8–10 precincts, and importantly, also included rural areas that Kerry ignored in 2004. He gave neighborhood team leaders a great deal of latitude in organizing their neighborhood networks as they saw fit, also encouraging them to spend the summer recruiting more volunteers rather than immediately start voter contact.[65] In fact, the campaign reported that they had as many as six million volunteers by Election Day, which if true, is a staggering number considering that only 130 million people voted.[66]

Obama was the first candidate in recent history to outline a fifty-state strategy. He was the first top-tier Democratic candidate, for example, to visit Idaho during the primaries.[67] The organization he built in forty-eight states in order to win the Democratic nomination was already in place and expanded on for the fall campaign. The campaign had paid staffers in every state in the union, and the campaign targeted twenty-two critical states for "large-scale operations." The campaign spent $4.3 million on rent and utilities for field offices in the month of August alone.[68] For many campaigns in years past, this would have been a respectable amount of money spent on television advertising. As one source noted, Obama employed "the largest full-time paid [campaign] staff in presidential history . . . well over twice the size of the Bush reelection campaign staff in 2004 and nearly three times the size of McCain's." By the end of May the amount of money Obama paid in staff salary was triple that of McCain.[69] One report further suggests that the Obama campaign contacted more voters than McCain nationally, as well as in sixteen of seventeen critical battleground states.[70]

CONCLUSION

Packaging, marketing, selling, or otherwise crafting and propagating presidential candidate images are not new to the television era. It is an old practice in presidential campaigns. What has changed with the rise of television are the tools with which a new breed of highly specialized election people, or campaign managers, can craft and sell these images to the public, using highly specialized election people, or campaign managers. This has most assuredly made image making in the television era more sophisticated, but this is a far cry from implying or intimating, by way of metaphor or otherwise, that the practice is new.

In addition, while image building has its importance, it should not detract from the fact that political campaigns are largely fought on the ground. In short, all of the slick advertisements designed to persuade voters are pointless if no one votes. This is not to suggest that image is irrelevant. Certainly in a close election, such Bush-Gore in 2000, every vote counts, and even the smallest details could potentially mean the difference between victory or defeat for a candidate, as the literature on campaign effects suggests.[71] Nevertheless, it is important to remember that behind every campaign are volunteers, workers, and other individuals who carry their message to others and remind people of the importance of their vote. In recent election cycles, turnout has been a prime determinant of victory. The Bush 2004 and Obama 2008 campaigns made innovative and aggressive use of information technology to mobilize supporters. This resulted in a national network of committed supporters who encouraged, cajoled, and otherwise persuaded others to register and vote for their candidate. The sales job was personal—one on one—and, in both cases, effective.

FOR MORE READING

Baumgartner, Jody. *Modern Presidential Electioneering: An Organizational and Comparative Approach.* Westport, Conn.: Praeger, 2000.

Dinkin, Robert J. *Campaigning in America: A History of Election Practices.* New York: Greenwood, 1989.

Melder, Keith. *Hail to the Candidate: Presidential Campaigns from Banners to Broadcasts.* Washington, D.C.: Smithsonian Institution Press, 1992.

Polsby, Nelson W., and Aaron Wildavsky. *Presidential Elections: Strategies and Structures of American Politics*, 11th ed. Lanham, Md.: Rowman & Littlefield, 2004.

Wayne, Stephen J. *The Road to the White House, 2004: The Politics of Presidential Elections.* Belmont, Calif.: Wadsworth, 2004.

11

✛

The Illusion of Competitive Congressional Elections

> If a group of planners sat down and tried to design a pair of assembl-
> ies with the goal of serving members' reelection needs year in and
> year out, they would be hard pressed to improve on what exists [in
> the U.S. Congress].
>
> —David R. Mayhew[1]

D emocratic theory specifies that in a democracy, citizens elect most of
their leaders in free, fair, and regular elections.[2] The notion that
these elections should be competitive is almost self-evident. There would
be little reason to hold an election if the outcome was a foregone conclu-
sion. Interestingly, and perhaps not surprisingly, most Americans believe
that congressional elections are competitive. According to a poll conducted prior to the 2006 mid-term elections, more than 71 percent of those
who had an opinion on the question anticipated a "close" contest in their
district for the U.S. House.[3]

However, a significantly smaller percentage of congressional races
actually are competitive. This chapter examines this lack of electoral competitiveness in congressional elections. We begin by showing that congressional elections have become less competitive in recent years,
especially elections to the House of Representatives. In particular, we
illustrate that incumbents rarely lose in their bids for reelection. As Ronald Reagan once quipped, there was more turnover in the former Soviet
Union's presidium than in the U.S. Congress.[4] In addition to winning,
incumbents are doing so by greater margins.

In the following section we examine the advantages incumbents have
in their bids for reelection. First, there are various institutional factors

associated with the job that give them an advantage. These include an organizational base for their campaign in the form of offices and staffers, a greater ability to easily communicate with voters and potential voters, as well as being in a position to solve problems constituents might be having with the federal bureaucracy. In addition, certain legislative norms in Congress itself help members enhance their reputations, and they have greater access to interest groups and political action committees (PACs) to help finance their campaigns. This greater ability to raise funds contributes to a "scare-off" effect, which in turn helps depress the entrance of adequately funded quality challengers. Finally, recent trends in congressional redistricting, greater name recognition, and voter loyalty advantage incumbents as well.

In the final section of the chapter we shift gears, discussing how incumbents can lose. We focus on the fact that the "scare-off" effect does not always work, on how presidential politics affect congressional elections, and on the occasional effect of "national tides" on what are essentially local congressional elections. We conclude that while American elections satisfy most of the conditions for a democracy, the lack of competitiveness in congressional elections poses some problems for a healthy democratic system.

BACKGROUND

For many years Congress was not considered a career. Until the 1900s it was quite common for a member of Congress, especially in the House, to serve only one or two terms (senators were not directly elected until after the ratification of the Seventeenth Amendment in 1913). There were a relatively high number of incumbents who did not seek reelection each election cycle. There are typically three general explanations given for this.

First, in earlier times, the notion of a "career" in Congress was not desirable to most ambitious professionals. Mediocre salaries, hot and humid summers in Washington, D.C., long stretches of time away from home, and the rather limited responsibilities of the federal government all combined to make the job of a U.S. Congressman less attractive than it is today. Second, even those who wished to stay in Washington for multiple terms were hard pressed to do so. Most congressional elections were highly contested, close races. Third, many members were prevented from running for more than one or two terms. In many states, especially nonsouthern states, party organizations had informal term limits that prevented members from seeking the nomination more than one or two times (during this time, political parties controlled the nomination process).[5]

However, as the century progressed, the percentage of House incum-

Table 11.1   House incumbents running for reelection and retirement rates, by decade (1850–1910)

Decade	Number Running for Reelection	Percentage Retiring
1850s	60	27.1
1870s	64	22.8
1880s	66	20.0
1890s	73	17.3
1900s	80	11.2

Sources: Samuel Kernell, "Toward Understanding 19th Century Congressional Careers: Ambition, Competition, and Rotation," *American Journal of Political Science* 21 (1977): p. 684, Table 2, and John B. Gilmour and Paul Rothstein, "A Dynamic Model of Loss, Retirement, and Tenure in the U.S. House of Representatives" (*The Journal of Politics*, 58:54–68, 1996), p. 57, Table 1.

Note: Data for the 1860s are not included because southern states did not hold elections to Congress during the Civil War years.

bents running for reelection increased, and the percentage of those retiring—voluntarily or otherwise—decreased. Table 11.1 shows that over time, considerably more House incumbents ran for reelection and a much smaller percentage opted to retire. Another way to look at this would be to track the number of first-term members (freshmen) in the House or the average number of terms served by House members over time.[6] As seen in table 11.2, the percentage of freshmen in the House dropped more than thirty percentage points (from 51.3 to 20.4), and the average number of terms that members served more than doubled (from 1.88 to 4.34) in the century after 1850. Together, tables 11.1 and 11.2 display a pattern of steadily increasing tenure in the House from the mid-1800s forward.

The pattern of increased numbers of incumbents running for and winning elections accelerated in the post–World War II era (see table 11.3). Since 1946, an average of 91.4 percent of House incumbents have sought

Table 11.2   Percentage of first-term members and average tenure, House of Representatives, by decade (1851–1949)

Decade	Percentage First-term Members	Average Number Terms
1850s	51.3	1.88
1870s	49.1	2.09
1880s	39.0	2.47
1890s	39.7	2.54
1900s	23.8	3.43
1910s	26.2	3.55
1920s	19.6	3.99
1930s	25.6	3.92
1940s	20.4	4.34

Source: Nelson W. Polsby, "The Institutionalization of the U.S. House of Representatives," *The American Political Science Review* 62 (1968): 9, 146, Tables 1 and 2.

Table 11.3 Reelection rates for House incumbents, 1946–2008

Year	Number of incumbents seeking reelection (%)	Sought reelection, defeated in primary (%)	Won primary, defeated in general election (%)	Total percentage reelected
1946	398 (91.5)	18 (4.5)	52 (13.7)	82
1948	400 (92.0)	15 (3.8)	68 (17.7)	79
1950	400 (92.0)	6 (1.5)	32 (8.1)	91
1952	389 (89.4)	9 (2.3)	26 (6.8)	91
1954	407 (93.6)	6 (1.5)	22 (5.5)	93
1956	411 (94.5)	6 (1.5)	22 (5.5)	93
1958	396 (91.0)	3 (0.8)	37 (9.4)	90
1960	405 (93.1)	5 (1.2)	25 (6.3)	93
1962	402 (92.4)	12 (3.0)	22 (5.6)	92
1964	397 (91.3)	8 (2.0)	45 (11.6)	87
1966	411 (94.5)	8 (1.9)	41 (10.2)	88
1968	409 (94.0)	4 (1.0)	9 (2.2)	97
1970	401 (92.2)	10 (2.5)	12 (3.1)	95
1972	390 (89.7)	12 (3.1)	13 (3.4)	94
1974	391 (89.9)	8 (2.0)	40 (10.4)	88
1976	384 (88.3)	3 (0.8)	13 (3.4)	96
1978	382 (87.8)	5 (1.3)	19 (5.0)	94
1980	398 (91.5)	6 (1.5)	31 (7.9)	91
1982	393 (90.3)	10 (2.5)	29 (7.6)	90
1984	409 (94.0)	3 (0.7)	16 (3.9)	95
1986	393 (90.3)	2 (0.5)	6 (1.5)	98
1988	408 (93.8)	1 (0.2)	6 (1.5)	98
1990	406 (93.3)	1 (0.2)	15 (3.7)	96
1992	368 (84.6)	19 (5.2)	24 (6.9)	88
1994	387 (89.0)	4 (1.0)	34 (8.9)	90
1996	384 (88.3)	2 (0.5)	21 (5.5)	94
1998	402 (92.4)	1 (0.2)	6 (1.5)	98
2000	403 (92.6)	3 (0.7)	6 (1.5)	98
2002	398 (91.5)	8 (2.0)	8 (2.1)	96
2004	402 (92.4)	3 (0.7)	7 (1.8)	98
2006	401 (92.2)	3 (0.7)	26 (6.5)	95
2008	399 (91.7)	5 (1.3)	22 (5.5)	95

Sources: Gary C. Jacobson, *The Politics of Congressional Elections*, 6th ed. (New York: Longman, 2004), 24, table 3.1. Data for 2004 from Michael Barone and Richard E. Cohen, *The Almanac of American Politics: 2006* (Washington, D.C.: National Journal Group, 2006). Data for 1982, 1992, 2002, and 2004 include races pitting one incumbent against another. Data for 2006 from Gary C. Jacobson, "Referendum: The 2006 Midterm Congressional Elections," *Political Science Quarterly* 122 (2007): 1-24, table 1. Data for 2008 from Gary C. Jacobson, "The 2008 Presidential and Congressional Elections: Anti-Bush Referendum and Prospects for the Democratic Majority," *Political Science Quarterly* 124 (2009): 1–30, table 1. Primary data from Center for Responsive Politics, 2009, www.opensecrets.org/bigpicture/casualties.php?cycle=2008.

reelection per election cycle, and the percentage of those seeking reelection has dipped below 87 percent only once. This occurred in 1992, in the aftermath of a major check-writing scandal, when only 84.6 percent of House incumbents sought reelection. During this period, very few of those seeking reelection were defeated in either the primary or general elections. An average of 1.7 percent of incumbents per election cycle did not win their party's primary, and the average number defeated in the general election was just 6 percent.

Most incumbents who survive their primaries win in the general election. In only six elections since World War II has the percentage of incumbents winning reelection fallen below 90 percent, and in the past four decades, the number has not fallen below 88 percent. Ninety-eight percent of incumbents seeking reelection won their races in 1998 and 2000; only six were *not* reelected. Even in 1974, a bad year for Republicans tainted with the scandal of Watergate, a full 77 percent of the Republicans seeking reelection were returned to office.[7] From 1982 through 2002, an average of 15.4 percent of incumbents faced no major-party opposition in the general election (see table 11.4). In 1998, almost one in four incumbents (23.4 percent) had no major-party opposition. Races like these are clearly uncompetitive.

While the House returns a very high percentage of incumbents, the Senate is slightly more competitive. In the post–World War II era, 82.7 percent

Table 11.4   House incumbents with no major-party opposition in general election, 1982–2008

Year	Running unopposed, number (%)
1982	49 (12.5)
1984	63 (15.4)
1986	71 (18.1)
1988	81 (19.9)
1990	76 (18.7)
1992	25 (6.8)
1994	54 (14.0)
1996	20 (5.2)
1998	94 (23.4)
2000	63 (15.6)
2002	78 (19.6)
2004	34 (7.8)
2006	34 (8.4)
2008	36 (9.0)

Sources: Paul S. Herrnson, *Congressional Elections: Campaigning at Home and in Washington*, 4th ed. (Washington, D.C.: CQ Press, 2003), 30, table 1.3. 2006 and 2008 data from Gary C. Jacobson, *Political Science Quarterly* 122 and 124, 2, table 1.

Table 11.5 Reelection rates for Senate incumbents, 1946–2008

Year	Number of races	Sought reelection (%)	Sought reelection, defeated in primary (%)	Won primary, defeated in general election (%)	Total percentage reelected
1946	37	30 (81.1)	6 (20.0)	7 (29.2)	57
1948	33	25 (75.8)	2 (8.0)	8 (34.8)	60
1950	36	32 (88.9)	5 (15.6)	5 (18.5)	69
1952	35	31 (88.6)	2 (6.5)	9 (31.0)	65
1954	38	32 (84.2)	2 (6.3)	6 (20.0)	75
1956	35	29 (82.9)	0 –	4 (13.8)	86
1958	36	28 (77.8)	0 –	10 (35.7)	64
1960	35	29 (82.9)	0 –	1 (3.4)	97
1962	39	35 (89.7)	1 (2.9)	5 (14.7)	83
1964	35	33 (94.3)	1 (3.0)	4 (12.5)	85
1966	35	32 (91.4)	3 (9.4)	1 (3.4)	88
1968	34	28 (82.4)	4 (14.3)	4 (16.7)	71
1970	35	31 (88.6)	1 (3.2)	6 (20.0)	77
1972	34	27 (79.4)	2 (7.4)	5 (20.0)	74
1974	34	27 (79.4)	2 (7.4)	2 (8.0)	85
1976	33	25 (75.8)	0 –	9 (36.0)	64
1978	35	25 (71.4)	3 (12.0)	7 (31.8)	60
1980	34	29 (85.3)	4 (13.8)	9 (36.0)	55

Table 11.5 (Continued)

Year	Number of races	Sought reelection (%)	Sought reelection, defeated in primary (%)	Won primary, defeated in general election (%)	Total percentage reelected
1982	33	30 (90.9)	0 —	2 (6.7)	93
1984	33	29 (87.9)	0 —	3 (10.3)	90
1986	34	28 (82.4)	0 —	7 (25.0)	75
1988	33	27 (81.8)	0 —	4 (14.8)	85
1990	35	32 (91.4)	0 —	1 (3.1)	97
1992	36	28 (77.8)	1 (3.6)	4 (14.8)	82
1994	35	26 (74.3)	0 —	2 (7.7)	92
1996	34	21 (61.8)	1 (4.8)	1 (5.0)	90
1998	34	29 (85.3)	0 —	3 (10.3)	90
2000	34	29 (85.3)	0 —	6 (20.7)	79
2002	34	27 (79.4)	1 (3.7)	3 (11.5)	85
2004	34	26 (76.5)	0 —	1 (3.8)	96
2006	34	29 (85.3)	2 (6.9)	7 (24.1)	79
2008	35	30 (85.7)	1 (3.3)	7 (23.3)	83

Sources: Gary C. Jacobson, *The Politics of Congressional Elections*, 6th ed. (New York: Longman, 2004), 24, table 3.1. 2004 data from "US Senate/Complete Results," CNN, November 2004, www.cnn.com/ELECTION/2004/pages/results/senate. Data for 2006 from Gary C. Jacobson, "Referendum: The 2006 Midterm Congressional Elections," *Political Science Quarterly* 122 (2007): 1–24, table 1. Data for 2008 from Gary C. Jacobson, "The 2008 Presidential and Congressional Elections: Anti-Bush Referendum and Prospects for the Democratic Majority," *Political Science Quarterly* 124 (2009): 1–30, table 1. Primary data from Center for Responsive Politics, 2009, www.opensecrets.org/bigpicture/casualties.php?cycle = 2008.

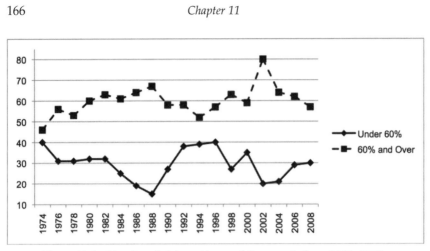

Figure 11.1   Margins of victory, House of Representatives, 1974–2008.

Source: Data from Roger H. Davidson and Walter J. Oleszek, *Congress and Its Members,*
12th ed. (Washington, D.C.: CQ Press, 2010), 143.

of Senate incumbents sought reelection (see table 11.5). Approximately one in twenty (4.8 percent) lost their primary bids, and of those who gained their party nomination and stood in the general election, less than one in five (17.7 percent) lost. Taken together, 79.1 percent of incumbent senators seeking reelection were successful. While there is more variation in reelection rates than in House races, the general trend of elections becoming less competitive is similar. For example, in the eleven election cycles from 1982 to 2002, only 3 of 306 Senate incumbents lost in their party's primary.

Congressional incumbents are not only winning, but they are doing so by larger margins. In 1974, political scientist David Mayhew noted that fewer elections in the postwar era could be classified as competitive. Mayhew dubbed this trend "the case of the vanishing marginals," a reference to the fact that close races in the House were becoming rare (Senate races tend to be more competitive, for reasons we will discuss shortly).[8]

As figure 11.1 shows, this trend has become more pronounced over time, especially in the House. The dotted line in the figure represents the percentage of House races in which the winner received more than 60 percent of the vote (traditionally defined as an uncompetitive election). It shows, for example, that the winning candidate received more than 60 percent of the vote in an astonishing 80 percent of all U.S. House elections in 2002—a high for the post-Watergate era. In addition, 18 percent of all U.S. House elections were uncontested in 2002—equaling the high mark set in 1988 during the post-Watergate era.[9]

To be fair, it is worth noting that open-seat elections to Congress are in fact quite competitive. But, not only are more incumbents running, they are winning, and doing so by greater margins. Some scholars have attempted to quantify the value of incumbency in an election. Various measures suggest that incumbency in the House was worth between 2.1 to 3.3 percent of the vote from 1946 to 1966 and jumped to between 7 and 8.6 percent from 1968 to 2000. In the Senate, from 1914 to 1960, incumbency was worth a bit more than 2 percent of the vote and jumped to 7 percent from 1962 to 1992.[10]

Why are congressional elections so noncompetitive? There are several contributing factors, most of which revolve around the various advantages incumbents enjoy by virtue of being the current officeholder. This is the subject of the next section.

THE ELECTORAL ADVANTAGES
OF INCUMBENCY

Our discussion of the advantages of incumbency is divided into several sections. The first section deals with various institutional factors, or perks, of the office. These advantages include a large staff working for members of Congress as well as office space, computers, and so on. In addition, members of Congress employ various ways to communicate with their constituents at the taxpayer's expense. Incumbents also aggressively solve various bureaucratic problems for members of their district in hopes that these favors will be returned on Election Day. Finally, there are certain norms guiding legislative activity itself that favor incumbents, allowing them to build and present their record in a favorable light.

In addition to these institutional advantages, there are other aspects of incumbency that give incumbents an edge over challengers. One is an overwhelming edge in raising campaign funds, which can sometimes scare off quality challengers.[11] Congressional redistricting efforts have also helped incumbents in recent years. Finally, the criteria that people use to make their voting decisions favor incumbents as well. Together, these factors provide the current officeholder with an enormous edge in a reelection bid.

Office and Staff

Institutional advantages are those associated with doing the job of a congressperson. Congressional office comes with various perks, often referred to (e.g., in American government textbooks) as "in kind" advantages, some of which aid in the reelection efforts of members. One advantage is the fact that each member of Congress has a staff that also serves as the nucleus of a permanent campaign organization, and the number of these staffers has increased dramatically in the past century.

The number of employees in the House of Representatives has increased approximately sevenfold since 1930. In 1950, the House employed slightly fewer than two thousand staffers. By 1990, that number exceeded 7,500. Individually, the average member has fourteen employees (staffers) but is allowed eighteen full-time and four part-time employees.[12] Total staff growth of the Senate has been slightly less. In 1955, there were approximately one thousand staffers in the Senate and, by 1990, four thousand. However, the average is thirty-four staffers per senator, from as few as thirteen to as many as seventy-one. There are no limits to the number of staffers a senator may employ.[13] Beyond serving as an unofficial nucleus for their campaign organization, members of Congress use staffers for casework in their home districts, especially if it looks to be a tight race. The percentage of total staff working for House members in their districts nearly doubled from 1972 to 1992 (22 to 42 percent), and for senators the percentage almost tripled during the same period (from 12 to 32 percent).[14]

Members of Congress are also given allowances for "travel, communications, office rental, stationery, computer services, and mail."[15] House members average about 2.3 offices in their districts, while senators average four offices per district (state).[16] All of this comes at the expense of the taxpayer. While these staffers technically cannot be used for the campaign, the member's press secretary is especially important helping to generate favorable news about the congressperson at the local level.[17] In addition, staffers help with constituency service, which creates a favorable impression that may translate into a vote on Election Day.

Direct Communications

Members of Congress take full advantage of what is known as the "franking" privilege. This is the right of members of Congress to send letters to their constituents informing them about what is happening in Washington, at government expense. The rationale for this is straightforward. The health of a representative democracy depends in part on an informed citizenry, and central to this is knowing what our representative is doing in government. In fact, the precedent for this practice dates back to 1660 in the British House of Commons and was granted by the Continental Congress to members in 1775. Subsequently, the first U.S. Congress passed a law granting its members the privilege in 1789.[18]

One widely circulated account suggests that new members are urged to "use the frank,"[19] and by all accounts, they do so. Members of Congress send mass newsletters to all constituents as well as more narrowly tailored messages to different segments of their electorate. Often recipients are invited in these messages to send their thoughts to their member of Congress. Estimates suggest that from the mid-1960s to 1990, the volume of franked mail has at least tripled and perhaps quadrupled. Importantly, the amount of franked mail is higher during election years.[20] In 1990, Congress enacted new regulations limiting the amount of franked mail to one piece per address per state for a senator and three pieces per address per House district. Other regulations, such as prohibiting personal photographs of or references to the member and integrating franking costs into the members' office expenses were added. However, at a minimum, these communications keep the incumbent's name fresh in voters' minds and present a favorable image of him or her.

Bureaucratic Ombudsmanship: Casework in the District

It is not unusual for an ordinary citizen to need assistance from time to time navigating or circumventing the bureaucracy that makes up modern government. Citizens might contact their member of Congress for any number of reasons, which could include requests or questions about an expired passport only days before a planned trip or a tax problem with the Internal Revenue Service. Here, the member would be acting in a capacity analogous to that of an ombudsman (or ombudsperson), a government-appointed individual who looks after the rights and needs of citizens in disputes with government. Originally a Scandinavian concept, ombudsmen are found in virtually all modern bureaucracies (including some larger corporations). Members of Congress take this type of work—referred to as casework—very seriously.

Each member of Congress receives thousands of such requests each year. While it is impossible for members to handle each request personally, much of the staff work handled in district offices is devoted to resolving citizens' problems and answering requests. This is an extremely effective way to win the loyalty and votes of citizens and others. A favor done for a constituent makes it more likely that he or she will repay the kindness come election time—and perhaps even tell others. This type of interpersonal, word-of-mouth advertising is invaluable.[21]

Favorable Local Media

Incumbents have certain advantages with various media that make it easier to boost name recognition among their constituents as well as communicate and cultivate a favorable view among supporters and potential supporters. First, all members of Congress have their own web sites, which allow interested parties to learn about what they are doing in

Washington.[22] The government pays for these web sites, and members use them to publicize their achievements, downplay their shortcomings, and invite visitors to send comments and feedback.

Second, both parties in each house of Congress, as well as the chambers themselves, have state-of-the-art audiovisual studios. Members can produce short statements to the press, interviews, and other types of programming. Along with satellite link technology, this allows incumbents to feed the local media, which is always looking for story material, especially on 90- or 120-minute evening newscasts.[23] Some members are regular guests on various local programs; others have their own local programs (e.g., a call-in show). Almost all produce press releases on a fairly regular basis that local news organizations print or air unedited, presenting them as news.

The link with local media outlets is important because studies show that local news organizations are rarely as confrontational as the national press. When members are featured in a thirty-second spot answering a few questions, the questions are rarely difficult and the answers rarely challenged. This is in part because the news organizations in question (typically the electronic media) are in need of material and want to make sure they have access in the future, so they work at not offending the member. In addition, local reporters are often less well prepared for the interview or versed in national politics in general. The result is generally favorable coverage in local media, which is especially helpful for members of the House, who mainly run on local issues.[24]

Legislative Norms

In a representative democracy, an assumption exists that there is a link between what people want and what elected officials work to accomplish. Members of Congress understand this, and understand that this is what people expect. Therefore, it is not surprising that their legislative activity is geared toward working—or at least appearing to work—for the people in their district. With so many decentralized committees and subcommittees in Congress, new members have almost no trouble seeking out and receiving an assignment on a committee that deals with policy concerns important to their district. For example, if the legislator is from Washington state, he or she might seek assignment on the Merchant Marine and Fisheries Committee; if from the Midwest, on agriculture. Because the details of most policy is worked out in committees, this allows the legislator to go back to the district and claim to be doing something for the district.[25]

Another legislative norm is that a member is not required or expected to vote with his or her party if that vote will damage them electorally.

Weak party discipline allows members to protect themselves if the party's position contradicts what constituents expect. Finally, most members cooperate with other members when it comes to distributive legislation. If there is "pork" (government projects that benefit a specific locale) to be spread around, everyone gets a piece to take home to the district. Additionally, a member will support another member's bill with the expectation of reciprocity. This reciprocity is referred to as "logrolling," and allows members at the end to claim credit for passing legislation that is popular back home.

Financial Advantages

Congressional elections cost a great deal of money. One estimate suggested that in 2008 congressional elections would cost a total of approximately $2.9 billion.[26] In three of the most competitive House races in 2008, candidates alone raised an average of $10 million. In the Senate, candidates in three of the most competitive races raised an average of $34 million.[27] Unlike other incumbent advantages, financial aspects of congressional campaigns are easy to quantify, and a good deal has been written on this subject.[28] Since the 1970s, the United States has had the most transparent campaign finance system in the world.[29] This provides a detailed understanding of the financial advantage incumbents have over their challengers.

Most incumbents start their campaigns with money left over from the previous campaign. This is referred to as their "war chest." In 2002, the average returning House member had three hundred thousand dollars left in their campaign coffers after the election.[30] But even with this advantage, incumbents continue to raise enormous sums of money. They do this because reelection is never a certainty,[31] and raising large amounts of cash can scare off challengers.

Beyond having a head start in the money race, incumbents can raise money more easily than most challengers. This is especially true when soliciting funds from Washington-based PACs (see chapter 4), who are six times more likely to give to an incumbent.[32] One reason for this is that PACs know that incumbents are more likely to win, and they want to ensure future congressional access by backing the winning candidate. Incumbents also have financial backing from congressional party campaign committees (one for each party, in each chamber of Congress), as well as access to money from state party organizations. In addition, individual donors who give large sums of money are more likely to give to incumbents. The point is that most campaign dollars go to incumbents, making it difficult for challengers to raise the necessary resources to be competitive.

During the past two decades, the financial advantages of incumbency have grown tremendously. In 1990, for example, House incumbents had a four-to-one financial advantage over challengers, while in the Senate the ratio was two-to-one. By 2004, that ratio had grown to almost six-to-one in the House and almost nine-to-one in the Senate (see table 11.6 for 2008 figures).

Lack of Quality Challengers

Another reason why incumbents enjoy high reelection rates is the lack of quality challengers. A quality challenger is an individual who can mount a viable campaign and possesses a combination of characteristics that can convince voters that he or she is qualified to be their representative. These qualities include, but are not limited to, having previously held public office (either elective or otherwise), being a celebrity (show business, sports, etc.), or being a prominent local business, religious, or community leader. At minimum, a quality challenger usually enjoys some name recognition in the community (or district/state) and has enough ties to support fundraising efforts to raise the money necessary to challenge a congressional incumbent.[33] A quality challenger usually possesses some political experience as well.

Most challengers in congressional elections are amateurs, or lesser-quality candidates. They lack some, or all, of the various characteristics, background, and experience mentioned above. Importantly, experienced politicians or prominent leaders—potential quality challengers—have enough political savvy to know that the chances of beating an incumbent member of Congress are slim. Generally, open-seat races are more likely to attract quality candidates, leaving most incumbents to face off against relative amateurs. Fundraising efforts by incumbents further deter quality candidates. Raising early money, as well as being active in the district,

Table 11.6   Incumbent financial advantage in congressional elections, 2008

Type of candidate	Number of candidates	Total raised	Average raised	Ratio
House				
Incumbent	435	$590,069,349	$1,356,481	4.0:1
Challenger	652	$218,835,955	$335,638	
Senate				
Incumbent	36	$314,645,503	$8,740,153	7.6:1
Challenger	104	$119,826,912	$1,152,182	

Source: "The Big Picture, 2008 Cycle: Incumbent Advantage," *Center for Responsive Politics*, at www.opensecrets.org/bigpicture/incumbs.asp?cycle=2008.

goes a long way toward deterring potential challengers. This is the so-called "scare-off" effect,[34] and while it is clear that anything can happen in a campaign, most challengers pose little threat to incumbents.[35]

Congressional Redistricting

House district boundaries in almost every state are redrawn every ten years following the census. This ensures that districts within each state contain approximately equal numbers of people. Few voters know about or pay much attention to this process.[36] Redistricting is a very contentious exercise because it almost always gives an advantage to a certain party or group.

To illustrate how districting could advantage one group over others, imagine a state with twelve equal geographic divisions (for example, counties), with each division containing equal numbers of straight partisan voters. In other words, all voters in each geographic division vote the party line in every election. From this state, four congressional districts, each containing roughly equal numbers of voters and three of these geographic divisions, is drawn. Box 11.1 shows this, as well as which geographic divisions belong to which party (D = Democrat, R = Republican) in the left-most column, under "Partisan Distribution." In "Districting Plan #1," Democrats and Republicans will each win in two districts. However, if district lines are drawn slightly differently, as seen in "Districting Plan #2," Democrats win in only one district, while Republicans win in three.[37]

Drawing district lines to maximize the electoral advantage of a group, party, or faction is known as "gerrymandering." The term, first used in 1812, characterized the salamander-like redistricting plan drawn up by Massachusetts Governor Elbridge Gerry. Partisan gerrymandering, or redistricting that favors a specific party, enjoys a long history in the

---

BOX 11.1

EXAMPLE: PARTISAN EFFECTS OF DISTRICTING

Partisan Distribution				*Districting Plan #1*				*Districting Plan #2*			
R	R	R	R	R	R	R	R	R	R	R	R
R	R	D	D	R	R	D	D	R	R	D	D
D	D	D	D	D	D	D	D	D	D	D	D

United States. While not an exact science, since the 1990s gerrymandering has evolved into a practice of incumbent-based, or "sweetheart," gerry-mandering. This is a true bipartisan effort where district lines are drawn to ensure that there is a high concentration of each party's supporters in "their" respective districts.[38] Thus, the status quo (incumbents of each party) is protected. While some recent research suggests that the effect is minimal, many suggest that incumbent-based districts lead to a decline in the number of competitive elections, at least in the House, as more districts are "packed" on a partisan basis.[39]

Voting Behavior

To round out our discussion, we should also note something about voting behavior, or how people vote. A few aspects of voting in congressional elections are important with respect to incumbent advantages. First, the electorate usually knows the incumbent better than the challenger. Second, with more campaign funding, incumbents can advertise more, beyond the free advertising they receive from franking, local media, and so on.

In House elections from 1980 to 2002, on average, respondents were almost twice as likely to recognize the incumbent's name as opposed to the challenger's name (92 to 53 percent) and more than twice as likely to be able to recall—unprompted—the incumbent's rather than the challenger's name (46 to 17 percent). For Senate candidates, the percentages are more even, but incumbent names are recognized and recalled more than those of their challengers (97 to 77 percent recognition, 58 to 35 percent recall). While people do not always cast their votes for the better-known candidate, the converse of this is probably a fair assumption: people are less likely to vote for an unknown candidate.[40] This is especially true in midterm elections where interest is lower than in presidential election years. For example, turnout in midterm elections of the voting age population has decreased from approximately 47 to 37 percent from 1962 to 2006.[41] Generally, lower turnout benefits incumbents.

Another factor favoring incumbents is the party loyalty of voters. Ticket splitting, or casting one's vote for the presidential candidate of one party while voting for the congressional candidate of the other party, increased consistently throughout the middle part of the past century. This trend seems to have reversed itself. In 1972, 192 districts split their votes in this way. In 2000, only 86 did so. In 2004, the number fell to 59, the lowest number since World War II (it rose again to 83 in 2008).[42] In short, voters, who are packed into increasingly partisan-leaning districts are voting to support their party. But since recent redistricting efforts have generally protected incumbents, "their party" is more likely to be the party of the incumbent.

Finally, it should be noted that members of Congress pay special attention throughout their careers, and especially during the campaign, to the way in which they present themselves. Here, the landmark study of Richard Fenno is informative.[43] Fenno followed and observed a number of House members, concluding that they self-consciously adopted a style or persona that was compatible with the culture of their district. He labeled this their "home style." For example, a House member from rural Georgia would be hard pressed to win an election if he traveled the district in a three-piece Brooks Brothers suit. In a district like this, a candidate would likely present himself as a common member of the local community, hoping to establish a connection with the majority of voters. This example is a bit exaggerated, but according to Fenno's work, not by much. And it seems to pay off.

To conclude this section, we will simply restate what has become clear: incumbents have any variety of advantages in their bid to be returned to Washington. The next section briefly reviews some of the situations that might contribute to an incumbent *defeat* and offers some concluding thoughts.

CONCLUSION: CAN INCUMBENTS LOSE?

Challengers clearly face uphill battles. However, there are some factors that make it more likely that a challenger can be competitive. First, the scare-off effect does not always work.[44] Incumbents sometimes show signs of weakness or are weakened by circumstance. This can be the result of any number of factors including unfavorable redistricting, a small war chest, press criticism, or scandal. All of these can make incumbents look vulnerable, attracting quality challengers to the fray. Or, more simply, any of these factors can actually make an incumbent more vulnerable, giving challengers a better chance to win.

Second, presidential politics sometimes affect congressional elections. The two most obvious ways in which this occurs are either the "coat-tail" effects of a popular presidential candidate or the historic tendency for a president's party to lose seats in midterm elections. In the first case, an extremely popular presidential candidate can increase the popularity—and thus the chances for victory—of the congressional candidates in his party. This happened, for example, in 1980, when Ronald Reagan's popularity helped the Republicans win control of the Senate for the first time since 1954. Many Democratic candidates were helped by Obama's popularity in 2008.

Alternatively, it is also historically the case that the president's party loses seats in the midterm elections (see table 11.7). Some midterm elections bring greater losses than others, but in most, a fairly significant number of the president's party loses. Some of these losses are inevitably suffered by incumbents. In 2006, Republicans lost their majorities in both the U.S. House and Senate, in part because of their association with President George W. Bush whose popularity gradually and steadily dropped following his reelection in 2004.

The final factor is the occasional effect of what scholars refer to as "national tides" on congressional elections. Local elections generally favor incumbents. Congressional elections are primarily local affairs, more so in the House than in the Senate. However, sometimes congressional elections are influenced by national political factors, favoring one party over the other. This was the case, for example, in 1974, when an anti-Watergate sentiment swept the country, and the Democrats made large gains. In 1980, anti-Carter sentiment and a national recession helped produce a significant number of victories for Republicans. Anti-incumbent and anti-congressional feelings in 1992 (surrounding various congressional scandals and the Clarence Thomas hearings) helped 110 newcomers win election to Congress. Republicans won both houses of Congress for the first time in more than four decades in 1994, partly as the result of an anti-Congress and anti-Clinton mood prevailing in the country. In 1998, anti-impeachment sentiment helped the Democrats reverse historical

Table 11.7   Mid-term losses for presidential party

Year	President (Party)	House	Senate
1946	Franklin Roosevelt & Harry Truman (Dem.)	45	12
1950	Harry Truman (Dem.)	29	6
1954	Dwight Eisenhower (Rep.)	18	1
1958	Dwight Eisenhower (Rep.)	48	13
1962	John Kennedy (Dem.)	4	(3)
1966	Lyndon Johnson (Dem.)	47	4
1970	Richard Nixon (Rep.)	12	(2)
1974	Richard Nixon & Gerald Ford (Rep.)	48	5
1978	Jimmy Carter (Dem.)	15	3
1982	Ronald Reagan (Rep.)	26	(1)
1986	Ronald Reagan (Rep.)	5	8
1990	Gorge H. W. Bush (Rep.)	8	1
1994	Bill Clinton (Dem.)	52	8
2006	Gorge W. Bush (Rep.)	30	6

Source: Jacobson, *The Politics of Congressional Elections*, 104, Table 4-2.

Note: Numbers in parentheses were gains for the presidential party.

trends and gain seats, and in 2002, national security concerns helped Republicans do the same. In all of these cases, a prevailing mood in the country overcame local concerns to help oust a significant number of incumbents.

In short, incumbents rarely lose, although challengers can sometimes capitalize on national conditions that might be in their favor (as in 1994 and 2006). The word "campaign" was originally used to refer to military operations and adopted for political use later. To use this metaphor, challengers face an overwhelming disadvantage given that their opponents have been gearing up for months, are already on the field, and have an arsenal in place.

Certainly, we are not the first observers to note that congressional elections have become less competitive over the course of the last century.[45] However, many Americans do not realize or appreciate how uncompetitive congressional elections have become. While the high rate of incumbent victories might, to some degree, equate to voter satisfaction, it more likely reflects the numerous advantages that incumbents have. This has undoubtedly increased the number of noncompetitive congressional contests, which, as noted earlier, has democratic consequences.

FOR MORE READING

Fenno, Richard F., Jr. *Home Style: House Members in Their Districts*. New York: Longman, 2003.

Herrnson, Paul S. *Congressional Elections: Campaigning at Home and in Washington*, 4th ed. Washington, D.C.: CQ Press, 2003.

Jacobson, Gary C. *The Politics of Congressional Elections*, 6th ed. New York: Longman, 2004.

Mayhew, David R. *Congress: The Electoral Connection*. New Haven, Conn.: Yale University, 1974.

12

✛

"Kingmaker" and Battleground States and the Myth of National Presidential Elections

The idea that presidential candidates wage a national campaign to win the presidency is likely shared by most citizens. In many respects the race for the White House is a national campaign. Presidential candidates and their parties fund, build, and mobilize campaign organizations in literally hundreds of locations throughout the country. Candidates and their surrogates (wives, children, parents, and more) take the campaign message to countless towns, villages, and hamlets. They, their parties, and other groups craft messages designed to persuade voters and air these messages on national media. National news organizations spend enormous amounts of money gathering news about the campaign and reporting it to a national audience. Indeed, presidential campaigns seem to be as national an event as the celebration of Independence Day.

In other respects, however, presidential campaigns fall short of being truly national contests. As we will illustrate in this chapter, presidential campaigns in both the primary and general election season focus their efforts on a handful of states and relatively few voters. The chapter is divided into two main sections. The first deals with presidential nominations. After a brief history of presidential nomination systems our focus will turn to the primary system of presidential nominations. Although far more participatory than previous nomination systems, relatively few citizens vote in primaries or participate in caucuses. We then turn to a discussion of the general election season, which is geared to and reaches only a limited audience. The Electoral College system all but forces presidential campaigns to spend disproportionately greater resources on a minority of voters in only a few battleground states.

THE NOMINATION: A BRIEF HISTORY OF
PRESIDENTIAL PRIMARIES AND CAUCUSES

There have been three systems for selecting presidential nominees throughout our history, each more democratic or inclusive than the previous. The first, the legislative caucus, functioned by having legislators from each party select their presidential candidate. The second, the convention system, allowed party leaders and party regulars to select the nominee. The third and current method, the primary system, permits voters to select their party's presidential nominee.[1]

During the colonial period and immediately following ratification of the Constitution, state legislators selected their party's candidates for local and state offices. Shortly after the ratification of the Constitution, many state legislative caucuses began selecting party candidates for national offices as well. Although they were not identifiable as parties, two informal national caucuses emerged in Congress in 1796. The first, a pro-administration faction, supported the presidential candidacy of John Adams, while the second, an anti-administration faction, backed Thomas Jefferson. In 1800, the same informal caucuses supported each of these candidates again. Following the ratification of the Twelfth Amendment in 1804, congressional caucuses began to nominate tickets comprising both a presidential and a vice-presidential candidate. This system, known as "King Caucus," was used to nominate presidential candidates until 1824.

In 1824, the splintering of the dominant Democratic-Republican Party led to a contested nomination between William Crawford, Andrew Jackson, John Quincy Adams, and Henry Clay. This was the beginning of the end of King Caucus. By 1828 there was no discernable nomination system in place. This, as well as growing pressure for increased popular participation in the nomination process, led to the first national party nominating convention. In 1831, leaders of the Anti-Masonic Party met in convention in Baltimore to choose their presidential candidate. The two major parties (the Democrats and the Whigs) adopted the practice shortly thereafter, and the convention system of presidential nominations was born.

One objective of the convention system was to widen the circle of participation in the nomination process. Under this system, state party leaders, party activists, and party regulars gathered in the summer of the presidential election year in a national meeting lasting several days. The main function of the meeting was to select the party's presidential candidate. Parties used this system well into the twentieth century. But, since relatively few party leaders seemed to control conventions, the system had its detractors.

One alternative that promised greater participation was the state nominating caucus. Started in 1846 in Iowa, a presidential nominating caucus is actually a series of caucuses held to select delegates to the national convention. The first round is held at the local level at schools, public buildings, and in some cases, private homes. Winners of this first round participate in the next round, which in Iowa is at the county level, and those winners go on to the next round at the congressional district level. The final caucus is a state-level caucus. Because the evolution of state-level presidential nominating caucuses is less important to our story of nominating systems than primaries, our focus will be on primaries.

Another alternative that emerged was the party primary, where voters directly or indirectly select their party's candidates. The first primary was held in 1842 by the Democratic Party of Crawford County, Pennsylvania, as a way of mollifying party members who wanted more say within the party. The "Crawford County System," as it became known, spread to other states, including California, Virginia, Ohio, and New York, but were not as yet used to select presidential candidates.

By the start of the twentieth century parties in several states held presidential primaries. Some were non-binding presidential preference votes, while in others, convention delegates who pledged to vote for a particular presidential candidate were selected. In 1912, five more states held primaries as the result of the Republican Party nomination battle between former president Theodore Roosevelt and then-president William Howard Taft. By 1916 the number of states holding primaries peaked at twenty. For the next sixty years candidates selectively used primaries to demonstrate their popularity and electability to their party. For example, in 1944, dark-horse Republican candidate Wendell Willkie used this strategy to help secure the nomination, as did Dwight Eisenhower in 1952 and John F. Kennedy in 1960. Kennedy's decision to enter the primary in heavily Protestant West Virginia was a strategic move designed to demonstrate that he, a Catholic, could win in a Protestant state.[2] Even though party leaders were leaning toward Lyndon Johnson, Kennedy's strong showing helped him secure the nomination.

The pivotal year in the move from the convention to the primary system was 1968. By the time the Democratic convention convened in Chicago the country had experienced growing protest against the Vietnam War and the assassinations of Martin Luther King Jr. and Senator Robert Kennedy of New York. Both Kennedy and Senator Eugene McCarthy from Minnesota had entered and won several primaries that spring. Vice President Hubert Humphrey, on the other hand, had not entered a single primary, but was the favorite of party leaders, and subsequently secured the nomination. Protest erupted in the convention hall and in the streets, and Chicago police responded with violence in their attempt to control the situation. The convention, in short, went poorly.

In order to unite the party for the general election party leaders agreed to reform their nominating procedures. To this end, the McGovern-Fraser commission recommended increasing the number of primaries. This led to six more states adopting primaries for the 1972 election season, bringing the total number of states holding primaries that year to twenty-one (including most of the more populous states). This made 1972 the first year that the majority of convention delegates (roughly two-thirds) pledged to support a particular candidate were selected by primaries. This effectively took the power to nominate presidential and other candidates out of the hands of party leaders and gave it to the party electorate.

Because the objective of a party primary is to win the pledged support of delegates attending the national convention, it is now impossible to capture the presidential nomination without competing in and winning presidential primaries and caucuses in many states. Almost all of the delegates to the national conventions in both parties are selected in primaries and caucuses.

The exact number of primaries and caucuses vary from one election year to the next. This is because states are responsible for conducting elections, and the national party organizations give state parties some latitude with respect to how they select their delegations to the national convention. In 2008 there were thirty-seven primaries and fourteen caucuses.[3] From these events, the Republican Party selected approximately 2,380 delegates. Of the 4,257 delegates to the Democratic convention, about 80 percent (3,434) were selected in primaries or caucuses.[4] The remaining 823 delegates were the so-called superdelegates, typically elected officials or other party leaders who come to the convention officially uncommitted to any particular candidate.[5]

There are three types of primaries and caucuses, distinguished according to which voters are allowed to participate.[6] In a closed primary or caucus, only those registered with the party may vote. For example, only registered Republicans are allowed to vote in a closed Republican primary. An open primary or caucus is open to any registered voter, and that voter may vote for either party's (but only one party's) candidates. Semi-closed primaries allow party members and independents to participate in the party primaries. Under these rules, only registered Republicans and independents may vote in a Republican primary, while only registered Democrats and independents may vote in a Democratic primary.[7]

PRIMARIES AND REPRESENTATION

While more citizens are now involved in the nomination process under the primary system than in King Caucus or the convention system, relatively few actually participate in any meaningful way. There are three main aspects of the system that make it less than fully representative: the disproportionate influence of the Iowa caucuses and the New Hampshire primary on the outcome of the race, the primary-caucus calendar, and the small number of citizens who actually vote in the process.

The Effect of the Iowa Caucuses and the New Hampshire Primary

Since 1972 the Iowa caucuses have been the first delegate selection event of the year. New Hampshire held its first primary in 1916 and has been the first primary of the nomination season since 1920. Democratic Party rules guarantee these prime positions on the nominating calendar for both states, and the Republican Party follows suit. Together, the delegate selection events of these two states are the first tests for those aspiring to the presidency, and doing well in at least one of these states is critical. Therefore, candidates pay an extraordinary amount of attention to each.

In 1987 the major-party candidates spent an average of fifty days in Iowa and thirty-seven days in New Hampshire.[8] From mid-March 1999 through July of 1999, fourteen presidential aspirants (from both parties) devoted approximately 35 percent of their campaign time to these two states.[9] From 2001 to 2002, 10 Democratic candidates spent a combined total of sixty-five days campaigning in New Hampshire and 300 days in 2003.[10] John Kerry spent seventy-three days campaigning in Iowa from January 2003 to January 19, 2004. Howard Dean spent approximately three million dollars in television advertising in Iowa in 2003 and early 2004.

National news organizations also pay an inordinate amount of attention to these two events. One analysis of the 1980 campaign by United Press International and CBS News suggested that 14 percent of the coverage of the nomination season was devoted to the Iowa caucuses. The *New York Times* ran approximately 120 stories in 1987 and 1988 about the Iowa caucuses. An analysis of the coverage by ABC, CBS, NBC, and CNN from January 1995 through June 1996 found that the 1996 Republican New Hampshire primary received one-fourth of the total coverage during the primary season.[11]

The results of the Iowa and New Hampshire contests tend to affect subsequent contests, and thus the nomination itself. From 1972 to 2008, the winner of the sixteen contested nominations won in New Hampshire ten times and placed second six times. During that same time period, eleven of the sixteen nominees finished first or second in Iowa.[12] George McGovern (1972), Michael Dukakis (1988), George H. W. Bush (1988), and Bill Clinton (1992) placed third, and, John McCain won his party's nomination after finishing fourth in Iowa in 2008.

Doing poorly in either or both of these contests can effectively end a campaign. No candidate placing third or lower in New Hampshire since 1972 ever went on to win the nomination. In 2004, Dick Gephardt withdrew immediately after the Iowa caucuses, after finishing fourth with 11.2 percent of the vote. Joseph Lieberman, who did not enter the Iowa caucuses, finished fourth in New Hampshire with 8.6 percent of the vote, and did not win a single one of the five primaries held one week later. He withdrew immediately afterward. Rudy Giuliani's biggest mistake in 2008 was deciding not to seriously compete in either Iowa or New Hampshire's events. In fact, given the history of presidential nominations since 1976, this strategy was incomprehensible.

Given their relative weight in the overall electoral process, it is arguably undemocratic that these states have such power over the nomination. Iowa and New Hampshire combined have a total of eleven electoral votes (Iowa, seven; New Hampshire, four). New Hampshire primary voters are responsible for choosing less than 1 percent of delegates to the Democratic Party convention. The relative number of votes that determine the winners in these events is even smaller. In 1976, Democratic nominee Jimmy Carter won thirty-five thousand votes in Iowa and New Hampshire, which as one account explains is "fewer than it takes to be elected city councilman in Cincinnati."[13] Carter's margin of victory in New Hampshire over second-place finisher Morris Udall was a mere 4,663 votes. That same year, Gerald Ford, the Republican nominee, received only 1,587 more votes than Ronald Reagan. In 2000, Al Gore defeated Bill Bradley in the New Hampshire primary by 6,395 votes.[14]

The Primary-Caucus Calendar

Although New Hampshire and Iowa may have a disproportionate influence on the nomination, geographic inequities among the nominating electorate do not end there. Many primaries and caucuses are actually held after the nomination has effectively been decided. One analyst divided states according to their role in the nominating process. "Kingmakers," the states holding the earliest primaries and caucuses, have the most influence. "Confirmers" come next, both chronologically and in terms of influence. In these states, leaders solidify their positions. The final category, "rubber stamps," speaks for itself. These states are the last to hold primaries and caucuses, held after the nomination has in effect been decided.

Twenty-six states were classified as "rubber stamps" in 2000, with delegate selection events held after March 7. This number declined to eighteen in 2004, but there were an additional twelve "confirmers" that held their events on the same day (March 2). In recent election cycles voters in as many as half of the states have no say whatever in the presidential nomination process. "Rubber stamp" state voters might participate in their state's nominating event, but they have no say in who their party's nominee will be.

A second less-than-democratic aspect of the nomination calendar is the increased tendency of states to "frontload," or schedule nominating events earlier in the primary season. In 1968, New Hampshire was the only state that held its primary before the end of March, but in 1988, twenty states did so. In 2008, thirty-six held nominating events (twenty-four primaries and twelve caucuses) prior to the end of February. Twenty-four of these states held their nominating event on February 5, dubbed "Super Tuesday."

This has tended to make the nominating season shorter. For example, Robert Dole had the Republican nomination secured by March 13 of 1996. Al Gore and George W. Bush effectively secured their nominations in the third week of March by winning greater than 50 percent of the pledged delegates in 2000. In 2004, John Kerry had the Democratic nomination cinched by March 3, and John McCain had all but won the Republican nomination in 2008 by February 5.

This dynamic exacerbates the winnowing effect of Iowa and New Hampshire and results in early withdrawals by many candidates. In 1988, only Pat Robertson remained to challenge George H. W. Bush for the Republican nomination after the end of March. In 1992 three of the five Democratic contenders had withdrawn by the end of the third week of March. In 2000, John McCain and Bill Bradley, the only serious challengers remaining for their respective party's nomination, withdrew on March 9. In 2004 it was essentially a two-man race between John Kerry and John Edwards for the Democratic nomination by February. The 2008 nomination season saw a similar dynamic. By the end of January all but two Democrats (Clinton and Obama) remained in the race, from an original field of seven. From a field of six Republican candidates, only McCain and Mike Huckabee remained after Mitt Romney withdrew on February 7; Huckabee ended his campaign on March 4.

The point here is simple. Whether we focus on the fact that only some states have a meaningful say in the nomination, or that the compressed schedule forces early withdrawals, it is fair to say that the nomination schedule results in a less than meaningful choice.

The Nominating Electorate

Our final point about the representativeness of the nomination process focuses on citizens. With the exception of New Hampshire, voter turnout in the primary season is low, even in states where participation has an effect on the outcome. Because these events are held in the late winter/ early spring, relatively few people have given much thought to the presidential race. In addition, voting in a primary is more challenging than in the general election, since the general election presents a choice between two candidates from different parties. The choice in a primary is between candidates of the same party. In order to choose, voters have to take time to learn something about each one.[15] Participation in caucuses is even lower because caucus participation can take several hours, and prior to the caucus, individuals typically spend time acquainting themselves with candidates and issues.

Voter turnout in primaries actually hovers at about 15 percent of eligible voters. While this seems low, not all of these 15 percent actually influence the outcome. For example, barely four million voters who participated in the Democratic and Republican presidential primaries in 2000 were "kingmakers." Almost fourteen million were "confirmers," and nearly fourteen million more voters were "rubber stamps." Put another way, 12.9 percent of those who cast primary ballots in 2000 had a major role in affecting the Democratic and Republican contests; 43.6 percent had bit parts; and 43.5 percent had no part at all. They were little more than spectators.[16]

Only one in three general-election voters in 2000 voted in a primary or participated in a caucus, and only one in six did so in the first six weeks, when their vote actually mattered. Only one in twenty-five could be considered "kingmakers," and one in two hundred participated in the influential Iowa or New Hampshire delegate selection events.[17] In other words, very few voters, from very few states, have much of a say about who the presidential nominees will be.

In addition, citizens who vote in primaries and participate in caucuses are less representative of the general public. They are generally better educated, come from higher income brackets, are more politically knowledgeable and interested, and are slightly older than the broader electorate. Furthermore, these voters are more ideologically extreme than the average voter. Democratic primary voters tend to be more liberal than the average Democratic voter in the general election. Republican primary voters tend to be more conservative than the typical Republican voter.[18]

To summarize this section about the modern presidential nominating system, we face a conundrum. Desire for greater public participation in presidential nominations created the primary-caucus system. Even if "only" thirty million people vote in primaries or participate in caucuses, this is many more than the several thousand that previously decided presidential nominations at the national party conventions. The process is clearly more open than it was previously.

However, full and equitable participation has not been attained. The influence of two states (Iowa and New Hampshire) on the outcomes is highly disproportionate to their population. After the delegate selection events in these two states, the nomination contest is effectively fixed so that a number of candidates cannot meaningfully compete. The compressed nominating season exacerbates this winnowing effect and dramatically reduces the number of states that actually have a voice in the process. Finally, of the citizens who do vote, few are actually participating in the decision of who will become the nominee, and even these are hardly representative of the electorate as a whole.

Of course this discussion about low voter turnout in presidential primaries ignores what happened in 2008. In most states that held primaries, voters, especially Democratic voters, showed up in record numbers to cast their ballots. Voter turnout *nationally* fell just short of breaking the record set in 1972, the first year that primaries decided the party nominations. This said, more than sixty million people voted in nominating contests in 2008, or almost 46 percent of the better than 131 million who voted in November.[19] By May 19, turnout records had been set in a total of twenty-three of the states that held primaries for both parties. In all but one state that held a primary, voter turnout exceeded numbers recorded in 2004. Turnout was also higher in states that held caucuses, especially Democratic caucuses.[20]

But in spite of the fact that it may sound pessimistic, there is ample reason to believe that 2008 was an anomaly in terms of voter turnout in presidential primaries and caucuses. High turnout in 2008 can largely be explained by the fact that Democrats were much more likely to participate in primaries and caucuses than their Republican counterparts. Average turnout in Democratic primaries was almost double that in Republican primaries (20.7 as opposed to 10.4 percent).[21] We can point to three reasons for this.

First, there was widespread dissatisfaction, especially among Democrats, with President Bush. Democrats, in general, were mobilized by the idea that Bush's term would soon be ending, and as importantly, that their party might be able to re-capture the White House. Second, many of these same Democrats were attracted to, and energized by, Barack Obama. This was especially true with younger voters.[22] The freshman senator from Illinois was exceptionally charismatic, delivered stirring speeches, and hammered home a message of change that resonated powerfully with Democratic voters. Finally, the Democratic nomination was not decided until Hillary Clinton withdrew on June 7, 2008, after the final primaries had been held. It was, in spite of the rhetoric and hyperbole that surrounded the nomination struggle, a competition until the end. This also makes the 2008 Democratic nomination an exception to the discussion above about short nomination races. Political science has long recognized that competitive races tend to see higher levels of voter turnout.[23]

The point is that it may be some time before factors converge again to produce such high participation in nominating contests.[24] Few presidents leave office as unpopular as Bush did; a politician like Obama might come along once in a generation; and few nominating contests are as close as the Democratic contest of 2008.

In the next section we take up the matter of the general election campaign. The focus here is on campaign strategy and organization. In particular, we examine how the logic of the Electoral College again skews the campaign toward a few voters in a few states.

ELECTORAL COLLEGE STRATEGY

"A presidential campaign, like a military campaign, relies on sound strategy."[25] One of the main elements of a sound campaign strategy is *where* to campaign. To what regions of the country should the campaign travel? What groups should the campaign attempt to persuade? At first the answer might appear to be straightforward: everywhere and everyone. Given limited resources, however, this would be foolish.

Campaigns group voters into three general categories. There is one group that will never vote for a particular candidate under any circumstances. These voters are typically hard-core or solid opposition partisans, people who strongly identify with the other party. Then there are those upon whose vote a candidate can likely depend on. These are the people who strongly identify with the candidate's party. These "base" voters are unlikely to vote for the candidate of the other party. The third group, known variously as "swing" or moderate voters (see chapter 3), is the group that campaigns try to persuade. How do these voting categories affect a campaign's strategy? Part of the answer relies on an understanding of how the Electoral College works.

Under the Electoral College system, each state has the same number of electors (votes) as it has members of Congress. For example, in 2008 North Carolina had thirteen members in the House of Representatives and two senators, giving North Carolina fifteen Electoral College votes. The District of Columbia is awarded three electors, two for the senators and one for the member of the House that they would have if they had representation in Congress. Forty-eight states (and D.C.) award all of their Electoral College votes to the candidate who wins (according to plurality winner rules) the popular vote in the state.[26] The candidate who wins the majority (not the plurality) of Electoral College votes wins the presidency. There are a total of 538 Electoral College votes, so a candidate must receive 270 Electoral College votes to win.

In terms of campaign strategy, it is not necessary to win the popular vote in every state or the popular vote in the country in order to win the election. In fact, a candidate can win the presidency by barely winning in eleven states, provided these are the states that have the largest number of Electoral College votes. This means that a candidate can lose, and lose by a wide margin, in the other thirty-nine states (and D.C.).

Table 12.1 is a hypothetical outcome of what this scenario might look like, using the actual number of votes cast in each state in 2008. Here the Democratic candidate received a bare majority (50.01 to 49.99 percent) of popular votes in the "Big Eleven," or the states with the most Electoral College votes. This gave the Democratic candidate all of the Electoral College votes in each of those states, while the Republican candidate received none. The Republican candidate got a larger margin of victory (55 to 45 percent) in the "Other Forty" Electoral College units, giving the Republican candidate every Electoral College vote in each of these forty. The net result, seen in the last row, is that the Democratic candidate wins the presidency with 271 Electoral College votes, with a margin of victory of only 1/10 of 1 percent in each of only eleven states. However, the Democratic candidate loses the nationwide popular vote (47.8 to 52.2 percent).

Of course, it is not likely that the eleven states that are richest in Elec-

Table 12.1 Hypothetical Electoral College outcome: Democrats win, losing popular vote in 40 states

	The "Big 11"*	The "Other 40"	Total
Democratic Candidate			
Percentage of Popular Vote	50.01%	45.0%	47.8%
Number of Popular Votes	36 million	27 million	63 million
Electoral College Votes	271	0	271
Republican Candidate			
Percentage of Popular Vote	49.99%	55.0%	52.2%
Number of Popular Votes	36 million	33 million	69 million
Electoral College Votes	0	267	267

* The "Big 11" consists of CA, TX, NY, FL, IL, PA, OH, MI, GA, NJ, and NC.

toral College votes would select the same candidate. The point is that a reasonable move by a campaign might be to target some states for more attention and others for less, based on (1) how competitive they might be and (2) how many Electoral College votes are at stake. The history of how different states have voted in the past suggests that putting too much emphasis on certain states is a potential waste of resources. Each party can typically count on certain states for electoral support. Table 12.2 is a very rough measure of this. It shows how many times each party has won in each state in the past five elections, and, in parentheses, the number of consecutive wins the party has had, starting with 2008 and moving backward in time.

Based on the electoral history of each state, state polling data, conditions within the state, and other factors, campaign strategists make a determination of how likely it is that a particular state will vote for the candidate. These states are classified as "safe." Table 12.3 (p. 192) is another simple measure of safe states for each party. It is derived by averaging the margin of victory for the winner for the previous three presidential elections. If the margin of victory is greater than 10 percent, we classified the state as safe for that party.

Using this measure, the Democrats have a slight advantage in Electoral College votes from safe states. In part this is because two states (California and New York) give the Democrats almost 32 percent of the 270 votes needed to win.

Beyond understanding where the base (of safe states) is located, there are a few general rules that guide an Electoral College strategy. First, small states, especially those in which the candidate has virtually no chance of winning, can be all but ignored. It makes little sense for a Democratic candidate to spend much time campaigning in Alaska, given (1) that the state has gone Republican in the past seven elections, and (2) there are only three Electoral College votes at stake. Similarly, a Republican candidate could safely leave Delaware and Rhode Island out of their campaign strategy.

A second rule is that large states (California, Texas, New York, Florida, Illinois, Pennsylvania, Ohio) almost always get at least some attention from both party's candidates. For example, in 1976, Jimmy Carter and Gerald Ford targeted seven of the same eight states. Despite the fact that Bob Dole knew that he had no chance of winning in California in 1996, he spent a good deal of time (and approximately four million dollars) during the last three weeks of his campaign in the state.[27] Presidential candidates cannot afford to ignore large states completely. This is because of the large number of Electoral College votes in these states and because there is a desire to ensure the party stays competitive in these states in the

Table 12.2 Electoral College outcomes by party, 1992–2008

State	E.C. Votes	Rep. Wins	Dem. Wins
Alabama	9	5 (5)	0
Alaska	3	5 (5)	0
Arizona	10	4 (3)	1
Arkansas	6	3 (3)	2
California	55	0	5 (5)
Colorado	9	3	2 (1)
Connecticut	7	0	5 (5)
Delaware	3	0	5 (5)
D.C.	3	0	5 (5)
Florida	27	3	2 (1)
Georgia	15	4 (4)	1
Hawaii	4	0	5 (5)
Idaho	4	5 (5)	0
Illinois	21	0	5 (5)
Indiana	11	4	1 (1)
Iowa	7	1	4 (1)
Kansas	6	5 (5)	0
Kentucky	8	3 (3)	2
Louisiana	9	3 (3)	2
Maine	4	0	5 (5)
Maryland	10	0	5 (5)
Massachusetts	12	0	5 (5)
Michigan	17	0	5 (5)
Minnesota	10	0	5 (5)
Mississippi	6	5 (5)	0
Missouri	11	3 (3)	2
Montana	3	4 (4)	1
Nebraska	5	5 (5)	0
Nevada	5	2	3 (1)
New Hampshire	4	1	4 (2)
New Jersey	15	0	5 (5)
New Mexico	5	1	4 (1)
New York	31	0	5 (5)
North Carolina	15	4	1 (1)
North Dakota	3	5 (5)	0
Ohio	20	2	3 (1)
Oklahoma	7	5 (5)	0
Oregon	7	0	5 (5)
Pennsylvania	21	0	5 (5)
Rhode Island	4	0	5 (5)
South Carolina	8	5 (5)	0
South Dakota	3	5 (5)	0
Tennessee	11	3 (3)	2
Texas	34	5 (5)	0
Utah	5	5 (5)	0
Vermont	3	0	5 (5)
Virginia	13	4	1 (1)
Washington	11	0	5 (5)
West Virginia	5	3 (3)	2
Wisconsin	10	0	5 (5)
Wyoming	3	5 (5)	0

Note: Figure in parentheses is the number of consecutive wins in the state by the party, starting with 2008 and moving backward in time. Data compiled by authors. Electoral College vote totals based on 2008 election. In 2008, Nebraska awarded four of its Electoral College votes to McCain and one to Obama. This is recorded as a Republican win.

Table 12.3   Safe states, by party

Republican States	E.C. Votes	Democratic States	E.C. Votes
Alabama	9	California	55
Alaska	3	Connecticut	7
Arkansas	6	Delaware	3
Georgia	15	Hawaii	4
Idaho	4	Illinois	21
Indiana	11	Maine	4
Kansas	6	Maryland	10
Kentucky	8	Massachusetts	12
Louisiana	9	New Jersey	15
Mississippi	6	New York	31
Montana	3	Vermont	3
Nebraska	4	Washington	11
North Dakota	3	Washington D.C.	3
Tennessee	11		
Texas	34		
Utah	5		
West Virginia	5		
Wyoming	3		
Total Republican: 145		*Total Democratic: 179*	

Source: Compiled by authors, based on the average winning margins of elections of 2000, 2004, and 2008.

future. However, it is generally pointless to spend much time in states where the candidate has little chance of winning.

Although some time must be spent bolstering support in areas where the candidate is likely to do well, the central element of presidential campaign strategy consists of identifying states where the candidate has some chance of victory and focusing efforts there. In 1964, Barry Goldwater devoted most of his resources to campaign in the Midwest and West, while all but ignoring the Northeast. Richard Nixon, in 1968, focused on New Jersey, Wisconsin, and Missouri where he thought he had a chance of defeating Hubert Humphrey, as well as in five border-South states to compete with George Wallace for the southern vote.

The decision on where to focus the campaign is fairly nuanced. Jimmy Carter's campaign manager, Hamilton Jordan, developed a complex formula that factored in state size, previous and existing Democratic support (based on control of elective offices), and state turnout. After identifying important states, each day of the campaign was scheduled according to state scores and the predetermined value of a Carter, Mondale, or a family member visit.[28] For example, "Carter's scheduler Eliot Cutler, convinced that Ohio was the key to the race, scheduled 65% of vice-presidential candidate Walter Mondale's time there in the last two weeks of the campaign

(Carter won Ohio by 8,000 votes)."[29] In 1996, Clinton pollster Mark Penn devised a seven-variable model that he used to allocate television advertising dollars, including electoral history, advertising costs, number of persuadable voters, and impact of prospective ads on House and Senate races.[30]

Political scientist Daron Shaw examined the electoral strategies of Democratic and Republican presidential candidates from 1988 to 2004, tracking the states that campaign managers considered to be important to their effort. States are divided into five categories: base Republican or Democrat, "lean" Republican or Democrat, or battleground. Base states, which correspond to safe states discussed above, require little attention from either party candidate's campaign. Each campaign focuses most of its efforts on the battleground states and those that lean toward one party or the other. Table 12.4 lists these states. What stands out in this table is that although the relative number of battleground and marginal states varies from one campaign to the next, there are only about fifteen states identified in each campaign year as being relatively competitive, and therefore important to the campaign.

How does this focus translate into campaign effort? Using various data, Shaw shows that from September 1 through Election Day during the campaigns of 1988 through 1996, the average amount of spending for campaign advertising in battleground states for three election cycles was more than quadruple that for each party's respective base states. Spending in leaning Democratic or Republican states was almost double that for spending in base states. Additionally, both Democratic and Republican candidates made more appearances in battleground or leaning states than in their base states. While the data show variation between election cycles and parties, a pattern of resources allocation favoring battleground or marginal states is clear.

A similar pattern emerges in 2000 and 2004. Table 12.5 (p. 195) shows data for spending for campaign ads and candidate appearances by presidential and vice presidential candidates during the fall campaigns of 2000 and 2004. In 2000, total spending on television ads was three to five times greater in battleground and marginal states than in the other thirty-six states combined. Presidential and vice presidential candidates visited battleground and marginal states two to three times more often than the other thirty-six. No money whatever was spent by the campaign for television advertising in a total of twenty-six states; thirty-two states received no visits from the Republican candidates; and twenty-three states did not see either Democratic candidate during the campaign.

Differences were more pronounced in 2004. Here, spending on television ads in battleground and marginal states exceeded that in the other

Table 12.4   Geographic focus, presidential campaign, 1988–1996

Year	Battleground States	Marginal*	Total
1988	California, Missouri, Ohio, Texas	Connecticut, Delaware, Illinois, Maine, Michigan, New York, New Jersey, Oregon, Pennsylvania, Vermont, Washington, Wisconsin	16
1992	Georgia, Michigan, New Jersey, Ohio	Colorado, Kentucky, Louisiana, Maine, Missouri, Montana, New Mexico, North Carolina, Pennsylvania, Wisconsin	14
1996	Louisiana, Nevada, New Mexico	Arizona, California, Colorado, Florida, Georgia, Kentucky, New Hampshire, New Jersey, Ohio, Tennessee	13
2000	Arkansas, Florida, Iowa, Maine, Michigan, Missouri, New Hampshire, New Mexico, Oregon, Pennsylvania, Tennessee, Washington, Wisconsin	Minnesota, West Virginia	15
2004	Florida, Iowa, New Hampshire, New Mexico, Ohio, Pennsylvania, Wisconsin	Maine, Michigan, Minnesota, Missouri, Nevada, Oregon, Washington, West Virginia	15

Source: Daron R. Shaw, *The Race to 270: The Electoral College and the Campaign Strategies of 2000 and 2004* (Chicago: University of Chicago Press), pp. 47–49, 64, 66.

* "Marginal" states are those that one campaign identified as a battleground state and the other campaign identified as leaning toward one party or the other.

thirty-six states by more than a factor of twenty. In fact, three states alone (Florida, Ohio, and Pennsylvania) accounted for approximately half of the spending on television ads in each party. Candidates visited the fifteen battleground and marginal states three to five times more than the other thirty-six states combined. In 2004 there was no campaign spending for television ads in more than half the states (twenty-six Republican, twenty-seven Democrat). Republican candidates ignored thirty-four states and Democratic candidates twenty-four in terms of campaign stops.

While there is a fair amount of variation between battleground and marginal states, the pattern is clear. The fall campaign is not a true national campaign but rather an effort disproportionately targeted to a few voters in a relatively small number of states. Other studies confirm this as well.[31]

Table 12.5 Resource allocation, battleground, marginal, and other states, 2000 & 2004

	Republican Spending	Democrat Spending	Republican Campaign Visits	Democrat Campaign Visits
2000				
Arkansas	$2,333,354	$2,050,697	6	5
Florida	$16,969,907	$10,272,868	21	26
Iowa	$4,025,441	$3,468,186	10	14
Maine	$1,801,045	$1,074,138	4	5
Michigan	$12,535,431	$12,403,378	27	12
Minnesota	$1,770,283	$1,281,082	2	3
Missouri	$9,080,218	$8,379,107	15	15
New Hampshire	$1,313,175	$279,605	4	3
New Mexico	$2,115,919	$1,896,791	7	5
Oregon	$5,256,798	$4,732,847	10	6
Pennsylvania	$14,193,775	$13,908,415	24	12
Tennessee	$2,176,429	$1,822,425	9	9
Washington	$8,392,058	$6,401,109	10	8
West Virginia	$1,823,112	$830,504	4	1
Wisconsin	$6,117,109	$5,943,895	13	18
2000, Total: Battleground & Marginal States	$89,904,054	$74,745,047	166	142
2000, Total: The Other 36 States	$26,536,704	$14,852,135	79	52
2004				
Florida	$26,418,059	$31,050,552	38	46
Iowa	$7,237,644	$7,094,758	18	20
Maine	$1,431,717	$2,168,756	1	2
Michigan	$7,716,070	$7,963,137	16	9
Minnesota	$5,952,380	$5,355,920	13	8
Missouri	$2,530,130	$894,830	6	3
Nevada	$4,459,255	$5,731,087	6	4
New Hampshire	$2,274,889	$2,107,049	5	7
New Mexico	$2,926,277	$3,348,814	6	7
Ohio	$17,746,015	$19,264,232	30	33
Oregon	$2,499,023	$2,469,950	3	4
Pennsylvania	$19,314,988	$18,518,841	21	15
Washington	$698,075	$2,744,041	0	0
West Virginia	$4,175,726	$4,257,790	4	6
Wisconsin	$8,904,241	$9,679,390	20	20
2004, Total: Battleground & Marginal States	$114,284,489	$122,649,147	187	184
2004, Total: The Other 36 States	$5,389,894	$5,066,019	51	41

Source: Shaw, *The Race to 270*, pp. 79–80, 86–87.

CONCLUSION

To be clear, there are some truly national aspects of presidential campaigns worth acknowledging. First, news about the primary campaign is certainly national in its scope and reach. Second, reporting the results of national polls about presidential preferences likely has some impact on voters in the early primary states. Third, during the fall campaign, all Americans are aware of, and can access information about, what the presidential candidates are saying. By this point in the campaign, news stories about the campaign are ubiquitous.

Our point, however, is that some are more equal than others with respect to the campaign. Attention and resources are maldistributed in the primary season and are heavily weighted toward the earliest delegate selection events. In the fall campaign, battleground states dominate. In short, while all citizens can participate, some have greater opportunities for meaningful participation.

FOR MORE READING

Baumgartner, Jody. *Modern Presidential Electioneering: An Organizational and Comparative Approach*. Westport, Conn.: Praeger, 2000.

Polsby, Nelson W., and Aaron Wildavsky. *Presidential Elections: Strategies and Structures of American Politics*, 11th ed. Lanham, Md.: Rowman & Littlefield, 2004.

Wayne, Stephen J. *The Road to the White House, 2004: The Politics of Presidential Elections*. Belmont, Calif.: Wadsworth, 2004.

Notes

1. There are, of course, a plethora of books that cover campaigns and elections in the United States. Focusing only on presidential elections, there is a fairly long tradition of journalistic accounts of specific elections that date back to Theodore White's *The Making of the President, 1960* (Cutchogue, N.Y.: Buccaneer Books, 1961). This tradition relies on the journalist (or a team of journalists) who are on the inside of the campaign traveling with the candidate. White's books present a detailed chronology of the campaign, relating many interesting anecdotes about the candidate, his family, entourage, etc. While others have made contributions using this approach (e.g., Timothy Crouse, *The Boys on the Bus*, Toronto, Canada: Random House, 1973), White was the pioneer, and continued the tradition for several election cycles.

More recently, various writers for *Newsweek* magazine have followed a similar approach (e.g., Jack W. Germond and Jules Witcover, *Blue Smoke and Mirrors: How Reagan Won & Carter Lost the Election of 1980* [N.Y.: Penguin Group, 1981]; Thomas M. Defrank and others, *Quest for the Presidency, 1992* [College Station, Tex.: Texas A&M University Press, 1994]; Evan Thomas, Eleanor Clift, and the Staff of *Newsweek*, *Election 2004: How Bush Won And What You Can Expect In The Future* [New York: Public Affairs, 2005]). All of these accounts are informative and interesting, but they contain a level of detail best suited for the most politically interested.

Another approach to the study of campaigns and elections is what some term the "practitioner approach." This approach is similar to the journalistic tradition inasmuch as it relies on insider perspectives. The best example of this is the series sponsored by the John F. Kennedy School of Government Institute of Politics. The Kennedy School invites campaign managers to a symposium for what amounts to a de-briefing about the strategies and tactics they employed during the previous campaign. The first of these books, titled *Campaign for President: The Managers Look at 1976* (Jonathan Moore and Janet Fraser, Cambridge, Mass.: Ballinger, 1977), was published in 1977 and has been produced every four years since. These books are also geared toward the politically interested and are also excellent insider accounts.

A final approach to the study of presidential campaigns and elections comes from the scholarly community. Many of these books are also produced immediately after a presidential election, and attempt to make some sense of what happened and why. Unlike the previous two traditions, the scholarly tradition is geared more toward scientific explanation rather than anecdotal and impressionistic conclusions. Most are, again, post-election quadrennial publications. James Ceaser and Andrew Busch have been authoring a post-election book since 1993 (*Upside Down and Inside Out: The 1992 Elections and American Politics* [Lanham, Md.: Rowman & Littlefield, 1993]). Many are edited volumes. Michael Nelson has been editing a post-election collection every four years since 1985 (the latest, *The Elections of 2008* [Washington, D.C.: CQ Press, 2009]). Other edited volumes include Gerald Pomper's collections (the last of which was *The Election of 2000: Reports and Interpretations* [New York: Seven Bridges, 2001]), relative newcomer Larry Sabato (*The Year of Obama: How Barack Obama Won the White House* [New York: Longman, 2009]), and William Crotty (*Winning the Presidency 2008* [Boulder, Colo.: Paradigm, 2009]). Some texts focus on upcoming elections (e.g., Michael Goldstein, *Guide to the 2004 Presidential Election* [Washington, D.C.: CQ Press, 2003]).

Other books are non-election specific. The most notable of these are Polsby and Wildavsky's *Presidential Elections* (Nelson Polsby and Aaron Wildavsky, *Presidential Elections: Strategies and Structures of American Politics* [Lanham, Md.: Rowman & Littlefield, 2007]), in its twelfth edition, and Stephen Wayne's *The Road to the White House* (*The Road to the White House 2008: The Politics of Presidential Elections*, [Florence, Ky.: Wadsworth, 2007]), in its eighth edition. Yet other texts examine congressional elections, most notably, *The Politics of Congressional Elections* by Gary Jacobson (7th ed. [New York: Longman, 2008]) and *Congressional Elections: Campaigning at Home and in Washington* by Paul Herrnson (5th ed. [Washington, D.C.: CQ Press, 2007]).

All of the books in these traditions are similar in that they take a fairly comprehensive look at campaigns and elections. Other books examine more specific aspects of the electoral process. For example, William Mayer's quadrennial edited book (*The Making of the Presidential Candidates 2008* [Lanham, Md.: Rowman & Littlefield, 2007]) is an excellent text for understanding the presidential nomination process. Kathleen Hall Jamieson's *Packaging the Presidency* (*Packaging the Presidency: A History and Criticism of Presidential Campaign Advertising*, 3rd edition [New York: Oxford University, 1996]) is one of many that examine presidential campaign advertising. These, and many others not listed here, are excellent sources for further reading on the subject.

CHAPTER 1

1. We wish to acknowledge the contribution to this chapter made by Michael P. McDonald and Samuel Popkin, "The Myth of the Vanishing Voter," *American Political Science Review* 95 (2001): 963–74.

2. See, for example, Morris P. Fiorina, Paul E. Peterson, with Bertram Johnson, *The New American Democracy*, 3rd ed. (New York: Longman, 2003), 164–65.

3. John Dean, "Why Americans Don't Vote—and How That Might Change," WritLegal Commentary, *CNN Interactive*, 8 November 2000, edition.cnn.com/ 2000/LAW/11/columns/fl.dean.voters.02.11.07/; "Voter Turnout May Slip Again," *Pew Research Center for the People and the Press*, 13 July 2000, peoplepress .org/reports/print.php3?PageID = 194; John Gray, "Trends in Increasing Voter Apathy Point to a Record Lack of Interest in Casting Ballots This Presidential Election," *Toronto Globe and Mail*, 28 October 2000, www.commondreams.org/head lines/102800-03.htm.

4. See Bryan Mercurio, "Democracy in Decline: Can Internet Voting Save the Electoral Process?" *John Marshall Journal of Computer & Information Law* 22 (2004), papers.ssrn.com/sol3/papers.cfm?abstract_id = 590441.

5. Ruy A. Teixeira, *Why Americans Don't Vote: Turnout Decline in the United States, 1960–1984* (Westport, Conn.: Greenwood, 1987); Ruy A. Teixeira, *The Disappearing American Voter* (Washington, D.C.: Brookings Institution, 1992); Frances Fox Piven and Richard A. Cloward, *Why Americans Don't Vote* (New York: Pantheon, 1988); Frances Fox Piven and Richard A. Cloward, *Why Americans Still Don't Vote: And Why Politicians Want It That Way* (Boston: Beacon, 2000); Mark Lawrence Kornbluh, *Why America Stopped Voting: The Decline of Participatory Democracy and the Emergence of Modern American Politics* (New York: New York University, 2000); Martin P. Wattenberg, *Where Have All the Voters Gone?* (Cambridge, Mass.: Harvard University Press, 2002); Lisa Hill, "Low Voter Turnout in the United States: Is Compulsory Voting a Viable Solution?" *Journal of Theoretical Politics* 18 (2006): 207–32; Arend Lijphart, "Unequal Participation: Democracy's Unresolved Dilemma," *American Political Science Review* 91 (1997): 1–14.

6. Walter Dean Burnham, "The Turnout Problem," in *Elections American Style*, ed. A. James Reichley (Washington, D.C.: Brookings Institution, 1987).

7. "About the Project," *Vanishing Voter Project*, www.vanishingvoter.org/ about.shtml.

8. This section draws heavily on David Lee Hill, *American Voter Turnout: An Institutional Approach* (Boulder, Colo.: Westview, 2006).

9. For a more complete treatment of this subject, see Mark N. Franklin, *Voter Turnout and the Dynamics of Electoral Competition in Established Democracies since 1945* (New York: Cambridge University Press, 2004).

10. Kei Kawashima-Ginsberg, Amanda Nover, and Emily Hoban Kirby, "State Election Law Reform and Youth Voter Turnout," *Center for Information & Research on Civic Learning & Engagement*, www.civicyouth.org/?p = 349.

11. In almost all elections in the United States, the Australian ballot is used, which lists each office separately. Another balloting system is used in parliamentary elections, where citizens are presented with a list of party candidates, from which they choose one party list.

12. G. Bingham Powell, "American Voter Turnout in Comparative Perspective," *American Political Science Review* 80 (1986): 17–43; Robert Jackman, "Political Institutions and Voter Turnout in the Industrial Democracies," *American Political Science Review* 81 (1987): 405–424.

13. Kawashima-Ginsberg, Nover, and Hoban Kirby, "State Election Law Reform."

14. Robert M. Stein and Patricia A. Garcia-Monet, "Voting Early but Not Often," *Social Science Quarterly* 78 (1997): 657–71.

15. Donald P. Green and Ron Shachar, "Habit Formation and Political Behaviour: Evidence of Consuetude in Voter Turnout," *British Journal of Political Science* 30 (2000): 561–73.

16. Eric Plutzer, "Becoming a Habitual Voter: Inertia, Resources, and Growth in Young Adulthood," *American Political Science Review* 96 (2002): 41–56.

17. John P. Katosh and Michael W. Traugott, "Costs and Values in the Calculus of Voting," *American Journal of Political Science* 26: 361–76; for more information about trust in government, see Joseph S. Nye Jr., Philip D. Zelikow, and David C. King, ed., *Why People Don't Trust Government* (Cambridge, Mass.: Harvard University Press, 1997).

18. Steven J. Rosenstone and John Mark Hanson, *Mobilization, Participation, and Democracy in America* (New York: Macmillan, 1993); Cornelius P. Cotter and others, *Party Organizations in American Politics* (New York: Praeger, 1984).

19. William H. Flanigan and Nancy H. Zingale, *Political Behavior of the American Electorate*, 11th ed. (Washington, D.C.: CQ Press, 2005).

20. Flanigan and Zingale, *Political Behavior of the American Electorate*.

21. Diana Burgess, Beth Haney, Mark Snyder, John L. Sullivan, and John E. Transue, "Rocking the Vote: Using Personalized Messages to Motivate Voting among Young Adults," *Public Opinion Quarterly* 64 (2000): 29–52.

22. Alan Gerber and Donald Green, "The Effects of Canvassing, Telephone Calls, and Direct Mail on Voter Turnout: A Field Experiment," *American Political Science Review* 94 (2000): 653–63.

23. McDonald and Popkin, "The Myth of the Vanishing Voter."

24. Philip E. Converse, "Change in the American Electorate," in *The Human Meaning of Social Change*, eds. Angus Campbell and Philip E. Converse (New York: Russell Sage, 1972).

25. For an excellent review of voter fraud in the 1800s, see Peter H. Argersinger, "New Perspectives on Election Fraud in the Gilded Age," *Political Science Quarterly* 100 (Winter 1985–1986): 669–87.

26. McDonald and Popkin, "The Myth of the Vanishing Voter," 964.

27. Jerrold G. Rusk, "The Effect of the Australian Ballot Reform on Split Ticket Voting: 1876–1908," *American Political Science Review* 64 (1970): 1220–38.

28. Russell J. Dalton, *Citizen Politics: Public Opinion and Political Parties in Advanced Industrial Democracies*, 3rd ed. (New York: Chatham House, 2002).

29. Richard Sammon, "Young Voters: A Rising Force in National Politics," *Kiplinger Business Forecasts*, 16 May 2008; Alexandra Marks, "For Election 08, Youth Voter Turnout Swells," *Christian Science Monitor*, 16 January 2008, 1; Jill Lawrence, "Young Voters Poised To Be An Election Force," *USA Today*, 6 May 2008, A1; Leah Chernikoff, "The Young & The Political," *Daily News*, 5 October 2008, 22.

30. Marks, "For Election 08."

31. This includes polls conducted by the Harvard Institute of Politics and the Pew Research Center. See Joe Garofoli, "Youth Vote," *San Francisco Chronicle*, 3 November 2004, sfgate.com/cgi-bin/article.cgi.

32. John Della Volpe, "Campus Kids: The New Swing Voter," *Harvard Univer-*

sity Institute of Politics, 21 May 2003, www.iop.harvard.edu/pdfs/survey/spring
_2003.pdf.

33. Figures were obtained from a LexisNexis Academic Reference Search of
Polls and Surveys, Roper Center, "Public Opinion Online," 24 January 2004, Question Number 073.

34. "Hillary Clinton tells P. Diddy 'Vote or Die' Slogan Hits Nail on the Head,"
MTV, 5 August 2004, www.mtv.com/chooseorlose/headlines/news.jhtml?id =
1489969.

35. Christina Nifong, "Candidates Court 'Twentysomethings,'" *Christian Science Monitor*, 6 March 1996, 4.

36. Figure was obtained from the Center for Information and Research on Civic
Learning and Engagement (CIRCLE).

37. "Youth Voting," Center for Information and Research on Civic Learning
and Engagement, www.civicyouth.org/?page_id = 241.

38. Michael Hoover and Susan Orr, "Youth Political Engagement: Why Rock
the Vote Hits the Wrong Note," in *Fountain of Youth: Strategies and Tactics for Mobilizing America's Young Voters*, eds. Daniel M. Shea and John C. Green (Lanham,
Md.: Rowman & Littlefield, 2007), 141–62.

39. Stephen Watson, "Younger Voters Came Out at High Rate, but Percentage
of Total Didn't Change," *Buffalo News*, 9 November 2004, B6.

40. Figures were obtained from the Center for Information and Research on
Civic Learning and Engagement (CIRCLE).

41. Martin P. Wattenberg, *Is Voting For Young People?* (New York: Pearson Longman, 2007); Mark Bauerlein, *The Dumbest Generation: How the Digital Age Stupefies
Young Americans and Jeopardizes Our Future (Or, Don't Trust Anyone Under 30)* (New
York: Tarcher Penguin, 2008).

42. Statistics reported in this section are derived by a method similar to deriving VEP statistics. See Mark Hugo Lopez, Emily Kirby, and Jared Sagoff, "The
Youth Vote 2004, with a Historical Look at Youth Voting Patterns, 1972–2004,"
Working Paper 35, Center for Information and Research on Civic Learning and
Engagement, July 2005.

43. Emily Hoban Kirby and Kei Kawashima-Ginsberg, "The Youth Vote in
2008," 17 August 2009, www.civicyouth.org/PopUps/FactSheets/FS_youth_Voting
_2008 eupdated_6. 22.pdf.

44. Ted Halstead, "A Politics for Generation X," *Atlantic Monthly*, August 1999;
The Institute of Politics at Harvard University, "Attitudes towards Politics and
Public Service: A National Survey of College Undergraduates," Cambridge, MA:
Harvard University, 2000.

45. Karon Reinboth Speckman, "Who Did a Better Job Informing Youth Voters
in the 2000 Election—TV Network News or Online News?" *White House Studies*
(Fall 2002).

46. Institute of Politics, "Attitudes towards Politics and Public Service."

47. See, for example, Chuck Todd and Sheldon Gawiser, *How Barack Obama
Won: A State-by-State Guide to the Historic 2008 Presidential Election* (New York: Vintage Books, 2009).

48. John R. Hibbing and Elizabeth Theiss-Morse, *Stealth Democracy: Americans'
Beliefs About How Government Should Work* (New York: Cambridge University
Press, 2002).

49. George Will, "In Defense of Nonvoting," in *The Morning After*, ed. George Will (New York: Free Press, 1986).

50. This was an argument advanced by many classical political theorists including Aristotle and John Stuart Mill.

51. For an excellent discussion on these last two points, see Richard Hasen, "Voting Without Law," *University of Pennsylvania Law Review* 44 (1996): 2135–79.

CHAPTER 2

1. Mayhill Fowler, "Obama: No Surprise that Hard-Pressed Pennsylvania Turns Bitter," *Huffington Post*, 11 April 2008, www.huffingtonpost.com/mayhill -fowler/obama-no-surprise-that-ha_b_96188.ht ml.

2. Tom Vanden Brook, "Clinton Brands Obama's Words as 'Elitist, Divisive,'" *USA Today*, 14 April 2008, www.usatoday.com/printedition/news/20080414/ a_bitter14.art.htm. See also Shailagh Murray and Perry Bacon Jr., "Obama Reinforcing Stereotypes, Clinton Asserts," *Washington Post*, 14 April 2008, www .washingtonpost.com/wp-dyn/content/article/2008/04/13/AR2008041302461 .html.

3. Thomas Frank, "Obama's Touch of Class," *Wall Street Journal*, 21 April 2008, A17, online.wsj.com/article/SB120873309012529689.html?mod = opinion_main _commentaries.

4. *American Rhetoric: Online Speech Bank*, "Patrick J. Buchanan: Address to the Republican National Convention (delivered August 17, 1992, Houston, Texas)," www.americanrhetoric.com/speeches/patrickbuchanan1992rnc.htm.

5. *Cornell University Law School*, "Romer, Governor of Colorado, et al. v. Evans et al. (94-1039), 517 U.S. 620 (1996) (delivered May 20, 1996)," www.law .cornell.edu/supct/html/94-1039.ZD.html.

6. Quoted in James Q. Wilson, "How Divided Are We?" *Commentary Magazine* (February 2006), www.commentarymagazine.com/cm/main/viewArticle .aip?id = 10023. The quotation does not reflect Wilson's own view of Republicans or Democrats but rather reflects what he believes are the extreme popular perceptions of them.

7. Quoted in E. J. Dionne Jr., "What Kind of Hater Are You?" *Washington Post*, 15 March 2006, A19. The quotation does not reflect Dionne's own view of Republicans or Democrats but rather reflects what he believes are the extreme popular perceptions of them.

8. Wilson, "How Divided Are We?"

9. Dionne, "What Kind of Hater Are You?"

10. Morris P. Fiorina, with Samuel J. Abrams and Jeremy C. Pope, *Culture War? The Myth of a Polarized America* (New York: Longman, 2005). See also Alan Wolfe, *One Nation, After All: What Americans Really Think About God, Country, Family, Racism, Welfare, Immigration, Homosexuality, Work, The Right, The Left and Each Other* (New York: Penguin Books, 1998); and Andrew Gelman, *Red State, Blue State, Rich State, Poor State: Why Americans Vote the Way They Do* (Princeton, N.J.: Princeton University Press, 2008).

11. Jonathan Rauch, "Bipolar Disorder," *The Atlantic Monthly*, January/February 2005, www.jonathanrauch.com/jrauch_articles/2005/01/bipolar_disorde .html.

12. William Beaman, "A Fractured America?" *Reader's Digest*, November 2005, www.rd.com/your-america-inspiring-people-and-stories/the-reality-of-party -affiliation-in-america/article28693.html.

13. Joe Klein, "America Divided? It's Only the Blabocrats," *Time*, 8 August 2004, www.time.com/time/election2004/columnist/klein/article/0,18471,67859 3,00.html.

14. Gary Karniya, "The Culture War: It's Back!" *Salon*, 15 September 2008, www.salon.com/news/feature/2008/09/15/palin_interview/print.html.

15. Bill Bishop, *The Big Sort: Why the Clustering of Like-Minded America is Tearing Us Apart* (New York: Houghton Mifflin, 2008).

16. James Davison Hunter, *Culture Wars: The Struggle to Define America* (New York: Basic Books, 1991).

17. E. J. Dionne Jr., "Why the Culture War Is the Wrong War," *Atlantic Monthly*, January/February 2006, www.theatlantic.com/doc/prem/200601/culture-war.

18. Ellen Chesler, *Woman of Valor: Margaret Sanger and the Birth Control Movement in America* (New York: Simon and Schuster, 1992).

19. Dionne, "Why the Culture War Is the Wrong War."

20. Dionne, "Why the Culture War Is the Wrong War."

21. Dick Meyer, "The Official Start of the Culture War," *CBS News*, 22 July 2004, www.cbsnews.com/stories/2004/07/21/opinion/meyer/main631126.shtml.

22. Bishop, *The Big Sort*, 116.

23. Clyde Wilcox, *God's Warriors: The Christian Right in Twentieth-Century America* (Baltimore: Johns Hopkins University Press, 1992).

24. Quoted in Linda Feldmann, "How Lines of the Culture War Have Been Redrawn," *Christian Science Monitor*, 15 November 2004, www.csmonitor.com/ 2004/1115/p01s04-ussc.html.

25. Scott Shepard, "Bush-Kerry Contest a Sharp Contrast in Charting America's Future," *Cox News Service*, 6 March 2004.

26. For example, see Fiorina, with Abrams and Pope, *Culture War?*; Gelman, *Red State, Blue State, Rich State, Poor State*.

27. Fiorina, with Abrams and Pope, *Culture War?*

28. Mitchell Killian and Clyde Wilcox, "Do Abortion Attitudes Lead to Party Switching?" *Political Research Quarterly* 61 (2008): 561–73.

29. Alan I. Abramowitz, "It's Abortion, Stupid: Policy Voting in the 1992 Presidential Election," *Journal of Politics* 57 (1995): 176–86.

30. Everett Carll Ladd, Jr., "The 1992 Vote for President Clinton: Another Brittle Mandate?" *Political Science Quarterly* 108 (1993): 1–28. See also Jonathan Knuckey, "A New Front in the Culture War?" *American Politics Research* 33 (2005): 645–71.

31. Kevin P. Phillips, *The Emerging Republican Majority* (Garden City, N.Y.: Anchor, 1969).

32. Carll Everett Ladd, Jr., with Charles D. Hadley, *Transformations of the American Party System: Political Coalitions from the New Deal to the 1970s* (New York: W.W. Norton and Company, 1975). See also Robert Huckfeldt and Carol W. Kohfeld, *Race and the Decline of Class in American Politics* (Urbana, Ill.: University of Illinois

Press, 1989); John B. Judis and Ruy Teixeira, *The Emerging Democratic Majority* (New York: Scribner, 2002).

33. Judis and Teixeira, *The Emerging Democratic Majority*, 2.

34. Charlie Cook, "Hard Knocks." *National Journal*, 17 May 2008.

35. Thomas Frank, *What's the Matter with Kansas? How Conservatives Won the Heart of America* (New York: Metropolitan Books, 2004), 8.

36. Frank, *What's the Matter with Kansas?* 5–6.

37. Larry M. Bartels, "What's the Matter with *What's the Matter with Kansas?*" *Quarterly Journal of Political Science* 1 (2006): 201–26; see also Larry M. Bartels, *Unequal Democracy: The Political Economy of the New Gilded Age* (Princeton, N.J.: Princeton University Press, 2008); and Mark D. Brewer and Jeffrey M. Stonecash, *Split: Class and Cultural Divides in American Politics* (Washington, D.C.: CQ Press, 2007).

38. Bartels, "What's the Matter with *What's the Matter with Kansas?*" 209.

39. Bartels, "What's the Matter with *What's the Matter with Kansas?*" 211.

40. Juliet F. Gainsborough, *Fenced Off: The Suburbanization of American Politics* (Washington, D.C.: Georgetown University, 2001); see also Peter L. Francia and Jody C Baumgartner, "Victim or Victor of the 'Culture War'? How Cultural Issues Affect Support for George W. Bush in Rural America," *American Review of Politics* 26 (Fall/Winter 2005–2006): 349–67; and Seth C. McKee, "Rural Voters and the Polarization of American Presidential Elections," *PS: Political Science & Politics* 41 (2008): 101–108.

41. Bishop, *The Big Sort*.

42. Bill Bishop, "No, We Didn't: America Hasn't Changed as Much as Tuesday's Results Would Indicate," *Slate*, 10 November 2008, www.slate.com/blogs/blogs/bigsort/archive/tags/Virginia/default.aspx.

43. Quoted in Bishop, "No, We Didn't."

44. Jonathan Rauch, "The Widening Marriage Gap: America's New Class Divide," 23 May 2001, www.theatlantic.com/politics/nj/rauch2001-05-23.htm.

45. Fred I. Greenstein and Raymond E. Wolfinger, "The Suburbs and Shifting Party Loyalties," *Public Opinion Quarterly* 22 (1958): 473–82.

46. Robin M. Wolpert and James G. Gimpel, "Self-Interest, Symbolic Politics, and Public Attitudes toward Gun Control," *Political Behavior* 20 (1998): 241–62.

47. Quoted in Bishop, "No, We Didn't."

48. Alan Abramowitz and Kyle Saunders, "Why Can't We All Just Get Along? The Reality of a Polarized America," *Forum* 3 (2005): article 1, www.bepress.com/forum/vol3/iss2/art1.

49. Abramowitz and Saunders, "Why Can't We All Just Get Along?"

50. Byron E. Shafer and Richard Johnston, *The End of Southern Exceptionalism* (Cambridge, Mass.: Harvard University Press, 2006).

51. Alan Abramowitz, "Diverging Coalitions: The Transformation of the American Electorate," *Larry Sabato's Crystal Ball*, 9 April 2009, www.centerforpolitics.org/crystalball/article.php?id = AIA2009040 901.

52. Knuckey, "A New Front in the Culture War?"

53. Abramowitz and Saunders, "Why Can't We All Just Get Along?"

54. Laura R. Olson and John C. Green, "The Religion Gap," *PS: Political Science and Politics* 39 (2006): 455–59.

About the Authors

Jody C Baumgartner, Ph.D., is assistant professor of political science at East Carolina University. He received his Ph.D. in political science from Miami University in 1998, specializing in the study of campaigns and elections. He has several books to his credit, including *Modern Presidential Electioneering: An Organizational and Comparative Approach* (2000); *Checking Executive Power* (2003), co-edited with Naoko Kada; *The American Vice Presidency Reconsidered* (2006); *Conventional Wisdom and American Elections: Exploding Myths, Exploring Misconceptions* (2007), written with Peter Francia; and *Laughing Matters: Humor and American Politics in the Media Age* (2007), co-edited with Jonathan Morris. He has also written or collaborated on two dozen articles and book chapters on political humor, the vice presidency, and other subjects.

Peter L. Francia, Ph.D., is associate professor of political science at East Carolina University. He is the author of *The Future of Organized Labor in American Politics* (2006) and coauthor of *The Financiers of Congressional Elections* (2003). Francia has written dozens of articles and book chapters on American elections, campaign finance, election reform, interest groups, and political parties, and has provided commentary for several media outlets, including CNN, National Public Radio, and the *Wall Street Journal*. He holds a doctorate in government and politics from the University of Maryland, College Park.

HAMMERING

HOt

IRON

for KENNETH GEORGE BULLOCK

HAMMERING

HOT

IRON

A SPIRITUAL CRITIQUE
OF BLY'S IRON JOHN

ChaRLeS
UPTON

QUEST BOOKS
The Theosophical Publishing House
Wheaton, Ill. U.S.A.
Madras, India/London, England

The Theosophical Publishing House
P.O. Box 270
Wheaton, IL 60189-0270

A publication of the Theosophical Publishing House,
a department of the Theosophical Society in America.

*This publication made possible with
the assistance of the Kern Foundation*

Library of Congress Cataloging-in-Publication Data

Upton, Charles.
　Hammering hot iron : a spiritual critique of Bly's Iron
John / Charles Upton.
　　　p.　cm.
　Includes bibliographical references and index.
　ISBN 0-8356-0697-X : $14.00
　　1. Bly, Robert Iron John.　2. Men—United States.
3. Men—United States—Psychology.　4. Masculinity
(Psychology)　I. Title.
HQ1090.3.U58　1993
305.31—dc20　　　　　　　　　　　　　　　　93-22749
　　　　　　　　　　　　　　　　　　　　　　　　CIP

9 8 7 6 5 4 3 2 1 * 93 94 95 96 97 98 99

This edition is printed on acid-free paper that meets the
American National Standards Institute Z39.48 Standard

Printed in the United States of America by Versa Press

 # Contents

 # Foreword

Fragmentation of the Soul: The Distortions of Archetypal Psychology

IT IS A COMMON NOTION that modern humanity is suffering from soul-loss, from the quantification and intellectualization of reality. The disillusionment with the Judeo-Christian religious traditions and scientific materialism has become so thorough among some people that we are seeing a reaction against them in the name of mythological and psychological polytheism, earth-centered paganism, and mystical eroticism. While reactions against religions that have abandoned their own wisdom tradition and a science which could not respond to the needs of the soul are understandable and to some extent justifiable, the reaction is in danger of being so extreme and unbalanced that it denies what has been known and practiced by authentic wisdom traditions for countless centuries.

When it is proposed that modern humanity has lost its soul, one meaning is that we have lost our ability to perceive with the Active Imagination which operates in an intermediate world, an interworld between the senses and the world of ideas, which Henry Corbin called the "imaginal realm" (*mundus imaginalis* in Latin, *alami mithal* in Arabic). The Active Imagination is the imaginative, perceptive faculty of the soul, and its function is to restore a space that sacralizes the ephemeral, earthly state of being. It unites the earthly manifestation with its higher counterpart on the imaginal level and raises it to, in Corbin's words, "incandescence." And isn't this what is being sought by most of those who are drawn to paganism, mythologies, and mystical eroticism?

The development of the soul depends upon our understanding of what the soul is and what its possibilities are. What has to be restored is the presence of the soul and its imaginative powers, but souls can be sick or healthy; souls can be created in this "vale of soul-making," and souls can also be destroyed.

❖   ❖   ❖

Integral to the present polytheistic reaction is the post-Jungian school of archetypal psychology. Considering the growing influence of this school, from its theoretical foundations according to James Hillman, to its popularization by people like Robert Bly and Thomas Moore, I feel it is time that some of its criticisms of spirituality and the monotheistic perspective be refuted. In some important respects, it seems to me, archetypal psychology diminishes and trivializes the human soul by reducing it to the terms and level of the social disease of our time: psychic fragmentation. I would further propose that archetypal psychology is a distortion and contradiction of Neoplatonism rather than its contemporary heir (as is sometimes claimed). I approach these matters neither in the name of "monolithic monotheism" nor any form of "religious conservatism," but from a wish to do justice to and preserve the attainments of those whose exploration of the Divine Imagination has not been in vain.

Monotheism need not be monolithic or abstract. Zoroastrian monotheism has its angels: an angel of the earth, angels of mineral and vegetable worlds, an angel of feminine wisdom, an angelic counterpart for each human soul. Islam has its Divine Attributes, and the polar categories of gentleness and rigor, of intimacy and awe, of hope and fear. And although Plotinus, the founder of Neoplatonism, did not reject polytheism out of hand, he saw the "gods" as manifestations of the Divine. Historically, however, his successors deviated further and further until their polytheism degenerated into superstition, magic, and theurgy, which are distractions from the One Spirit and

Source of all existence. Archetypal psychology could contribute to a similar degeneration.

What distinguishes polytheism from monotheism is not its willingness to admit diversity, but its lack of a center. And such uncentered polytheism is a not uncommon state in a contemporary world dedicated to an unconscious idolatry of appearances, a fragmentation and disintegration of the psyche. It is the state of one whose identity is without integration and so always shifting, till it becomes no more than a dissociation of voices and images, many of these absorbed from the mass media.

James Hillman and other archetypal psychologists would have us embrace this fragmentation, since they view any attempt at integration as a fantasy and ploy of the ego. Hillman's "polytheistic psychology" is supposedly derived, at least in part, from Henry Corbin's phenomenology of the Active Imagination and the imaginal world. But his misreading of Corbin's notion of the *mundus imaginalis* (*alami mithal*) is fundamental. Corbin was primarily elucidating Ibn 'Arabi and other Sufis, who represented a metaphysics of pure monotheism in which only God, in other words the Self, is real, and only the "I" that separates itself from this unified reality is unreal. The *mundus imaginalis* is a level of reality in which visions, which are simultaneously meanings, are experienced by a psycho-spiritual faculty, the Active Imagination, or what Sufis would simply call the "heart." It is important to realize that this level of perception was not considered to be available to any but the most "purified" souls; in its mature functioning it is certainly not conceptual, intellectual, or merely symbolic experience, but a visionary one of the kind which Jung himself had only a few times in his life, but which is the natural medium of genuine mystics.

One of Hillman's favorite targets of criticism is what he calls "pneumopathology," which is his own particular caricature of spiritual work as a kind of one-sidedness and inflation. This is not to say that such caricatures do not exist in reality; it is true that there are pathologies of spiritual aspiration. But the genuine realization of the spiritual is always allied with a realization of our own humanness in humility. It is the helplessness of our human situation, our weakness in relation to our subconscious complexes that lead us to surrender to the wholeness of the Self. Hillman is confused if he believes that the soul consists of the complexes which challenge the autonomy of the ego. The soul is precisely that presence and interiority which experiences both the ego and the unconscious complexes, on the one hand, and Spirit, on the other.

Hillman has introduced his own understanding of "soul" into archetypal psychology, which is confusing, because soul has commonly meant one's essential, spiritual identity, one's Self. Yet according to Hillman, soul is a catch-all term for deep, moist, feminine, imagistic energies that love to taunt, distract, and otherwise harass the rigid, self-serious ego and the well-meaning but rather dry and all-too-highbrow spirit. On the other hand, he also names soul "that unknown component which makes meaning possible, turns events into experiences, is communicated in love and has a religious concern." Meaning, love, religious concern—what is left over for poor old spirit but an impersonal bird's-eye view of the messy stuff of life? However, it is not among the realized saints of Spirit, who are the first to meet the salt of the earth on their own terms, that we find dryness and denial of the earthly, but among the pharisees and certain religious professionals and academics.

It is true that our greatest disease in this postmodern era is "loss of soul," and the dry abstractness Hillman distrusts is one face of this disease. The medicine he prescribes for it is the depth, moistness, and image-producing richness of his concept of "soul." But we are not subject to loss-of-soul because we have denied the image-making capacities of the psyche (our culture is dominated by images), nor because we have denied ourselves a soulful sensuality (we live in an era of unrepression), nor because we live at such a spiritually transcendent height. We have lost our soul, our interiority, to unconscious sensuality and materialism, reactive living, and mechanical thought. If we are to prescribe for this condition of soul-loss, we must be careful not to propose a remedy which is itself a symptom of the disease. The outcome of archetypal psychology's Felliniesque soulfulness is likely to be a further psychic fragmentation if not indulgent hedonism.

The world is a place for fashioning the soul: a presence which is the attribute of the Self, the center of the being, and which as center can integrate all the levels of the human being. That soul is not given to us automatically. Our soul, our presence must be created from within the distractions and forgetfulness of the outer life, from within the constant clash of pleasure and pain, happiness and loss. Our soul is the space of our experience; it makes the difference between being nominally human and fully human.

Kabir Helminski,
Mevlevi Shaikh

Acknowledgments

I WOULD LIKE TO TAKE this opportunity to thank Deborah Underwood, who keystroked the chaotic typescript of this book into late twentieth-century form; Jack and Leana Kornfield, for their constant reminders that our opponents are not targets in a shooting gallery, but real human beings; Brenda Rosen, my editor, for her strong Athena quality and her expertise in the traditional liberal art of rhetoric; and especially Leonard Lewisohn, who mitigated my battle-frenzy by placing me in the equivalent of three successive barrels of water (the first one burst; the second boiled over; but the third only became very hot) and, in so doing, made this book a stronger statement than it otherwise would have been.

The author also gratefully acknowledges the following: Poem by Antonio Machado reprinted by permission of the publishers from *Antonio Machado, Selected Poems*, translated by Alan S. Trueblood, Cambridge, MA; Harvard University Press, copyright © 1982 by the President and Fellows of Harvard College. "The peacock's excuse and the hoopoe's answer" reprinted from *The Conference of the Birds* by Farid du-Din Attar, translated by Afkham Darbandi and Dick Davis [Penguin Classics, 1984], copyright © 1984 by Afkham Darbandi and Dick Davis, 1984. Reproduced by permission of Penguin Books, Ltd. "Cuchulain Comforted" reprinted with permission of Macmillan Publishing Company from *The Poems of W. B. Yeats: A New Edition*,

Salut!

# Introduction

ROBERT BLY IS UNDOUBTEDLY the best-known living poet in America. His fame arises less from the popularity of his poetry, however, than it does from his position as "leader" of what has come to be called the Men's Movement. But this should not blind his followers to his stature as a poet pure and simple, nor to the groundbreaking work he has done in bringing poetry from Latin America, from Spain, from Sweden, and from Eastern Europe closer to the literary mainstream of the United States. And he has almost single-handedly created the first popular renaissance in classical Indian and Near Eastern sacred poetry—notably that of Mirabai, Kabir, and Rumi—since the New England Transcendentalists.

Bly is also one of our foremost popularizers of the sociological and psychological "truths of the day"; he occupies the identical niche in American culture that Emerson did in the last century. Through his lectures, his television appearances, and through such books as *Iron John*, his best-selling work on the mythology of the Men's Movement, he has carried a certain level of psychological understanding and social criticism farther into the public mind than perhaps any other figure of our time.

The Men's Movement is clearly filling a real social need; if this were not the case, I would not feel called upon to criticize the incomplete and sometimes contradictory intellectual framework for

1

the movement which Bly puts forward in *Iron John*. The work he is doing is so important, and the material he directs our attention to so essential, that I am impelled to give him all the help I can, including the surgical help of some sharp and pointed criticism.

As a poet, an activist, and a social worker of the "baby boom" generation, I have traveled through many self-contained worlds of belief, including hippie populism, psychedelic spirituality, yoga, Celtic lore, ad hoc sorcery of the Castaneda variety, Buddhism, Jungian psychology (and the mythopoeic school of poetry partly based on it), solidarity with the revolutions of Central America (including the Sanctuary movement), Liberation Theology, the global peace movement of the New Age, and service to the homeless. And while traveling this undulating road, I have learned at least two things: first, that psychic experience—no matter how fascinating and informative it may be—is not the same thing as an unfolding orientation to spiritual truth; and secondly, that it is possible to go beyond the need to see the world always in terms of a given set of beliefs and learn to see how beliefs themselves operate, both personally and collectively: to look through the eye, not with it.

I am a member of a fairly small group of Americans who believe that some ideas are true, and others false. I also believe that false ideas can pervert the best of intentions, because the ideas we hold determine which experiences we will admit and which we will deny, as well as how we understand and value our experience as a whole. To a great extent, what we see is a result of what we say.

Bly has done the best he could with the intellectual capital he has chosen to draw upon: the mythopoeic worldview derived from modern psychology, anthropology, art, and mythography. The myths he presents in *Iron John* are in some ways those of a fading liberalism and an all-but-dead counterculture in the process of being transformed into folklore; they are more or less the dominant myths of whatever sectors of society do not identify with the words *conservative* or *fundamentalist*.

Scholarly mythopoeia, as exemplified by the works of Joseph Campbell, is an interesting area. It's the place where secular scholarship meets the world of the traditional spiritualities—either to elucidate them or to complete their destruction, depending on the school of thought you subscribe to. In my own life, the study of mythopoeia was an extremely valuable introduction to the great spiritual traditions. But it wasn't until I really entered the field of these traditions that I began to see the limitations of writers like Joseph Campbell or Robert Graves (*The White Goddess*) or Sir James Frazer (*The Golden Bough*). Campbell himself said in his PBS documentary that his scholarly distance from his material and his unwillingness to choose and remain faithful to one tradition meant that he would never be a saint.

My view of reality has always been essentially religious, or metaphysical, which is why I must take issue with those who, like Bly and many others today, tend to put a psychological understanding of myth in the place of religion. I've even seen *Iron John* stocked in the religious sections of bookstores. Psychology and religion can dialogue with each other and inform each other, but religion necessarily deals with a higher and more complete level of being, whether or not it remains faithful to that level. In *Iron John* Bly shows a good deal of psychological understanding, but when it comes to metaphysical truth, to the *sophia perennis*, he is clearly elsewhere. So one of the purposes of this book is to untangle the confusion of levels in *Iron John* between the psychic and the spiritual—a confusion Bly cannot be blamed for, since it is endemic in all Western societies and many Eastern ones in this century. In doing this, it is my intent to remind the reader—and Bly, too—that God, by whatever name, is real.

Traditional metaphysics divides the human form and the universe it projects into three hierarchical levels of being: the material, the psychic, and the spiritual. This division is usually associated with the Gnostic or Neoplatonic triad of *soma, psyche,* and *pneuma,* but actually it is much more universal. In the Old Testament we find the triad of body, *nefesh* (soul), and *ruach* (spirit); in Egyptian religion, body, *ba*-soul, and *ka*-soul; in Tibetan Buddhism, *nirmanakaya, sambhogakaya,* and *dharmakaya,* as well as the *sidpa, chönyid,* and *chikhai bardos* (after-death states), etc. While the emphasis varies from tradition to tradition—the Egyptian triad being a kind of subtle anatomy, for example, and the Tibetan one an analysis of the three essential modes of the enlightenment-principle—all such visions of the three levels of being spring from a common archetype.

Hierarchy is not a popular concept nowadays, probably because we feel so fragmented that we instinctively react against any view of reality which threatens to divide us further. And *hierarchical* means "oppressive" in many of our vocabularies. But the real source of the

oppression and fragmentation we feel is the lack of any viable collective hierarchy of values. We have no stable orientation, no center.
Contemporary social mores require us to place all values on the same
level, and thereby force them to become rivals for our wandering
attention; this is why they are constantly attacking and wounding each
other. "One law for the Lion and the Ox is oppression,"[1] said William
Blake. We desert love for power, and then think we can return to the
values of love the next day without meeting the consequences. We
desert relatedness for self-aggrandizement, and then wonder why we
can't relate. In such a moral environment, conscious choice becomes
next to impossible. The necessity of clearly choosing one thing and
letting another thing go confronts us either as a crushing burden or
as a moment of blind caprice—and all because the dominant social
mores give us no way of putting first things first.

This is not true in traditional metaphysics. According to the
sophia perennis, Spirit comes first. It is our point of access to objective
truth, beyond the duality of subject and subjectively perceived object;
this is "the truth that makes us free." Psyche *is* that dual unity of
subject and object; it is the plane on which reality is composed,
not of objective truth, but of subjective experience. Psyche comes
second. And the material world, the world defined by our sense
organs, according to which we appear to be objects called "bodies"
contained in and presumably created by an environment made of
"matter," comes last.

Spirit, psyche, and body are not parts into which we are divided,
but levels of being which are also levels of consciousness, each one
less expansive than the last. Thus Spirit is not higher than psyche
in the sense of "idealistically exalted," nor psyche higher than body,
because each higher level includes and forms the substance of all
that is below it. Psyche includes matter because matter does not
exist outside our experience of it, and Spirit includes psyche and its
experience of matter because objective reality is absolute and infinite.
The universe and the witness of the universe are made of nothing
but the truth. Due to the requirements of survival, we are fairly adept
at distinguishing psyche from matter, but our ability to distinguish
Spirit from psyche tends to atrophy, since only divinely revealed truth
(scripture or tradition) can teach us how to make this distinction—
outside of individual inspiration, that is—and society is now turning
its back on divinely revealed truth. In the coming pages I have taken

every opportunity to establish criteria for making this distinction of levels, drawing on many of the revealed traditions to which every literate person in the world now has access.

My second major purpose in writing this book is to criticize the cultural beliefs and attitudes which work to destroy our sense of the sacred, and defend those which nurture it—in particular, that world of feeling, relatedness, and commitment which goes by the name of *romantic love*. As Frithjof Schuon has said, "The 'romantic' worlds are precisely those in which God is still probable. . . ."[2]

In my view of reality, religious values are the highest values and the source of all others, which is why corruption of spiritual truth necessarily corrupts human nature and society, and ultimately the natural environment. Religion today will tend to one of three moral, doctrinal, and emotional worlds: modernism, fundamentalism, or traditionalism. And this is true on a global level. The modernists are those who, since the Enlightenment, and ultimately since the Renaissance, have tried with great "success" to adapt religious doctrine to the advance of secular knowledge: astronomy, biology, physics, sociology, anthropology, psychology, and history. In North America they are best represented by liberal Christians (and by Muslims, Jews, and Buddhists), as well as by large sectors of the New Age. The fundamentalists are not so much conservative as reactionary, and modernism is what they're reacting against. They stand for a return to literalism in religion, which they see as fundamental, primordial. But the truth is, no religion has ever sprung from a literalist view of reality: "The letter killeth, but the Spirit giveth life." Modernists and fundamentalists are so violently opposed to each other they usually fail to see how much they actually agree upon. The modernists, such as Teilhard de Chardin and his many successors, base their theologies on the discoveries of the physical sciences; they are materialists. But when the fundamentalists insist on a literal interpretation of the Bible, they are in effect demanding a materialistic interpretation: if Jesus *really* walked on water, it means (to them) that he walked on the water *materially*. A symbolic interpretation (which does not exclude the possibility of a material manifestation of the symbol—in other words, a miracle) is of little interest to them. If someone were to tell a fundamentalist that for Jesus to walk on the water is a symbol of the eternal precedence of the human form over material nature, the fundamentalist would call this merely an intellectual interpretation, and not the real thing—forgetting that the whole function of religion is to remind us of the precedence of redeemed humanity over natural impulses and circumstances, and that a momentary suspension of the laws of nature with nothing symbolic behind it is no more than an act of magic, or a fluke. And what is the fundamentalist belief that spiritual growth must result in material success, if not materialism?

A recent traveler in Bali, an anthropologist, noted that both modernist and the fundamentalist Muslims saw nothing wrong in using a loudspeaker for the call to prayer, whereas the traditionalist Muslims relied on the unaided human voice. The traditionalists are those who claim to represent the perennial or primordial wisdom, a tradition that is as old as the human race. (According to the Muslims, Adam was the first prophet.) And as the outer or exoteric dimension of the various revealed religions has become more and more deeply invaded by modernism and fundamentalism, the traditionalists have moved to occupy the only territory left to them: the esoteric or inner dimension. Modernists will almost always see traditionalists as akin to fundamentalists; fundamentalists will tend to see them as heretics. But the truth is, traditionalists are the guardians of the essence of every religious tradition.

Traditionalism today is represented by a well-known school of writers on comparative religion, founded in this century by René Guénon, presently led by Frithjof Schuon (as first among equals), and including such authors—both living and dead—as Titus Burckhardt, Martin Lings, Seyyed Hossein Nasr, Marco Pallis, Louis Massignon, Henry Corbin, Ananda K. Coomaraswami, Leo Schaya, Huston Smith, and Philip Sherrard.

The traditionalists are by far the most reliable writers on the subject of religious esoterism. Though they seem to share with the fundamentalists an attachment to the past (I detect in some of their writings, though by no means all, a vein of royalist romanticism, which makes me grateful that most of the members of the school seem completely uninterested in politics), in reality they see the primordiality of religious tradition as based not on past values, but on eternal truth. Their allegiance is not to the old but to the always so, and to the old only insofar as it is a symbol of the always so.

At this point I can describe myself as a "mitigated" traditionalist. A pure traditionalist would never mention Carl Jung and his school except to dismiss them, while I believe that Jungianism is full of insights that are capable of being oriented to a higher level of truth than the psychological. And many pure traditionalists distrust democracy, seeing it as a kind of collective egotism which degrades truth to the level of majority opinion, whereas I believe that no matter how valid such criticisms may be from the purist perspective, democracy is still the least of four evils when it comes to contemporary modes of government.

I tend to be politically progressive, culturally moderate-to-traditional, and more traditional all the time—though radically unconventional when it comes to religion and spirituality. In this I number among my masters William Blake, that radical republican traditionalist and visionary, and Thomas Merton, who lived the life of a traditional Christian monk while breaking new ground in comparative mysticism and actively participating in the peace movement of the 60s.

When it comes to defending traditional values in the realm of religion and spirituality, I have no scruples against drawing my intellectual blade and using it. Since I believe in the separation of church and state, and abhor the use of political coercion in religious matters, I feel justified in writing at a white heat, in saying "true" to this and "false" to that, when it comes to defending my values. If this be fanaticism, then make the most of it.

In the Preface to *Iron John*, Bly states that his intention is to talk about male initiation alone. My intention is to try and situate this initiation in its greater context, that of the attainment of the fully human state. In traditional societies, there was no male initiation that was not also a human initiation, because social adaptation and psychological development had not yet been dissociated from the Spirit that gave them birth. To posit a male initiation outside the context of a human initiation into the reality of Spirit is an act of desperation—perhaps a necessary one. But if such an initiation is not in some way a secret response to Spirit, and therefore a step on the path of human return to the origin of the universe, then it is one more step on the road to hell. It is only because "hell is open before us and destruction hath no covering" in these days that nothing is finally lost, perhaps, in taking this risk.

We tend to believe nowadays that, in the absence of any clear spiritual authority, any spiritual risk is better than none. If there are no fathers, no elders, no wise women we can trust, then why not knock on just any door? When I was suffering through the initiations of my adolescence and young manhood, this was pretty much my attitude. And I have no way of knowing whether the scars I bear are those that anyone growing up in a vicious and dying culture must sustain, or if they are the results of true errors on the spiritual path, whether or not I bear personal responsibility for them. It is also possible (God, let it be so) that these scars are in some sense badges of wisdom and courage.

Yet since then I have discovered something that I can't transmit: that the truth has never been lost; that the spiritual path has never been broken. There is a *sophia perennis*, a universal expression of absolute truth which also functions as a way back to the core of that truth. It is hidden, but it is not dead. It is esoteric, but it is not to be identified with everything that passes for esoterism. It is subtle, invisible—and yet it is staring us in the face.

The initiation which Robert Bly proposes is in many ways a compensation for our botched puberty rites, coupled with the later initiation known as the midlife crisis. According to Hindu tradition, midlife is the stage at which the fully socialized householder begins to walk the spiritual path; in our secular culture, it often becomes a desperate attempt to regain our lost youth. And the initiatory ordeal Bly offers is not the deliberate scarring of the young warrior, but the breaking open of old and festering wounds, wounds that in some cases we never knew we received, in order to turn the blows dealt by life into emblems of integrity. There is no greater need, in this time, than that the wounds of men be transformed into wisdom and strength, but to situate this compensatory healing-initiation outside a living relation to the divine source of all life is a wound in itself.

At the end of his Preface, Bly quotes from a section of a poem by Antonio Machado, which, in a different translation, goes like this:

> Wayfarer, the only way
> is your footsteps, there is no other.
> Wayfarer, there is no way,
> you make the way as you go.
> As you go, you make the way
> and stopping to look behind,
> you see the path that your feet
> will never travel again.

Wayfarer, there is no way—
only foam trails in the sea.[3]

How poignant and beautiful this poem is. It is the cry of a
humanity that has lost the way to God, like a flower cut from its
root. It implies that we are alone, that no one has walked the road
to truth before us, or if they have, they have died or gone mad before
reaching the goal, or at least walked so solitary a road that they have
nothing to say to us, no way to guide us. It says, in effect, that there
are no fathers, no saints. In the place of "I am the Way, the Truth,
and the Life," all that remains is "Wayfarer, there is no way." Nothing
is left for us, in such a world, but the despairing gesture of self-
definition in the void, the constant, willful reinvention of ourselves,
moment by moment, out of nothing, or out of whatever cultural
flotsam may wash up on our beach, whether it be archaeological
plunder, the monkey-cleverness of technical brains operating on
divine truth as they would on market analysis, or the corpse of the
Judeo-Christian tradition. But if we believe that we can make our
path as we go like this, we have failed to take even the first step; we
will end up like the foam of the sea. No one can walk the path for
us, and yet the path is there, because God is the essence of every
form and because this essence has always sent messengers—captains
and shipwrights possessing all skill. The walking is our part—the
path is God's; though we may become master-navigators, we do not
command the wind.

What Antonio Machado says is beautiful, but it is not true.

❖   ❖   ❖

Bly's *Iron John* is built around his commentary on the Grimm's
fairy tale "Iron John" or "Iron Hans." Here is the tale in synopsis:

A king lives near a dangerous forest from which no one
who enters returns. A traveling hunter goes into the forest
and finds a pool, out of which rises a naked arm, which
snatches the hunter's dog and pulls him under. He reports
to the king, who orders the pool to be emptied; a hairy, rust-
red Wild Man is discovered at the bottom. The Wild Man is

locked in an iron cage in the king's courtyard, and no one is allowed to approach him.

The king's eight-year-old son, playing in the courtyard, lets his golden ball roll into the cage of the Wild Man, who says that he will return the ball if the boy releases him. The boy is afraid to approach; he says he doesn't know where the key to the cage is kept, but the Wild Man tells him that the key is hidden under his mother's pillow. He gets the key, releases the Wild Man, and in the process injures his finger. The boy, fearing punishment, asks the Wild Man to take him away into the forest, which he does.

The boy and the Wild Man make camp near a golden and crystal spring full of light. The Wild Man instructs the boy not to let anything fall into it, but he disobeys, first by putting his wounded finger into the water, next by letting a hair fall in, and finally by allowing his whole head of hair to drop into the spring. All turn to gold. He tries to hide his golden hair from the Wild Man but is found out and exiled from the spring into the world. However, the Wild Man promises that he will help the boy whenever he's in trouble and tells him his name: Iron John.

The king's son wanders through the world, comes to a castle, and is hired as a kitchen boy. He is ordered to serve food to the king of that castle, but since he refuses to bare his head in the king's presence, and so reveal his golden hair, he is dismissed and rehired by the gardener as his assistant. One hot day he takes off his headcloth, and the king's daughter, watching from her window, sees his golden hair. She asks him to bring her some flowers, and he brings wildflowers instead of the cultivated ones the gardener suggests. The king's daughter pulls off his headcloth against his will, sees his golden hair, and gives him some gold coins, which he gives to the gardener's children. The second time the king's daughter summons him, he will not show his hair; still, she gives him some more gold coins. The third time he is summoned, he will not accept the coins.

Then war comes, and the king's army is uncertain of success. The hero asks for a horse because he wants to go to battle and is given a three-legged nag. He rides out to the edge of the forest and calls for Iron John, who appears. He asks him for a war-horse, and Iron John sends him such a horse, plus a band of armed men, for which he trades the three-legged nag. He goes to war, vanquishes the king's enemies, returns the war-horse to Iron John for the three-legged one, and rides back to the castle.

No one knows the identity of the mysterious knight who saved the day, so the king holds a three-day festival, during which his daughter is to throw three golden apples, one each day, to the assembled knights. The hero wants to attend the festival and try to catch the apples, so he goes to the edge of the forest and calls Iron John, who gives him a red horse and red armor. He goes to the festival, catches the golden apple, and rides off before he is identified. The next day Iron John gives him a white horse and white armor, and the same thing happens. On the third day, the horse and the armor are black. For the third time he catches the golden apple thrown by the princess, but as he is riding away, the king orders his men to pursue and capture him, or at least wound him. They succeed in dealing him a sword-wound in the thigh, at which point his helmet falls off, revealing his golden hair.

Still, he escapes and returns undetected to his job in the garden. However, he shows the three golden apples he has won to the gardener's children, who tell the gardener, who tells the king's daughter, who tells the king. The king summons him. The princess snatches off his headcloth, and his golden hair appears. The king grants him a boon, and he asks for the hand of his daughter in marriage.

At the wedding celebration, to which the hero's parents are invited, the door flies open, and a great king appears with his retinue. He embraces the groom and reveals his own identity: he is Iron John, who has been living under enchantment in the form of a Wild Man. Due to the exploits of the hero, he is now freed from the spell. In gratitude, he makes a gift of all his vast treasures to the son of the king.

Jungian analyst Marie-Louise von Franz looks upon such fairy tales as "folk wisdom," emanating directly from the mind of the

people, which is identified with the collective unconscious. Other
commentators, such as Idries Shah, believe that many fairy tales
are consciously composed teaching-stories, disseminated among the
people of a given area by those whose role it is to do so. As for myself,
I can't pretend to know who is right, but I find it very interesting that,
according to J. G. Bennet, those who came to the "court" of G. I.
Gurdjieff at Fontainbleau were often required to begin as kitchen
boys or girls, after which they might be given outdoor work, and
that to start neophytes out as kitchen boys was also the practice of
the Mevlevi dervishes.

Bly reads the fairy tale of Iron John largely as a story of our need
to return to our own wild nature. I read it as a fable of the alchemical
refinement of the human soul through sacrifice of attachment—of
the development of the Wild Man from an *unnatural* state of nature
to a *natural* state of culture and refinement. While humanity remains
on the level of the natural elements, we lie under a spell. When this
spell is broken, we fill out the reality of the "Human Form Divine"
(in the words of Blake) and inherit our true kingdom.

This book is part metaphysical treatise, part social criticism, and
all autobiography. The reason I've chosen to write it as a response to
Iron John is that the themes Bly brings forward resonate, over and over
again, with important stages in my own development, though in many
cases my experience, or rather my way of utilizing that experience,
has led me to radically different conclusions. Thus I am, in a sense,
playing the part of Bly's shadow, both light and dark. I am his walking
blind-spot, as he may well be mine. My hope is that our opposing
visions will throw light into each other's darkness, purify and salute
each other, and open together upon a wider field of truth.

The serpentine motion of this book follows the course of Bly's argument, but the path it defines is straight: it is the path from psychic
multiplicity and polytheism to the unity of the Spirit. And insofar as
I have walked this path, I have had to deal with the many faces which
the psyche presents; consequently some of the experiences I record
have to do with encounters in the multiple realm, the world where
Maya rules. I can only hope that the strategic truths I learned while
traversing this realm may be of use to others struggling in the same
ocean and that the painful fragmentation I describe may serve as
a warning. The fascinating power of phenomenal existence, *avidya-
Maya*, is the essence of bondage and suffering—but somewhere in

this storm of images is the face of *vidya-Maya*, the fascinating power of truth. The more names we give to this one truth, the greater the chance that its voice will sometimes be heard, in the ten-thousand worlds.

In *Iron John* Bly says, "the disappearance of fierce debates is a loss" (p. 164). *Hammering Hot Iron* is written in part to redeem this loss, in line with the words of William Blake, from *The Marriage of Heaven and Hell*, "Without Contraries there is no Progression," and "Opposition is true friendship."

> O tongue, you are an endless treasure.
> O tongue, you are an endless disease.
> Rumi, *Mathnavi* (I, 1702)[4]

1

The Rejection of Transcendence

THE MEN'S MOVEMENT is a cultural phenomenon unique to our time. We've reached the point as a society where the assumption that men are the dominant sex no longer protects them from a sense of radical imbalance and alienation. As almost anyone who looks can see, the storm of cultural and technological change now assaulting us has called all traditional male roles into question and replaced them with cartoonlike caricatures. Caricatures, however, are not enough to live by. We men are "jocks"; we are "nerds"; we are "egghead intellectuals"; we are spiritual or artistic "flakes"; we are ruthless "hustlers" or oppressed and dehumanized "losers." But what would it be like if men were simply—men? This is the question the Men's Movement is trying its best to answer, on the wing in any way it can.

The tradition of working consciously to redefine masculinity in the face of radical social transformation goes back at least as far as D. H. Lawrence, and includes, among others, writers like Henry Miller and perhaps Jack Kerouac. But the tradition Lawrence began was then and is now inadequate to the task and, in many ways, self-defeating; it is the back-to-nature tradition which we've inherited from the eighteenth century, reinterpreted along more gender-specific lines. As a cluster of beliefs and sentiments, it includes the worship of sexuality, the tendency to seek understanding via the unconscious, the belief that automatic obedience to instinct is true spontaneity, the belief that the body *possesses* wisdom rather than acting as a mirror for the reflection of wisdom, and at least the beginnings of the belief that violence and barbarism are paths to spiritual and cultural renewal, as in Lawrence's book *The Plumed Serpent*. Most of these beliefs, minus the exaltation of overt violence, can be found in Bly's *Iron John*. (The best caricature of this belief system, however, remains *Zorba the Greek* by Nikos Katzanzakis.)

Taken together, these beliefs make up the world of modern nature-worship, the notion that the increasing artificiality of our social relationships and personalities, due largely to the insane course of technological civilization, can be made right again through a return to natural wildness. At its best, this trend represents the resurgence of a kind of Whitmanesque nature-mysticism, the vision of the divine nature in all things; but contemporary history, if not metaphysical principle, proves that if we try to unite with nature-as-God by abandoning the dignity and centrality of our full human stature in the name of freeing ourselves from repressive social conditioning, then the nature we encounter will be every bit as alienating—and ultimately every bit as mechanical—as technological society. In the incisive words of William Blake: "Where man is not, nature is barren." This is directly in line with the traditional esoteric wisdom of the *sophia perennis*, which declares that the Human Form Divine is both the center and the seed of universal cosmic manifestation, precisely because there is something in us which transcends this manifestation. We are given "dominion over the fish of the sea, and over the fowl of the air, and over the cattle, and over all the earth" (Genesis 1:26) not in terms of our power to manipulate and exploit them, but solely because humanity alone can contemplate them in their eternal forms, as emanating directly from the divine nature. In a very real sense, it is this power of contemplation which insures the continuity of life on the physical plane, if for no other reason than that as soon as we lose or betray this power, we start destroying everything we see. In the words of the Qur'an (XXXIII: 72): "Lo! We offered the Trust unto the heavens and the earth and the hills, but they shrank from bearing it and were afraid of it. And man assumed it. Lo! he hath proved a tyrant and a fool."[5]

One of the primary goals of all nature-worship, ancient or modern, is to heal the split between our subjective consciousness and the objective world by submitting our consciousness to the dictates of that world. (If we define *nature-worship* in these terms, then Marxism is one form of it.) But the enslavement of humanity to material conditions quickly becomes not a reconciliation but a crushing burden, and as soon as this burden is recognized collectively, we begin to long for salvation through transcendence of conditions rather than obedience to them. We begin to realize that submission to the will of the situation (if, that is, we experience this situation as a separate power) is not the same thing as submission to the will of God.

Those of us who live according to the transcendent religions of salvation—Christianity, Buddhism, Islam, and certain aspects of Hinduism, Judaism, and Taoism—have traditionally felt like sojourners in this world. We are not entirely at home here; we are just passing through. The Taoist master Chuang Tzu compared a human life span to a white colt on the run, glimpsed through a narrow space between two rocks. Among the possible attitudes toward life, this might be called the *realistic*. But few of us are realists. Through ignorance, based mostly on fear, we have become excessively attached to our precarious physical existence—much more deeply attached, I believe, than we were in those ages when the religions of transcendence were strong.

Historically, religions of transcendence have tended to be patriarchal, while religions which see the divine in the forms of the material world have made more room for matriarchal elements. I don't believe that this polarity is metaphysically necessary, since the transcendent can be symbolized as well by a feminine figure and the immanent by a masculine one, but it has been the established view for millennia, and so (for good or bad) it carries a lot of weight. This is why it's true to say that the alternate rule of the masculine and feminine principles in world history (primarily within a context of male dominance, however) is tied to the analogous alternation between the vision of God *beyond* the world and that of God *in* the world.

In terms of a much shorter wavelength of historical time, the alternation between times when Yang energy dominates and those dominated by Yin energy can be traced in terms of decades—especially today, caught as we are in an avalanche of chaotic change. In terms of the past twenty-five years—at least from my own more-or-less counterculture point of view—the wave looked something like this: the mid-to-late 60s were a time of what the *I Ching* calls "Old Yang"—the point at which the energy becomes so Yang that it invokes an inrush of Yin energy. It's as if the first touch of that Yin quality brought out all the Yang we men had in the bank and forced us to spend it. The world was full of inflated male culture-heroes and loud self-expression; men were spending their psychic masculinity like it was going out of style.

And then, when the 70s came along, it did go out of style. Men were no longer powerful and interesting enough for women to put up with their childish, irresponsible, and domineering ways; the new wave of feminism came in with a vengeance. This was the time of Yin proper. Women felt an inrush of new power, which was there to compensate for, and in part hide, a feeling of profound desolation in the face of the shattering of our most cherished collective myths of heterosexual love. And men were becoming painfully oversensitive and contracted. For women as well as men, this period was expressed in terms of muddy introverted poetry and gay liberation.

Here's where I begin to lose the thread, because this is the point where I dropped out of the counterculture; I no longer had that fascinating laboratory from which to view the dance of American society. But at one point, probably during the Carter administration, we undoubtedly went into a period of "Old Yin," which flipped over into the Yang proper of the Reagan years. Yet this reassertion of Yang was undermined by the major underlying shift of Western culture in a Yin direction according to a scale of centuries, not decades, and has now been seriously dampened by the loss of cultural and economic dominance on the part of the United States. Part of the violence of American culture right now can be put down to a Yang reflux that has been denied any viable field of creative expression. There is undoubtedly a new influx of truly spiritual Yang energy waiting in the seed-world a couple of generations down the road; but there is also a powerful transpersonal will, on the part of both sexes, to transcend the blind alternation between Yang and Yin, establish true polarized sexual equality, and develop beyond the level where our identity is limited to our sexual self-image. If we can attain the level of our own *humanity*, our sexual identities will naturally come into balance.

Breaking the Charmed Circle

The theme of the first chapter of *Iron John*, "The Pillow and the Key," is the primary separation of the young male from the maternal principle, which leads to, and is also precipitated by, the liberation of the Wild Man. This separation has been a major struggle for my generation and several previous ones. If we look at the problem in mythic terms, we can say that in a time when the dominant myth is the ruthless domination of and/or the sentimental worship of the natural environment, the sense that there could be any viable reality at all outside of the charmed circle of the mother is hard to come by. As the religions of transcendence have lost cultural force, the full separation from the personal mother has become increasingly difficult to accomplish.

This difficulty is compounded by the fact that the stresses of modern life act to overstimulate our mental activity (which, parenthetically, doesn't mean that we necessarily know how to think), while simultaneously stunning our senses. Consequently we feel cut off from our bodies and the natural environment, and so tend to idealize sense experience as a lost paradise—a paradise we drive even further away by running after it obsessively. And since sense experience is conventionally identified with the feminine principle, we increasingly project our lost wholeness on the figure of the Great Mother and on those spiritualities which make her the center.

During the commune movement of the 60s, for example, those men of my generation who identified with the counterculture did a kind of mass anima-projection on nature, hoping that nature or the country or the land would somehow magically create, or act as a substitute for, the stable love-relationships we no longer knew how to make. But what we ended up with was a goddess too big to marry and too impersonal and indifferent to act as the protective mother we hoped she would be for us, the nurturing bosom that would shield us against the negative father-world of raw technological society.

The lesson we needed to learn was that the Great Mother as an image is not the same thing as the Earth as an experience. We "come to our senses" not by worshiping the idea of sense-experience, even in the most idyllic surroundings, but by quieting the mind. And, for a man, an imbalance in the direction of the feminine principle will not necessarily produce that quiet.

In "The Pillow and the Key," Bly deals with the son's need to break with the maternal influence, and says, quite rightly, that many 60s' males took their primary initiations from women and consequently learned a lot more about their feminine sides, and about feminine values in general, than they did about their own masculinity. (I would, however, place the peak of this syndrome in the early 70s, not the 60s.) He then goes on to assert that no woman can initiate a man into his own masculinity, but, as we'll see, this may not be quite accurate.

Sexual Polarity as Male Initiation: The Dark Mother

It was in the early 1970s, at the point where the Old Yang culture of the classic hippie era was flipping over into Young Yin introversion, that many men of my generation—or at least the counterculture wing of it—encountered what I will call the *Dark Mother Initiation*. We men had used up a lot of our psychic maleness, our "Neal Cassidy energy," in reckless sexual, artistic, and just plain adolescent self-expression, fueled by psychedelics. The energy that normally would have gone into founding families and establishing careers was used instead to penetrate new states of consciousness, as well as new and undreamed-of levels of self-indulgence. And so by, say, 1972, men were in a state of energy-debt, and the Dark Mother was there to collect. It was in those years that many counterculture males developed the serious Yang deficiency which was to determine their basic character development for many years to come.

A man with insufficient Yang will necessarily be threatened by women; and it was men in this condition who became the "soft males" noted by Bly in his men's work. Now a soft male can relate to a woman as a servant-consort, a role which mythically derives from the son-lover of the Great Goddess—the sensitive, beautiful adolescent who is usually castrated and killed by her, like Attis or Adonis, or by her other servant, his dark, fierce, more masculine brother. But he can also rebel against the limitations of this role and become a tyrant—either a violent abuser, or the more subtle kind of tyrant who knows how to impersonate a woman's spiritual animus and dominate her intellectually.

Most women, in my experience, are willing to accept a man's male charm and expansiveness (even if he's a bit full of himself sometimes) as long as he is willing to accept real responsibility. But as the 60s ended, the women of my generation began to encounter more and more men who expected to be worshiped for their charm, while at the same time demonstrating a total lack of character.

How many hippie households were kept together—physically, emotionally, and even financially—by the women alone? In thousands of such households, it was the woman's role to work and the man's to entertain. Nothing makes a woman more violently and justifiably angry than a man who expects to bowl her over with his masculine charisma and then leave her to take care of the details, like food and shelter. How deeply some women long to love a man like this—while their unconscious anger grows—and how hopelessly they always fail; at which point, by unbreakable cosmic law, they turn into the Dark Mother. Many women of my generation became "witches" against their will, simply because they had little or no experience of complete men. (Note that I'm using the term *witch* not in the religious sense, to mean "a practitioner of Wicca," but in the slang pejorative sense as "a woman on a destructive power-trip.") The following is a poem of mine which expresses this particular imbalance:

Second Hymn to the Goddess

One day I went to Magda's house,
her cabin at Purple Gate
where many sad and manless women
came to eat power & play witch.

I danced until I sweated,
but I did not yet have a body
in which to dance.

so I smoked her dried mushrooms
I smoked her coca leaves
I ate her cactus—

and then the lightning opened his eye
in the corner above my head,
and the young lyric sorcerer
danced on the smoky rafters
like a puppet on a navel-string.

"I gave birth to a salamander once"
said Magda, staring into the fire—

so I picked up the rattle but the rattle shattered,
and the gourd seeds peppered the floor,
and the dog was barking,
and the bad woman was coming down the hill.

"Let's not invite any men to the
        next peyote meeting," she said—
"Let's just have *pictures* of men."

"You don't want our bodies there,"
        I said,
"You just want our souls."

What can a man do who finds himself depleted of Yang energy (and so confronting the Dark Mother) if he is unwilling to become either a *puer aeternus* or a tyrannical abuser? Bly's answer is that he needs to take his male initiation in the exclusively male world of the Men's Movement. In many ways this is a good answer, up to a point, but it is by no means the only one.

As the Jungians point out, both material and psychic history move by *enantiodromia,* the tendency of any extreme to swing to its polar opposite. This is also the philosophy of the *I Ching* mentioned above, where excess or Old Yin flips over into Yang, and Old Yang becomes Yin.

The same principle is at the basis of homeopathic medicine. Where the allopathic approach is to compensate for an excess by introducing the opposite element—by prescribing, say, "cooling" herbs for a fever and "warming" ones for a state of contraction and debility—the homeopathic way is to apply a tiny amount of an agent which in larger amounts is known to cause a condition similar to the one that needs to be cured. A little more warming brings the fever to a crisis until it breaks (Old Yang becomes Yin); a little more cooling stimulates the system to produce heat (Old Yin becomes Yang), in the same way that a positively charged (electron-deficient) pole draws a spark from a negatively charged (electron-excessive) pole.

This law operates psychically as well. In this time of vast energy imbalances, we have to learn how to allow one side of a polarity to posit the existence of the other side. If we see nothing around us but

Yin energy, it means that somewhere in the situation there must exist an equal amount of Yang energy. If we confront the Dark Mother and survive, apparently on willpower alone, we have already invoked the Father of Light. And as soon as any polarity is established, it naturally moves toward resolution—if, that is, we know enough not to cling to one side or the other, and have enough faith to surrender totally to the energies of change, a surrendering which sometimes includes surrender to the power of saying "no." But attachment to either affirmation or denial is the work of the ego, and for the two halves of the soul to meet and marry, the ego must die. The following lines were written out of a dream of mine, which illustrated this principle:

> He lay back, gave up, expired, and
> was gone.
> He breathed his last. *We saw him die.*
> And she & I, kneeling above that
> grateful corpse, embraced:
> Ecstatic—Joyful—Rising together—
> Married by his death we were going
> away
> Into a depth, a finality, a hum and
> flood of Purple . . .

Instead of building up the old masculine ego here, it is allowed to die, after which the two sides of the male soul embrace. When masculine and feminine energies in the male psyche are not confused but are fully polarized and then united, the same polar union becomes possible between that man and a woman in the outer world. If we men are attached to our masculinity, the Dark Mother will destroy it. If, instead, we are willing to let go of it, then the Dark Mother will have destroyed not our masculinity, but only our attachment to it, at which point that masculinity is reestablished, from its deepest source, in polar relationship to the feminine. Male narcissism dies, and manhood is reborn in love. This is the central principle of the troubadour ideal, that the right woman can "make a man" out of an unformed male by calling up in him the ego-killing and soul-resurrecting power of passionate true love.

I am not recommending the Dark Mother initiation to the men of America; I am simply saying that they may encounter it. Life is the

mystagogue here, and the initiations proposed by life can neither be
sought nor avoided.

Hatred of Christianity

In "The Pillow and the Key," Bly speaks of 60s and 70s men
as "soft males," which he says make up about half the people who
attend his workshops. But while he is aware of the far-from-soft male
violence now ravaging the United States, he sometimes seems to
imply that so-called soft males are the dominant character type in
contemporary America. They are not. The long hair of the 60s—
outside of a few hippie-revival pockets in the younger generation—is
now worn not by white collar or service workers but by carpenters
and truck drivers. There was, in fact, a lot of downward mobility in
the baby boom generation during the 70s. Plenty of hippies met,
and in a sense became, the Wild Man; and a lot of those who did
are probably not going to Robert Bly's workshops.

The "matriarchal" space in American culture no longer produces the soft males of the 60s and 70s type. It produces gang
members. Recent statistics show that one out of every five teenagers
now commonly carries a weapon. A 1988 study by Douglas A. Smith
and C. Roger Jarjourq[6] correlates crime not with poverty, nor with
race, but with single-parent households, most of which are headed
by single mothers. The space of the soft male, the "momma's boy" in
the older sense, the overcivilized aesthete, is fast disappearing. And
perhaps, via Bly and his colleagues, the Wild Man is here to apprise
the last of us overcivilized aesthetes of this uncomfortable fact while
there is still time.

Bly identifies the space of the soft male with the Virgin Mary and
"Gentle" Jesus of popular Christianity (p. 8) and clearly implies that
we need "wilder" gods, like Dionysus or Shiva. But the young men
now fighting in the street wars and drug wars already worship such
gods—sometimes overtly. The Dungeons and Dragons mythology is
being lived out in the streets of America with relentless literalism.
Perhaps the young corporate executive needs to make friends with
these darker gods, while there is still time. On the other hand, many
of these gods are actually company employees; they look after the
interests of the multinational corporations in places like El Salvador

and South Africa; they are already on the payroll. So are we talking here about the need to regain our lost masculinity by integrating the dark male shadow, or about calling a spade a spade by worshiping the gods who actually are dominant in this society? Undoubtedly, a little of both. But let us not forget that Dionysus was, literally, a "drug-lord," to whom alcohol was sacred, as well as the scarlet *amanita muscaria*, the hallucinogenic mushroom of the temperate and sub-arctic zones, which was also used by the death-devoted Viking *berserks* to spark their battle frenzy. And who but Shiva danced at Hiroshima, or Chernobyl? People like George Bush may talk Episcopalianism, but their real deities are the gods of the abyss.

Bly says that popular Christianity does not support the Wild Man, but he may be a little behind the times. In the mid-80s, for example, I attended a Wild Man Dance at a Presbyterian Church I had joined to participate in the Sanctuary movement for Central American refugees. The mystagogue in this particular instance was Ralph Metzner, colleague of Timothy Leary and Richard Alpert from the old LSD days, and a very professorial Dionysus. If I remember correctly, he transformed us into trees. One of the most influential voices in the Catholic Church right now is Matthew Fox, who is at least half a neo-Pagan. Another influential figure, the witch Starhawk, is in great demand as a speaker at liberal seminaries from coast to coast, or was a few years ago. Certain congregations within the Unitarian Church have officially come out as Pagans. And now, from a more conservative perspective, we are hearing of a Christian Men's Movement.

Nor is it accurate to portray the Pagan gods as only formidable and Jesus as only gentle. For many fundamentalists, the imitation of Christ is in no way a gentle affair, and anyone who has read the gospels as they are will encounter a portrait of a truly formidable spiritual warrior. As an introduction to this aspect of Jesus, I recommend Pier Paolo Passolini's powerful motion picture, *The Gospel According to St. Matthew*.

Why do social critics rush to attack, as if it were dominant and powerful, the social myth that is just now dying? For the same reason, I would say, that wolves attack the weakest members of a caribou herd—because it is easier. Feminists like to pretend that they are being oppressed by Victorian values, singles by the dominance of the values of married life, and Bly, apparently, by "mainstream" Christianity.

Wrong. All three. Liberal Christianity is dying and being replaced by fundamentalism, by the theologies of political liberation, and by a neo-Paganism which is either a valid response to, or an actual example of, the barbarism and social breakdown which surrounds and penetrates us. I would even go so far as to say that neo-Paganism is fast becoming the orthodoxy of anyone in North America who is not an atheist, a fundamentalist, a traditionalist, or a believer in the Social Gospel. And to the degree that Social Gospel Christians are involved in the ecology movement, they must at the very least coexist with neo-Paganism, since it has to some extent become the movement's religious expression. And the New Age spiritualities which worship subtle physical energies—the resonance of crystals, the electro-chemistry of the brain, the emanations of the galactic core—are neo-Pagan in all but name and style.

Why do so many of us hate Christianity, with its doctrine of a transcendent God? Perhaps because we see transcendence as totalitarian somehow, or antiwoman, or destructive to the Earth. Or perhaps because by now society has sunk below the level where Christian courage, compassion, and self-mastery have any meaning, and we hate to be reminded of how much we have lost.

In the world of pop mythopoeia, anyone who takes the Bible as orthodoxy and holy writ is in danger of being ridiculed, but if someone justifies a practice by saying "the Sioux Indians do it" or the Yoruba or the Maoris or the Australian Aborigines, he or she is met with automatic and pious approval. Why do we feel that the myths and practices developed by the natives of Australia are automatically relevant to us in the high-tech America of the 90s? Maybe they are. After all, the human race lived for a much longer period at the cultural level of the Aborigines than we have under industrial or post-industrial conditions, but the fact remains that this is an assumption, one that is dismissed by some social groups and accepted without question by others.

In challenge to this automatic dismissal of our Christian tradition in the name of Earth-based spiritualities, I quote the following statement by the Oglala Lakota priest, Black Elk, who not only became a Catholic, but a teacher of Catholic doctrine as well:

We have been told by the white men, or at least by those who are Christian, that God sent to men His son, who would restore order and peace upon the earth; we have been told that Jesus Christ was crucified, but that he shall come again at the Last Judgement, at the end of this world or cycle. This I understand and know that it is true, but the white man should know that for the red people too, it was the will of *Wakan-Tanka*, the Great Spirit, that an animal turn itself into a two-legged person in order to bring the most holy pipe to his people. . . . I shall explain what our pipe really is. . . . Then they will realize that we Indians know the One true God, and pray to Him continually. (From *The Sacred Pipe*, recorded and edited by Joseph Epes Brown.)[7]

Christianity is one of the high religions, as is any spirituality which recognizes God as One (or as void in the Buddhist sense of "not even One"), and which knows this divine reality as both infinitely beyond, and as the very substance of, the forms of the universe. Religions which do not accept the above formulation in one way or another, and which therefore believe in a fundamental plurality of divine beings, are what I—and not I alone—call *Pagan*. Defined in this way, Paganism cannot necessarily be identified with Goddess-worship; nor are all spiritualities which deal with invisible, nonphysical realities necessarily of the high religions. The person who says, "Kali is the universe and the Womb of the universe" is not a Pagan. The one who says, "Who's your favorite angel? Mine's Michael" (as I actually heard someone say) most likely is.

Some years ago I attended a Spiritual Directors' Institute sponsored by the Catholics and liberal Protestants of the San Francisco Bay area. It was there that I learned to what degree Jungian psychology now functions as a *de facto* element of Catholic orthodoxy. Insofar as this represents an attempt to integrate into the Christian tradition a knowledge which, while psychic, is still spiritually oriented, it is a good thing. Speaking historically rather than in terms of the metaphysical essence of the religion, Catholicism failed to find a place in its worldview for many psychic realities as anything other than demonism, largely due to its need to define itself as separate from the moribund Paganism of late antiquity. But insofar as this psychologizing of religion represents a return to something very much like this decayed Paganism, to a matter-worship and implied polytheism which effectively cuts us off from the higher spiritual worlds and the transcendence of God, then it is a disaster.

Which way will it go?

Carl Jung had faith in God. James Hillman, one of the most influential of the post-Jungians and a source of many of Bly's ideas, does not seem to, in my opinion. (I'll deal with him below.) While exploring the empirical multiplicity of the psyche, Jung still posited a real center: the archetype of the Self, which is not in his estimation simply one archetype among others, but the central and synthetic reality to which every archetype points, the *omphalos* or navel of the psyche, the point where it is intersected by the Divine Spirit. True, he denied that psychology as an empirical science could make any definitive statement about the nature or existence of this Spirit, but he also said (in a filmed interview conducted by Laurens Van der Post): "I don't *believe* in God—I *know*." As Marie-Louise von Franz puts it, in her *Introduction to the Interpretation of Fairy Tales*:

> After working for many years in this field, I have come to the conclusion that all fairy tales endeavour to describe one and the same psychic fact, but a fact so complex and far-reaching in all its different aspects that hundreds of tales and thousands of repetitions with a musician's variations are needed until this unknown fact is delivered into consciousness; and even then the theme is not exhausted. This unknown fact is what Jung called the Self, which is the psychic totality of an individual and also, paradoxically, the regulating center of the collective unconscious.[8]

James Hillman, on the other hand, speaks in defense of polytheism. He tends to emphasize the multiplicity of the psychic archetypes and distrusts the idea of individuation. He does not seem to believe in pre-existing potential in the psyche for attaining unity. Perhaps the terror and disintegration of our times have proved the abstract idea of unity to be powerless in the face of the concrete reality of psychic fragmentation, but true unity is not an abstract idea: it is concreteness itself. It was Blake who pointed out that the divine unity is not an abstract concept but a reality which is incarnate only in the "minute particulars" of our experience. In the words of Allen Ginsberg, from his LSD poem, "Wales Visitation": "The vision of the great One is multiple." Will Christianity—a monotheistic religion— side with those Jungians who posit psychic unity and a transcendent function through which it manifests? Or with Hillman and those like him?

Much rests on the outcome.

Hatred of Christianity as Hatred of Love

In addition to traditional Christianity, our culture is also losing a major facet of Christianity's "light Shadow"—the world of romantic love. As Christianity was our door to the transcendence of God, so romantic love was our particular way of accessing the immanence of God. Bly says that the 50s male wants a woman to return to him the golden ball, the image of wholeness, but heterosexual love has been a Western path to psychic wholeness—and a human one—for a lot longer than that. The universe of romantic love has worked as a compensatory movement to Christian asceticism for almost a thousand years. (I recommend to every man who still believes he can retain his masculinity in a passionate heterosexual relationship the two greatest classics of Western romance: *Gawain and the Green Knight* by the Poet of the Pearl, and *Parzifal* by Wolfram von Eschenbach.)

The knights we encounter in the European romances may not have been real men, but they do represent the conscious ideals of real men. And like the men who sometimes tried to pattern themselves on these ideals, the knights of romantic literature had faced and passed plenty of male initiations: prowess in combat, personal honor, fealty to their lord. It was only after they had proved themselves on the field of social competence that they felt called to take the deeper initiation into the feminine mysteries of the Grail. (Perhaps one of the tragedies of my generation is that we were forced to confront this second initiation before we had passed the first.) In Jungian terms, the confrontation with the Shadow—to a warrior, cowardice; to a knight, dishonor; to a vassal, disloyalty—usually precedes a man's encounter with his anima, the feminine image of that man's very soul. Is the Men's Movement of today preparing men for such an encounter? One of the tests of the validity of the movement as a whole—for heterosexual men, that is—is whether or not it ultimately leads to the renewal of a deep and fertile love between the sexes. In the words of George Oppen:

Love in the genes, if it fails—
We will produce no sane man again.[9]

But it is not really our genes that are failing us. It is our heart that is failing us. The central value of Western romantic chivalry was *courtesy*—a refinement of feeling which is capable of leading romantic love to the threshold of divine love and mystic union. And complementary to courtesy was courage, which is a lot more than guts or raw nerve. The man with courage does not lose his humanity in the face of fear, anger, and suffering. The word *courage* means "heart."

Liberal Prejudice

Bly writes: "The story [of Iron John] hints that we won't find the golden ball in the forcefield of an Asian guru or even the forcefield of a gentle Jesus" (p. 8). Of course not, since the tale of Iron John comes from a cultural place and time that had no access to Asian gurus, and is, as Bly says, "pre-Christian." Bly is implying, if not directly stating, that Christianity, Hinduism, and Buddhism cannot bring us to wholeness. But what does he suggest we replace them with? Jungian psychology? The Men's Movement? Jung always advised his clients to try their best to reintegrate themselves into whatever religious traditions they were closest to, while admitting that this is not always possible for people of the twentieth century. The truth is, the golden ball will be found where it is to be found, and where it is to be found is in the hands of God.

Liberal culture holds as an unshakable dogma that it itself is not capable of prejudice. When Bly says, referring to primitive male initiation rites, that no rabbi, minister, or guru is capable of initiating a man into the reality of "soul" (p. 9)—in Hillman's sense, something "wet, dark, and low"—he may be right in specific cases. Yet how is this assertion different from any other form of religious prejudice, which says that "all Jews" or "all Christians" or "all Muslims" are this or that? Plenty of ministers and rabbis are students of Jung; some even lead men's groups. And what about the Asian guru Nityananda, who spent years living in a tree with the monkeys? Or the Shaivite sadhus who roam India even today, naked, bearing tridents, and smeared with ashes? They are the Wild Man incarnate.

Bly himself compares the Wild Man to a rabbi teaching Kaballah (p. 55) and mentions the Shaivite sadhus in the context of the Wild Man (p. 241). How then can he justify this dismissal of the rabbi and guru as carriers of Wild Man knowledge? Obviously two contradictory belief systems are operating here. We ought to remember that such scorned Christian ascetic practices as fasting, vigil, and self-torture are praised by the liberal/counterculture world when practiced, say, by an Eskimo shaman and seen as pathological when practiced, say, by Heinrich Suso, a major interpreter of Meister Eckhart and a classic Christian ascetic. Such fierce forms of asceticism will most certainly bring up whatever is wet, dark, and low in the human psyche. The shaman who immerses himself in freezing water for a week through a hole in the ice; the Sufi who hangs himself head downward in a well, fasting and praying for forty days; the Christian ascetic who wears a hair shirt and sleeps on broken glass are simply saying: better to face the abyss of the psyche now and move beyond it (which often translates as: better to face it in this life). Now I realize that certain statements I have made and will make below about Paganism will be interpreted as prejudice. My intent is not to offend, but to tell the truth as I see it. I realize that this course of action is not without consequences, but I am willing to meet them, in the knowledge that anyone who speaks the truth as he or she sees it, without collective sanction, must pay for the privilege.

Bly recounts a pre-Classical creation myth in which cosmos is formed out of chaos by the agency of a sword that divides high from low, light from heavy, land from water, salt water from fresh (p. 166). He rightly describes this myth as "a history of discriminations," and then he says: "We can feel how different this story is from 'And God created the heavens and the earth.'" But, actually, it is quite similar. In the Genesis account, God creates the world by dividing day from night, the upper waters from the lower, land from sea; the parallels far outweigh the differences. Perhaps this extremely common reluctance to give Judeo-Christianity its due simply comes from our being too close to our own Western tradition to see it clearly, something like the difficulty an actor feels in performing the "to be or not to be" soliloquy from *Hamlet*: familiarity breeds contempt, or at least poor focus. I can't really call Bly anti-Christian, since he has at times professed Christianity; nor is it healthy to consider the churches to be above criticism. But he swims in a world where unconsidered anti-Christian statements are socially acceptable, if not hip—a world that is willfully blind to the real shape of the Christian universe. But if we can't recognize the value of our Judeo-Christian tradition, how can we approach other traditions without ultimately exploiting them?

The Theological Ignorance of Carl Jung

One of C. G. Jung's central errors was to identify Christianity per se with the "nice" liberal optimistic progressive Christianity of his time, which he judged as lacking in "Shadow-integration," and therefore not up to the encounter with radical evil, such as Nazism. Choosing to ignore the bulk of Christian theology and history—the doctrine of original sin, the belief in satanic forces, the fierce asceticism of the medieval saints, the Crusades—as well as the example of some of his own contemporaries, heroic Christians, like Dietrich Bonhoeffer, who opposed Hitler and died for it, Jung (following Nietzsche) arrived at the belief that Christianity has never been in touch with the dark side of reality, a belief I even heard echoed by Tibetan Buddhist teacher Chögyam Trungpa on one occasion. But if the crucifixion is not "dark" then what is? Disease, torture, betrayal, madness, political oppression—the Gospels are full of these dark realities of human life. (To say that Christianity has never been fully able to integrate eros into its cosmology is probably more accurate.) It is true, however, that some contemporary liberal Christianity does not like to see this side of things as an essential part of human life. The biggest New Age-Liberal-Congregational Church in my hometown even took down the cross in the sanctuary because the congregation was not "comfortable" with it, as if a religion to which divine sacrificial suffering is integral could be revised according to a simple criterion of comfort. But mindless optimism is more a problem of nineteenth- and twentieth-century Western culture as a whole than it is of Christianity. It is disease of rationalism, not a disease of faith.

Bly, like so many others, echoes this misconception:

it is good that the divine is associated with the Virgin Mary and a blissful Jesus, but . . . how different it would be . . . if we lived in a culture where the divine was also associated with mad dancers, fierce fanged men, and a being entirely underwater, covered with hair (p. 26).

Yes, it would be different. But when Bly refers to a "blissful" Jesus, he falsifies two thousand years of Christian experience at one stroke. Jesus is the man of sorrows, the child born in a cow trough, the whipped, the crowned with thorns, the crucified. He is portrayed as suffering and as triumphant, but never as blissful.

Exploration of the Unconscious? Or Worship of Unconsciousness?

Bly says: "Conversing with the Wild Man is not talking about bliss or spirit or mind or 'higher consciousness,' but about something wet, dark and low—what James Hillman would call 'soul'" (p. 9). The number of assumptions and contradictions in this statement is so large that the work of disentangling them reminds me of the famous task, imposed on many fairy tale heroes, of sorting bushels of mixed seeds strewn on the ground within a space of twenty-four hours. Therefore I call upon the Ant King and his subjects to help me in this work, and upon that mode of knowledge which Lorca called *duende*, which rises up from the soles of one's feet, like battle fury, or erotic love.

If conversing with the Wild Man is not about mind, what is it about? Without mind there is no experience—no Men's Movement— no human life. Without mind there is no experience of body, and so, effectively, no body. And "bliss"? Why do we often, like Bly, associate bliss only with the higher mentality? There are dark, savory, and abysmal blisses which our "bowels yearn for," and our genitals too. Dionysus, one of the deities Bly associates with the Wild Man, is also a god of bliss. And "higher consciousness"? If by *higher* we mean deeper, more comprehensive, more whole, and if such higher consciousness is not the goal of our conversation with the Wild Man, he is not worth conversing with, because he is a fool, and only fools take fools as their mentors. But clearly he is not a fool; he is the holder of a valid form of consciousness, of wisdom. (Shiva, patron of yogis and ascetics, and other of Bly's Wild Man gods, is also a god of higher consciousness.) And "Spirit"? Spirit is the breath of life. It is not opposed to the soul—it is the environment and substance of the soul and its center too. Was not Christ, whom the Sufis call the Spirit of God, born in a cave? And did he not harrow hell? "If you make your bed in Hell," says Jehovah, "behold I am there." The "high" is necessarily also the profound.

Now it's true that in the course of our psychological development, sometimes we need to explore the lower reaches of our psyches in the name of self-knowledge. But from a spiritual point of view, to believe, with the Jungians, that archetypal truths *rise* into consciousness from the direction of unconscious nature is false. The archetypes exist not in the unconscious but in the world of Spirit, which is a subtler and more comprehensive world than the individual or even collective psyche. They do not rise; they are simply *unveiled*— contemplated as eternal realities by the spiritual intellect. What we see rising are the reflections of these realities in the shifting sea of the psyche.

As more than one person has pointed out, the unconscious, collective or otherwise, is a misnomer. What we are talking about when we use this term is another form of consciousness, another kind of mind. To name the depth of the psyche the *unconscious* is to imply that we can never become conscious of it. But if this were true, we would have no word for it, not even the word *unconscious.* Let us beware of the attraction to ignorance and unconsciousness, to which individuals and societies exhausted by barren rationalism are extremely vulnerable. The reason we find this darkness so fascinating is because it is the satanic counterfeit of the unknowable essence of God. We project infinity on that darkening of the mind and long to hurl ourselves into the abyss of that infinity, hoping to find wisdom there—or at least relief.

Without the higher consciousness which allows us to know Spirit as an objective reality, we have no way of telling the difference between what is below consciousness—the abyss of matter—and what is above consciousness—the Abyss of Divine Spirit. In Spirit, these two are one, but this truth can only be effective in our lives if we reject materialism and take the divine as our center. And if we fail in this, if we begin to see blind abstract matter as the great reconciler of opposites—then God help us.

2

The Four Living Creatures

THE TALE OF IRON JOHN is about the development of consciousness, and the proof of this is found in the spring of which Iron John is the guardian. It is crystal; it is golden; it is full of light. Gold is the universal symbol of the solar principle, the spiritual intellect. Whatever is touched by the direct intuition of the divine realities turns to gold. But, as with King Midas, this truth will act as a curse as long as we retain our unconscious spiritual possessiveness.

In a sense the tale of Iron John is an analysis of this possessiveness and a story of how it can be overcome. To begin with, our original wholeness, our natural, given contact with the origin of our being, must be lost. The golden ball must roll beyond our grasp. To get it back we will have to fight for it; we will not be allowed simply to possess it. The attempt to retrieve it before we have done some basic character development results in a wounded finger—the consequence of our possessiveness. And those who are wounded in the finger or the hand find it hard to "get in touch with" or "come to grips" with life.

But later, when we dip our hand into the sacred spring, that same wounded finger turns to gold. And so this wound turns out to be a *felix culpa*, a "fortunate fault." Our possessiveness must emerge in order to be mortified, and through this mortification, a fault or crack is produced in our natural soul, through which the gold of the

35

Spirit can enter. To the degree that self-will is sacrificed, spiritual intellect dawns.

The symbol of this spiritual intellect is the hero's golden hair. But since this intellect has not yet penetrated to the center of his being, it must be hidden. If it is revealed to the world before it has taken root, it will burn itself away in a shallow, inflated, aesthetic spirituality. The hero will become a glib intellectual who never puts his ideas to the proof or a brilliant artist who dies young—a martyred Adonis, a sacrifice to the Great Mother. (When Keats published *Endymion*, he showed his golden hair too soon.) The hero must first cook awhile in a hermetically sealed vessel—the kitchen of the King.

The Track of the Red Fox

Somewhere in the psyche of every human being, there is something that hates the truth, that hates God. Christians call it "the Old Adam," or, when speaking of it as a transpersonal force, "the Devil." The corresponding Sufi terms are the *nafs* and *Eblis*. This force is often most active in those who are actively striving to realize God, to know and serve the truth. It tricks them, trips them up, sabotages their efforts. This is why saints in Christian paintings are often shown surrounded by demons. Thus when Bly says, referring to primitive male initiation rites, that "religion here does not mean doctrine, or piety, or purity, or 'faith,' or 'belief,' or my life given to God" (p. 38), he may be succumbing to such sabotage.

Let the Ant King, the Spirit who swarms beneath our feet in the solid ground we walk on, come to my aid again: The Australian tribal elders who initiate the young men transmit to them doctrine—the myths of the ancestors. The neophytes are influenced by every art known to their initiators to believe this doctrine. For this to happen, the young men must be purified of the childishness or dullness or selfishness or cowardice that might prevent the initiation from taking hold. (Try telling a Lakota at the door of his sweat lodge that religion is not about purification!) And the fool who is not pious, who laughs at the doctrine instead of respecting it, will earn the enmity of the Spirit of the tradition and of the elders who guard it. And rightly so. When Bly, in the same passage, says that religion is a willingness to live in the sacred water till we are fished for and caught by the Divinity, he is obviously talking about faith: "the presence of things hoped for, the evidence of things not seen." And when Bly says that religion is not about giving our lives to God, in a sense he is right, because we have never belonged to anyone else, and all religion requires is that we acknowledge this fact. If we fail in this requirement, if we fail to know ourselves as originating from a Source higher than our ego, then we are on our way to becoming mad dogs, sunk in viciousness and vanity, who destroy everything we touch, both the natural Earth and human society, in our greed.

Perhaps Bly is only trying to avoid terms and expressions that secular society sneers at, like *doctrine* and *piety* and *faith*. But once a society that denies the divine is conceded the right to repress any language that is adequate to divine realities, then, in my opinion, the game is up.

The Myth of the Four

Some fish we keep, some we throw back, and one fish we definitely need to put in our bag (pp. 42–44) is Bly's statement that, in addition to a masculine power identified with the sky and a feminine power associated with the Earth, there is also a celestial feminine power, a Sky Mother, and a chthonic masculine power, an Earth Father. I would even go so far as to assert that no mythic image of the spiritual world can be complete without all four figures. The Greeks had a quaternity like this; so do the Kabbalists. And my own rendition of the theme, based on a Gnostic revisioning of the Christian myth, forms the structural basis of my epic poem, *The Wars of Love*, in which the celestial masculine is Jesus; the celestial feminine, the Sophia incarnate as Mary Magdalene; the chthonic (earth- or underworld-related) feminine, Eve; and the chthonic masculine, Adam—or, in other words, the Wild Man.

When Jung identified wholeness with the number *four* (structural wholeness, that is, not dynamic wholeness, which is based on *three*) he was right on the mark. If we try to deal with a polar duality on the basis of the number *two*, we fall into hopeless contradiction. But if we render such a polarity in terms of *four*—as in the Yin/Yang symbol, where the black surge contains a drop of red, the red surge a drop of black—then the poles are balanced and united. It is a universal law of mythic algebra that "the *two* are made *one* by means of the *four.*"

This law is nowhere more applicable than in the field of gender. If we see women only as sensitive and refined and men only as hard-headed and materialistic, like the Victorians did, then we have not yet attained the level of the human form. And the same is true when we identify the masculine principle strictly with Spiritual Sky and the feminine with Maternal Earth. It is possible to identify the formless Absolute with the masculine principle—Shiva as the eternal witness—and universal manifestation with the feminine principle—the matrix of all worlds, gross or subtle, which appears on the material plane as the totality of matter, energy, space, and time. That's how the Hindu Tantrics do it. But the Tibetan Buddhist Tantrics do it the other way around. For them the formless Absolute, or *prajna* (transcendent wisdom) is feminine, while the manifestation in form of the means (*upaya*) of realizing this wisdom is masculine. Both myths are equally valid. And if we are familiar enough with the different ways the myth of gender can be played out, we may begin to understand that sexual polarity is in no way opposed to sexual equality and so stop mutilating ourselves by repressing gender differentiation in the name of an abstract equality of the sexes.

Bly says that the chthonic masculine and the celestial feminine have fallen into oblivion in the West. In many ways this is true; in others, it is not. After all, Christian myth portrays the Virgin Mary as Queen of Heaven, and who is Satan if not the chthonic masculine power, the Father Below? It is Protestantism which has really suppressed the Sky Mother by rejecting the cult of the Virgin; and it is liberal culture as a whole which has forgotten the Devil and so called up fundamentalism and satanism to bring him back into consciousness. But it is still true that the Sky Mother as a distinct hypostasis of the divine has been repressed, and the fact that the chthonic masculine could only be viewed as evil in the Christian universe (though with some exceptions) is another case of repression.

The chthonic feminine is fairly well represented among contemporary character types, as is the celestial masculine. And the chthonic masculine is pretty obviously returning with a vengeance. But what about the celestial feminine? From where I stand, it looks as if this particular transpersonal power, and the character type that's based on it, is the most repressed of all. Women (to use Bly's adjectives) are supposed to be "savvy" and "outrageous"; either hot and earthy, or cold and ruthless, or both. But if a woman exhibits a degree of refinement or sensitivity or wise innocence and still refuses to be physically or spiritually subordinate to a man, she drops out of sight. She doesn't fit the contemporary mythology. Women of this character type appear as a kind of terrifying hole in the dominant worldview, a hole that is immediately filled in with projections of weakness, stupidity, or pathetic naivete. This is because they call into question the deepest assumptions on which most contemporary personalities are built and are thus experienced, in a profoundly unconscious way, as the presence of death. Our first experience is fear—so swift we are likely to be unaware of it—and our second, a split second later, is righteous anger: the denial of fear. And we project weakness, stupidity, naivete on these women because, in terms of any recognition or integration of the qualities of sensitivity, refinement, or wise innocence, contemporary American society is weak. And stupid. And naive.

Given this state of affairs, I suggest that it may be the mission of the Men's Movement, based on its integration of the energies of the Wild Man, to recognize and liberate the celestial feminine from her prison of collective blindness, slander, and lies. The Gnostic myth of the Sophia—the fallen wisdom of God who is forced into prostitution by the rulers of the darkness of this world—and the myth of the knight who slays the dragon (in other words, integrates the Wild Man) and rescues the princess, are precisely stories of this unmet need. While we fail in this mission, our kingdom remains a wasteland.

Bly is doing an extremely valuable service in consciously resurrecting the chthonic masculine, the Wild Man. But we have to be clear on the fact that the Wild Man needs to be redeemed, not simply returned to. If we only sink in the direction of the Wild Man, in such a way that we lose the power to help him rise, then he is the Devil indeed. When Jesus harrowed hell during the three days between his death and resurrection, his mission was to redeem Adam and, by extension, all the human ancestors from a repressed and subhuman existence. In other words, he was there to free the Wild Man.

If one part of our psyche is too high, too ungrounded, it means that another part is too low, forced to live underground. In Freudian terms, this is the polarization between ideals and repressed impulses,

between superego and id. For every period of time we spend identifying with that in us which flies above the Earth, we will have to
spend an equal period beneath the Earth. And the force which splits
our psyche into high and low in the first place, which alienates our
intellect from our affections, is the ego: our obsessive self-definition,
our addiction to one set of self-images and our fear of all the others. When this ego is dissolved, our alienation and inner division
are overcome. The repressed energies of feeling and will, which in
alienated form make up the chaotic id, rise into conscious expression and empower us. And the intellectual faculties of creativity and
contemplation come down out of their equally alienated superego
state and move into relationship with these rising energies as their
organic principle of order. This is redemption on the psychic level:
Apollo choreographs; Dionysus dances.

But the psyche cannot redeem itself, because it cannot transcend
itself. Nor can the ego either purify itself or kill itself. Only when
Spirit dawns and becomes the conscious field of all psychic transformation can Sky and Earth marry within the human soul.

3

The Wisdom of
Serpents

HERE IS A TOWER which reaches up to God, but we did not build it, nor can we climb it. The Spirit of God pours down the shaft of this tower like a "rushing, mighty wind," and when it touches us, our soul rises up and flies off into that ocean of air, trying to reach God in the distance.

Then it returns to its perch, because every alchemical sublimation must be balanced by a precipitation and recrystallization, because the soul cannot reach God, no matter how far she flies.

The tower does not reach up to God; it lives in the heart of God. And humanity did not build and cannot climb it, because humanity *is* this tower. At the touch of the Spirit, the human psyche is transfigured, crucified, buried, resurrected. It is purified, refined, till it becomes the mirror of the light it swims in and from which it has never fallen. The soul does not reach God; God reaches the soul, and the soul, the psyche, only begins to know this when it finishes its struggle and rests at peace.

But we do not transcend struggle without struggling, which is one of the things William Blake meant when he said, "If the Fool would persist in his Folly, he would become wise."

Icarus

In Chapter Two of *Iron John*, "The Road of Ashes, Descent and Grief," Bly talks about the *puer aeternus*, the one he calls the "grandiose ascender." And he knows what he is talking about, both, as he says, from personal experience and because the *puer aeternus* is one of the main character types attracted by the Men's Movement.

Puer aeternus means "eternal youth." The psychic archetype of the eternal youth is an emanation of that aspect or name of God by which God continually renews all things in the eternal present: "Behold, I make all things new." Those addicted to linear time and the idea of progress, like the process theologians, will tend to see eternity as static, frozen; as a state of stagnation and paralysis; as a kind of obstructionism, a reactionary will to resist change. But eternity in itself is both infinitely stable, like a crystal, and infinitely motile, like the leaves of a great tree shaken by the wind. Eternity does not resist change, but encompasses it. In eternity, time unfolds, but it doesn't pass; it exists in a state of dynamic equilibrium. Eternal time, in other words, is just like music; it has no past or future; it is all presence.

The baby boom generation is the youth generation par excellence, which may be why it made its major artistic expression in the field of music. It grew up under the sign of the eternal youth. But when the eternal youth enters the field of linear time—and material existence is inseparable from linear time, since matter is a synthesis of linear and cyclical duration—then he or she becomes the most ephemeral of realities. As I used to say back in the 60s: "Eternity won't last." The flower children sprang up and withered in a day, just like flowers. When, in adolescence, we identified with the archetype of the *puer aeternus* or *puella aeterna*, we placed ourselves under the tyranny of passing time; in a certain sense we were driven further and further away from eternity by eternity itself.

When I visited the Egyptian room at the British Museum, I was struck by a horrible sense of moribund adolescence. The Egyptian religion, when it was spiritually alive, was probably more successful than any other sacred universe in bringing the feeling of eternity into the stream of passing time. But the outer shadow of this great achievement, the petrified and time-bound husk of it (which is all that's left in the British Museum) is a sickening mixture of eternal immaturity and eternal stagnation: images of wispy narrow-waisted adolescents carved on the hopeless stone of the sarcophagi. Now the Jungians have discovered that the *puer* archetype is often paired with that of the *senex*, the old man. In its higher sense, this represents the truth that, in eternity, the ever new is not essentially other than the always so. But in a more degenerate yet equally relevant sense, the pairing of *puer* with *senex* shows how the attempt to hold on to vanishing youth creates a terrible condition of senility and stagnation. (For Blake's treatment of these themes, see *The Book of Thel*, which is about the *puella*, and *Tiriel*, which deals with the *senex*.)

Whoever integrates the archetype of eternal youth will be able to see and respond to the freshness of each new moment, even into old age. But to be possessed by this archetype is to be hopelessly swept by the winds of change. Flexibility and stability are divided from each other, till all that's left of flexibility is flightiness, and of stability, paralysis. This radical split between possibility and actuality was the central psychic wound sustained by my generation.

The baby boom came of age at the peak of the social idealism and economic expansiveness of post-World War II America. Society projected upon us the highest expectations that any generation of young Americans has ever had to carry. And in most cases, we couldn't live up to them. Our parents, who remembered the Great Depression, saw our future as glorious and open-ended; whereas we, who had grown up in the shadow of the bomb, weren't always convinced that there would even be a future. And since our consciousness and desire were blocked from easily expanding into future time, the past of which this future would be a continuation also became less relevant to us. So we concentrated all our energies on the present moment, by which we meant either the eternal present of the mystics or the obsessively grasped (or avoided) blip of passing time of the hedonists (or the paranoiacs). Instead of working to become future consumers of material goods, the hippie sector of my generation (and also, interestingly enough, those who served in Vietnam) became consumers of experience instead, a tendency which eventually spread, in attenuated form, through society as a whole. At the same time, both mediated and distorted by psychedelics, we were experiencing a mass influx of archangelic energy, if not divine grace: "In those days I will pour out my spirit on all flesh, and your sons and daughters shall prophesy; your young men shall see visions, and your old men dream dreams." The result of all this was a hopeless confusion between the mystical ethos which calls us to live *in* the present and the hedonistic one which demands that we live *for* the present, that we "eat, drink and be merry, for tomorrow we die." This identification of mystical experience with self-indulgence (of which, perhaps, Rajneesh was the most recent example) may have been great advertising for popular mysticism, but it damaged the ability of many of us to walk the path to its final end. As more and more of us were being called, fewer and fewer (or so it often seemed to me) were being chosen. As a good friend of mine said when I asked him what he learned from LSD: "I learned that everything is possible, but nothing is likely."

Those baby boomers who entered hippiedom from the white middle class—and the United States as a whole was much more middle class in the 60s than it is today—were pulled in two directions as soon as they left the "Leave It to Beaver" world of their parents: upward, toward social and spiritual idealism, and downward toward lowlife, the ghetto, revolutionary violence, and the criminal under-world. And the truth is, having been raised in the cultural wasteland of the white middle class, we really did need to get both more earthy and more spiritual if we wanted to live anything like an authentic human life.

But for the more extreme members of the baby boom at least, the pull of these diametrically opposed needs was too much to deal with. Either we opted for the spiritual pole and became *puers*, or we went the other way and ended up crazy, prematurely aged, in prison, or dead. (And plenty of *puers*, choosing to leave this vale of tears by the upper route instead of the lower, also died young.) This meant in effect that we were forced to split ourselves in two; either our spirituality or our earthy masculinity had to be thrust into the personal and collective shadow. And even those fortunate enough to be able to carry some of the values of the 60s intact into the 1980s, into the era of New Age spirituality, found themselves alternating between subtle psychic explorations and gross political and/or eco-nomic struggle. We learned to cultivate out-of-body experiences, and we took massage workshops to try and get back in touch with our bodies. We were fascinated by accounts of near-death experiences, while dreaming that rebirthing or cryonics would bring us physical immortality. And that percentage of my generation who made it to the yuppie stratum—in the late 70s I heard estimates that about a third of us were upwardly mobile, and the rest moving down—included many who had left political and spiritual idealism behind to fight for economic dominance.

So our collective attempt to become more whole by cultivating the various sides of our nature in many cases resulted in even deeper contradictions. And, as Bly makes clear, those of us who became "grandiose ascenders" through spiritual or artistic idealism, later had to undergo what he calls *katabasis*: a fall like that of Icarus from too high and inflated a position to one that was, ultimately, too low to do us justice. On the other hand, that's precisely what *katabasis* is: justice—a balancing of accounts.

One of the wisest things Carl Jung ever said was that God comes to us through our weakest psychic function. If we are as much at home in the realm of intuition as, say, a farmer is in the world of sensation, then we are not usually overtaken by God through that function. We are too good at it, too much at home in the realm of subtle perceptions and energies. Instead of real mystics, we become skilled channelers or expert meditators. It's all part of our uninteresting daily identity.

Herman Hesse, in *The Glass Bead Game*, imagined a kind of quasi-ecclesiastical society dominated by a mysterious organization, which exists to play the entire repertoire of the artistic, philosophical, and spiritual intellect as a kind of game. The representatives of this organization choose a young boy to be initiated into their order. We follow his entire subsequent life within the Bead Game, during which he ascends through various initiations, till at last he becomes Grand Master. At one point, however, he decides to abdicate. He leaves the Bead Game, feeling liberated and reborn, goes for a swim in a cold mountain lake, and immediately dies. One touch of the physical world is deadly to the person who has spent his life playing the games of the mind, but this death is also transcendence, also an encounter with God.

This is exactly what happens to the *puer* when he encounters, not nature necessarily, but the world of work, responsibility, and social adaptation. It can be like a death to him or an incredible miracle or a slow and painful liberation. If the polarity between his idealism and earthly reality is extreme enough, he may even die physically. And grandiose ascension is precisely the attempt to avoid this potentially lethal contact.

One of the perennial controversies about the nature and goal of spiritual practice can be phrased like this: Is God to be found at the zenith or at the center? In terms of yoga, the question becomes: Is the crown chakra or the heart chakra the seat of enlightenment?

The Kundalini yogis choose the crown, the highest of the high, a blast of pure white light. The goal of this type of yoga, at least according to some schools, is to concentrate all one's psychophysical energy in the brain center to such a degree that the crown of the skull becomes hot like a coal, and the rest of the body cold like a corpse. And while this is a valid spiritual practice in its own right, it can be misused. If one is in a state of grief and loss, for example, the concentration of energy in the crown chakra can be used to deny one's feelings by denying, in effect, that one has a body in which to feel them. In the following lines I render one aspect of this state:

> Divine Hierarchy is cut
> within my own body:
>
> as the lower orders
> wink out
> in darkness —
>
> climb the Jacob's Ladder
> into cold,
>
> indifferent,
>
> shining
>
> Cloud.

In the spiritual sense, *ascension* can only mean an expansion and purification of the intellect, leading to a fuller submission and deeper dedication of the will to the truth this intellect presents us. As we ascend the hierarchy of being, we attain fuller degrees of spiritual development; we become more human, more what we really are. What then is grandiose ascension? And how is it different from ascension in the more traditional sense of the word?

In grandiose ascension, we ascend with only part of ourselves. Our head floats away into the higher spheres, where, since it is separate from the rest of our being, it can only be a spectator, while our feeling-nature sinks, like Euridice, into the depths of the Earth. External agents of psychic transformation such as psychedelics, or visionary art, or yogic or shamanic practices—when they are employed outside the informing context of an integral spiritual tradition, that is—can only exalt certain parts of the psyche at the expense of others, and so produce grandiose inflation; whereas any true spiritual path will orient us to the transcendent center from day one, and so allow the psychic faculties and psychophysical energies to unfold in a balanced way, a process which, to the grandiose ascender, will seem terribly tedious and time-consuming. To walk a valid spiritual path, then, is to climb, or be drawn upward, with the whole weight of our being, to ascend with all we are. The first step is to shoulder full responsibility for our own spiritual development, to "take up your cross and follow Me," after which we will discover, God willing, that it is God and no one else who is bearing that burden, and consequently that "my yoke is easy and my burden light."

Once again, the fact that Carl Jung was more ignorant than he had to be of theological and spiritual lore has created a mass of misconceptions. The particular error which needs to be dispelled here is Jung's disastrous separation of *wholeness* from *perfection*. Arguing from the naive and optimistic Christianity of his time, he criticized the Christian goal of perfection as excessively idealistic and posed against it his concept of psychic wholeness, to be attained by facing and integrating our shadow material. By so doing, he took self-knowledge and self-acceptance as ends in themselves, rather than as ways of establishing, and fruits of, an orientation toward what is hierarchically more exalted than the human psyche—the Divine Spirit. When Jesus said, "Be ye perfect, even as your Heavenly Father is perfect," he was not setting up an impossible ideal of perfect obedience to a meticulous legal code, or of lifelong avoidance of sin, but declaring that the only perfection is that of the God-self within us, which is why he responded to adulation by saying, "Why do you call me good? No one is good except my Father in Heaven."

Wholeness is horizontal stability and capacity; *perfection* is vertical exaltation and sublimity. They can be compared to the base and the apex of a pyramid. Perfection without wholeness is unstable; wholeness without perfection is useless. To demand exaltation without self-knowledge and self-acceptance is to build a house of cards, but to make self-knowledge and self-acceptance ends in themselves is to justify the avoidance of psychic refinement and purification and condemn the human personality to an endless course of incremental growth with no end in sight, no hope of self-transcendence. As San Juan de la Cruz said, "But if the motion of going were to continue forever, one would never arrive." Only an orientation to transcendent perfection can empower us to divide, synthesize, and integrate the psychic substance and so move toward wholeness. And the essential purpose of such wholeness is to better enable us to triangulate that perfection which is both the source and the center of our being.

❖   ❖   ❖

When the subtle intellect, the intuitive thinking function, is separated from the feeling nature through grandiose ascension, it is transformed from a guide into a tyrant. Instead of giving our feelings an open space of intelligence and perception to expand into, this "higher mind" now oppresses and torments them. For a man, this amounts to an oppression of his own feminine soul. And if he is narcissistically in love with his subtle intelligence to the exclusion of his feelings, they will undermine him, attack him from within. Because the parts of the psyche we choose to ignore react very much like people do in similar circumstances, they become profoundly hurt and angry. Of the following two poems, the first expresses grandiosity itself, and the second, some of its karmic consequences:

POEM ON A VELVET DRESS

I stepped up the rain, raised my fist,
And split the lightning's door:
    it dropped away as stone.
(That headstone has not made my history,
    nor do I steer by the palm—)

I am a satyr dancing
    beyond the Fire;
I am the notes of a flute
    through a wall of flames,
across the pastures of vengeance
    where graze the lambs,

the milk-white and milk-black lambs,
   whispering in their dreams
that vengeance is accomplished
   and fire sweet as grass . . .

I am an arrow
   that never misses
and has no name:

the Seraph in my forehead
   is naked now.

YEARS AMONG MYSELF

four years
a twist of smoke in
   inhuman places—

made no friends,
only passing acquaintances there—
   those of Fire—
those of Air—
   gnashed & fisted in Stone—
long-haired sleepers in the
   River lips on my
eyes before I
   saw them I
slept—

drew me through the
   strings of the elements,
   numbered my bones,
wove the threads of my
   blood in languages—

four years wandering thus
thought I could lose
   the sorrow

which formed my body, a
profile always there
   against the platter of
   Twilight

Phantom armed against me—
Vault-guard of the Law—

   once lay Flaming,
   Beautiful, in the
   lap of Summer—

   now an agéd child
excised from his mother-tongue;
   bald, shivering
     goat-sinewed giggler in
   ashes & poverty,
     gladly breaking—

ah what must I look like
   now that he is so old,
  now that he
     dies so well?

In neither poem does the soul-figure appear in her true form. In the first she is completely reified and dehumanized: not a woman, but a woman's dress. The pastures here are "pastures of vengeance" because for a man to identify his feminine soul with external nature is to repress her and earn that vengeance. And in the second poem the soul-figure still hasn't been redeemed from that subhuman existence, but remains "long-haired sleepers in the River" or "mother-tongue" or "the lap of Summer."

The grandiose ascender, having lost touch with his earthy masculinity, can only relate to the feminine principle via the numinous inner image which the Jungians call the anima figure. And sometimes this image is so powerful that it can effectively cut him off from relationships with real women, since he can only relate to them via a projection of this image. Flattered at first to be seen as goddesses, the women in the life of the grandiosely ascended male will eventually be driven away by the very intensity of his anima

In the higher sense, the law is simply what is. It is the Tao of things, the kingdom where cities are built not of bricks and girders, but of objective truths, each of which is a unique symbol of the One. Enacted civil or criminal law is obviously valid only insofar as it conforms with objective reality. And revealed religious law is valid because it conforms to a higher, transcendent objectivity, within the limits, that is, of the religious culture and world-age it is destined to create, and with the proviso that other revealed laws are equally valid in their own worlds.

Bly defines the *law* as "the rules we need in order to stay alive" and speaks of the *legends* as the "moist, the swampish, the wild, the untamed," a "watery" realm we can enter only after we've been through the "dryness" of the law (p. 140). But "the wild, the untamed" is not what we get after we have gone beyond the law in this sense, but the state we exist in before the law has even come into play. Here we can see a clear example of the modern tendency to identify the elemental with the transcendent, the rawness which precedes cultivation with the ripeness which follows it (and this is the error which so often leads us to confuse psychology with esoterism). But if Parzifal had stayed in his "moist, swampish" uncouthness, if he had never encountered his first mentor Gurnemanz, who taught him the laws of chivalry, he would never have found the Grail. True, he ultimately had to transcend these rules, but he did not do so simply by discarding them (since we obviously reject "the rules we need in order to stay alive" only at our peril), but by achieving a higher alchemical union between the "quicksilver" of his raw spontaneity and the "sulfur" of the chivalric code. It is ultimately foolish to reject the explicit law for the legends or the legends for the law; it is only the synthesis of the two which produces the alchemical gold.

Bly identifies the legends with "the world of dragonish desire, moistness, wildness, adult manhood" (p. 140). He then says something all too true: "So we move from St. George toward the Dragon" (p.141). Now the Dragon, in most Western mythologies, is precisely the lower self. No longer are we to kill or tame this Dragon; we are to obey it, even become it. This can only mean that we are now commanded to surrender to our lowest impulses, to that "dragonish desire" that is presently laying our planet in ruins. Clearly Bly does not intend this outcome; nonetheless, this is the ultimate mythic implication of what he is saying. On the other hand, he also says that "trying to be the Wild Man ends in early death, and confusion for everyone" (p.227). This is not a paradox, however, but a contradiction: we can't have it both ways.

When Bly says that we are moving away from St. George toward the Dragon, he's right. We are moving away from human responsibility and character development and toward a monster who holds our soul, "The Woman with the Golden Hair," in bondage. Our unconscious aspiration is to become the Dragon—to possess our own souls not by marriage, but by rape.

This mass identification with the lower self was the great reconciliation, the great release from *angst* which Hitler offered the German people: the end of the painful and humbling Christian struggle for moral and spiritual development and full capitulation to the mystery of iniquity. I know that Bly is not proposing such a capitulation, but I maintain that his words are. Very often our words are not our own but only channeled voices from the collective unconscious of society.

Since the publication of *Iron John*, on the other hand, Bly has lectured on the theme of battling the Dragon, and in the book itself he speaks of our dangerous tendency to romanticize chaos—in other words, to identify with the Dragon (p. 154). But ambiguity on such a crucial issue will not help us; once again, we cannot have it both ways.

The slaying of the Dragon and the rescue of the woman who is the soul from those psychic forces which are blind, and therefore evil, is one of the primordial legends. And one of the things the legends have always taught is that objective spiritual laws really exist. In a certain sense, the human form is composed of these laws. Just as our body unfolds from a specific genetic code, so our unique and eternal identity is woven on a loom of transpersonal norms.

The Bondage of the Sophia

Bly compares the Woman with the Golden Hair (the Princess in the story), who is the soul figure rising from the depths of the male psyche, with Mary Magdalene and says that they are similar in their "impulse to cause trouble" (p. 142). Not surprisingly, if the Dragon devours the Princess because the dragon-fight has been shirked through cowardice or ignorance, then the Dragon will begin to appear to us *as* the Princess, and a very troublesome Princess at that. But where in the Gospels was Mary Magdalene shown as "causing trouble"? The answer is, nowhere. She is shown as a penitent sinner, not a troublemaker. Legend has identified her with the "sinful woman" (Luke 7:36–50) who anointed Jesus' feet when he was taking dinner at a Pharisee's house, washed them with her tears, and dried them with her long hair, but even this, at least according to Jesus, was no more than a superb act of hospitality. It was the Pharisees who accused her of "causing trouble." And Mary Magdalene is also sometimes identified with the "woman taken in adultery" (John 8:1–11) although this is not according to scripture. Jesus' answer to the accusers in this case was: "He that is without sin among you, let him cast the first stone." If these stones take the form of backhanded compliments, so much the worse.

From the Gnostic Gospel of Philip [23] and from the greater mythic context of the Old Testament (especially Proverbs), we can discover who Mary Magdalene really is: she is the Sophia, the Holy Wisdom of God. In this world, that wisdom, intimately related to the celestial feminine principle, is in bondage to slander and accusation. We use her, rape her, throw her away, and if she protests, we accuse her of causing trouble. Our tendency to see her as an outrageously rebellious Wild Woman, rather than an embodiment of contemplative insight and divine justice, in no way supports her liberation; it is, in fact, the essence of her oppression. And this is true no matter how high a value we put on the Wild Woman concept, because that's not who she is. The following section from my *The Wars of Love* was written in her voice and in her defense. In it, Mary Magdalene speaks precisely as a woman who finds herself "too great for the eye of man." Students of Robert Bly will be able to pick out the part I stole from him, theft among poets being the sincerest form of tribute:

> I walk among you daily, and openly, in the streets
>   of Jerusalem;
> I buy food at the same market;
> I draw water from the same well as the other women;
> My face is not unknown to you—
> I appear veiled and discreet as the wives of the rabbis,
> And yet I am naked before you—why can't you see me as I
>   am?

Because nakedness is not part of your tradition, you say—
Because it has been exiled into the desert with the Goat—
Because it is hungry for children, the legends say—

But he who enters my house
Must enter naked. He must leave at the door
His family body; his social body; his private body;
    the body of his gods—
He must adorn himself for me: I am the Ark.
I am the Ark who was never stolen as the records claim,
But was trampled under your feet, sold from street to street.
I am the Temple of my Lord, I am the true Jerusalem,
A city you turned into a whorehouse—a place for you
    to buy and sell the blood of your people—

And I walk among you every day.
The stations of the day are not denied to me.
I am seen in the public places.
And still I am invisible to you—shall I tell you why?

It is because you are terrified of Beauty,
Exactly as much, and in the same way
As you are afraid of the Truth. Only one among all of you
Has seen me in these streets,
And he is my Beloved—whom you crucified.

It's true; we *are* terrified of beauty, which is why we rush to drown
ourselves in cheap glamour whenever beauty threatens to dawn. And
if she dawns anyway, breaching all our defenses, pouring through
our walls, "terrible as an army with banners," then we are judged,
horribly and pitifully judged for all the innocence, tenderness, refined emotional wisdom, and simple human love we have trampled
upon. If we want to escape this judgment, the only way is to learn
how to discriminate between *vidya-maya* and *avidya-maya*, between
the beauty that leads to truth and the glamour that leads to the pit
of materialism. As my wife Jennifer Doane has written:

Beauty is a way to spiritual Truth. Nothing compares with beauty—with that beauty which attaches itself to the Truth, the Real, that is, and not that "beauty" which participates almost completely in the world, and demands that we love this crass, habitual world, even if we have to swallow our truest feelings. That beauty breaks our hearts by putting up a wall between us and God, and finally tries to convince us that we no longer can reach God, and that God no longer wants us. How that beauty hates the other more beautiful beauty, and does everything in its power to keep us from seeing it. It even puts out our eyes. But the other beauty, the paradisiacal beauty still comes to us, and when we are blind it penetrates the pores of our skin, for nothing in this world can deny us the vision of Paradise.[24]

And to speak of the hell that lies under the signature of this paradise, the one reserved for those who willed to hide themselves in worldly glamour, the punishment there is to be tortured by a relentless, inescapable, heartrending beauty, under whose eyes those who saw love as shameful will be ashamed and those who saw innocence as foolish will be exposed as fools.[25]

6

Love and War

CHAPTER SIX OF *IRON JOHN*, "To Bring the Interior Warriors Back to Life," deals with the episode in the fairy tale in which the hero goes to battle against the King's enemies. In this chapter Bly speaks mysteriously and delightfully out of his own wisdom and integrity. Clearly, the archetype of the warrior abides in his value center.

Bly writes that to be a true warrior is to fight in the service of a real King, of a transcendent cause. A wise thing! As soon as he takes this stand, the whole hierarchy of being comes back into focus: it was never broken. As the warrior serves the King, so the psyche serves the Spirit, and in so doing gains the power to face the hardships of the material world.

Bly says that it is the business of the warrior, as opposed to the soldier and the murderer, to enforce real boundaries. A wise thing! Only when the ego rules does the warrior degenerate into a psychopath or an imperialist. When the heart rules, the values of courtesy (respect for boundaries) and courage (loyalty to the center) are paramount, and the sword of the warrior is drawn to defend the values of love, life, and the Spirit.

The defense of boundaries is traditionally the defense of the home (and by extension the homeland), and the home, traditionally, is the woman's world. Whoever ultimately takes responsibility for raising the children, such work cannot be done surrounded by the clash of swords, anymore than a garden can be raised when the deer and cattle are allowed to roam through it. In terms of the male psyche, warriorhood entails wielding the sword in order to make a space for subtle perceptions, for delicacy of feeling, and for compassion—the attributes of the feminine principle, the source of all the forms of life. This is why it will always be the responsibility of a man to defend womanhood, no matter how successful women become in defending themselves. Such defense represents the warrior's commitment to life, the dedication of his war-making power to values beyond the battlefield. Far from being an act of condescension, such defense is the only clear test of whether the sword-carrying man is a warrior or a bandit. If women are now being forced to enter the world of martial arts, for example, it is in part because so many men have failed this test. Women have every right to defend themselves. They also have every right to shame us into standing up for the values of perceptual refinement and emotional fertility which are the basis of any human life worthy of the name.

One view of the origin of the troubadour tradition—a limited view, but a very interesting one—is that various Sufi brotherhoods during the Crusades deliberately sent representatives to try to soften the barbarism of Western Christendom by introducing the cult of the Divine Feminine—a completely delightful form of psychological warfare. (Be that as it may, the lore of the Celts was ripe to respond to the Arabic-Persian influence on the basis of a deep affinity, and so bring forth the genre of Romance.) In Japan, a comparable development, in a comparable time of feudal chaos, was the Tea Ceremony. In addition to warcraft, the Samurai warrior learned to develop his delicacy and simplicity of soul through the art of sitting with companions in silence or in courteous and refined conversation, drinking tea. The warrior defends delicacy, but delicacy also empowers the warrior. The Celtic motto quoted by Bly is perfectly correct: "Never give a sword to a man who can't dance." When the medieval knight wore an article of his lady's clothing into battle, he was reminding himself of, and drawing effective power from, the values he fought for.

The Greater Jihad

As of Chapter Six, Bly knows—and may he fix it firmly in his memory—that the greater Holy War, the dragon fight, is the war against the passional soul, which is why the hero of the fairy tale hides his triumph over the invading army from the King's men. His is an inner victory, whose trophy is a value higher than public acclaim or glory. If this war is lost, the result is chaos, both in the soul and in society. And how right Bly is to say that we aren't sure if we really want the forces of order, represented by the savior-god Krishna, to triumph (p. 154). This is because we identify order with regimentation. But the truth is, chaos and regimentation create each other. If we suffer from repression, we will be attracted to chaos because we believe that chaos is freedom, and the resulting massive disorder will seem to justify even more repression, both in terms of character rigidity and of political tyranny. The choice between regimentation and chaos is the choice between death by multiple sclerosis and death by cirrhosis of the liver. But when the Hindus celebrate the victory of Krishna over the demons, they are not celebrating the triumph of authoritarianism over self-indulgence, but that of an all-embracing, limpid harmony over an agony of discord and self-contradiction. How rightly Bly quotes the line from the Mithraic bull sacrifice in this context: "Just as God kills the Bull, so I kill my own passions." The triumph of conscious responsibility over blind passion both invokes and lives as an emanation of the eternal precedence of the solar Spirit over the lunar psyche, the moon-horned bull. (And this is not, necessarily, the precedence of male over female. The archaic moon was masculine, as in the case of the moon-god Sin, after whom Sinai was named; and the sun of Japan, personified as *Amaterasu-no-omikami*, is feminine still.)

The World Mountain

As soon as Bly posits the warrior as a man in service to a transpersonal value, the true distinction between Spirit, soul, and body starts to become clear. He recounts the Pelasgian creation myth, in which an egg is floating in the ocean, before the dawn of time. A sword arrives, cuts the egg in two, and out springs Eros. Then the Great Cutter comes again and divides matter into heavy and light; the light rises, the heavy sinks. The Cutter goes on dividing and dividing until *cosmos* ("order") as we know it is born.

The sword is Spirit in its active mode. The ocean is the World Soul, which holds the egg, the hidden potentiality for manifestation.

And Eros here is what the perennial wisdom calls the Primordial or
Universal Man, who is also the Adam Kadmon of the Kabbalists, the
Insan al-Kamil of the Sufis, the cosmic Christ of St. Paul, and the Giant Albion of William Blake, who "anciently contained in his mighty
limbs all things in Heaven & Earth."[26] In terms of the "three forces"
of Gurdjieff, the sword is the creative First Force; the ocean-with-egg
is the receptive Second Force, the fertile womb of Being which brings
the creative impulse into manifestation by "resisting" it (not by trying
to repel it, but by providing it with a natural limit); and Eros is the
Third Force, the force of reconciliation that both encompasses and
neutralizes all polarities. All this happens in the spiritual or Divine
realm. Then, when the Great Cutter (the Spirit) moves again and
divides subtle matter into heavy and light, the action takes place not
in the spiritual but in the psychic realm. Eros, who represents (like
Mercurius) the *prima materia* of the alchemists, the subtlest form of
material existence, by his division produces the various worlds of
the psychic dimension, the light substances of the higher chakras,
the dense substance of the lower. With the next division, the four
elements appear; and with the next, the material world. Everything is
now put in its place; true hierarchy is re-established; order is born out
of chaos. The World Tree is risen; the World Mountain is established;
the King has arrived. The essence of chaos is the attempt to force
primal realities from different levels to occupy the same level, thus
placing them in conflict, and the essence of order is to allow each
primal reality to assume its natural hierarchical position, to let the
Sun shine down from above, the rain fall from the middle air, the
tree rise from the earth and put down roots, and the earth support
the tree.

    This myth is truly ancient. The hierarchy of being it reveals
was elaborated by the Neoplatonists of late antiquity, but the same
essential mythologem appears in the first two books of Genesis and in
many other contexts all over the world. It is primordial and universal,
because it is true.

The Tantric Polarity

    Bly has a lot of interesting things to say in Chapter Six about
copper and iron, about how the "man made of copper" becomes a

conductor for the intense and violent feelings of the people around him. Very true. The man whose father (or mother) was stuck in First Force, or self-assertion, and whose mother (or father) was mired in Second Force, or passive aggression, will be in danger of impersonating the Third Force for the rest of his life. He will be the reconciler, the man who can bring the opposites together. But he may never hold the power to say either a generous *yes* or a firm *no.*

The problem with this kind of man, however, is not that he is a conductor. Our ability to transmute the poison or ground the violence in the persons or situations we meet may decide whether or not we survive the next confrontation. And the capacity to conduct strong psychic currents with a minimum of heat-producing resistance is the key to both psychic and physical health and healing as well as to the inner alchemy of yogic or psychophysical development. It is also the basis of all empathy. The problem is not conductivity, but lack of insulation, of the ability to open consciously to the surrounding psychic energies and then consciously to close. The man whose "copper" is not well-insulated is too permeable to the psychic emanations of others—unconsciously permeable. He is forced to act as a scapegoat for other people's unresolved conflicts, a vicarious saint, who may believe he is compassionately taking on the karma of others, when all he is really doing is interfering with their development, robbing them of their chance to become conscious through creative suffering. And when such a man receives the call to establish the inner polarity, to allow himself to be the field for the current that flows between the inner King and Queen—the alchemical sulfur and quicksilver of his own being—he will not be able to answer this call because he is too attached to other people's energies and to the subtle dramas they create.

But no matter how conductive we are, as the current increases there will be heat. Resistance—hidden egotism—will surface. The heat arises specifically to burn that egotism away. To live between the opposites (in Bly's phrase) is to exist in an environment of intense psychic forces, since, in both electrostatics and tantric yoga, polarity is the primal source of energy. If we are well enough insulated— if, in alchemical terms, we have enough salt—then these powerful energies will work to synthesize the chaotic elements of the psyche, purify us of ego attachments, and nurture real spiritual growth. If, on the other hand, our supply of salt fails, we will not be able to retain our water or stand the heat. Our alchemical vessel will crack, resulting in dissipation or reactive violence.

The alchemical vessel, the *athenor*, is compounded of wisdom, courage, strength of character, and, ultimately, of love. It is what allows us to stand the tension between the polar opposites and the fierce currents such polarity must create. And, among *athenors*, few are as transformative as the state of marriage, provided that love is fire.

Joyeuse Gard

In this regard it is is essential to discern the outlines of a "sunken continent," whose true shape is deeply repressed in this culture: the domain of romantic love. "Romantic love involves a great deal of merging" (p. 172) says Robert Bly, and he goes on to cite the example of a character from Chekhov, a wife who seemed to have no soul content beyond the shop talk of her three successive husbands. They talk carpentry, she talks carpentry; they talk veterinary medicine, she talks veterinary medicine. But what could be less romantic than this? The essence of romance is not a flaccid unconscious merging, but polar relatedness and passionate union, as in the flamenco metaphor Bly uses further on. When I use the term *romantic love*, I'm not talking about cozy sentimentality as portrayed in the romantic movies of the 40s and 50s, but of the unsentimental passion of the original medieval romances, a passion we can still hear the ring of in the poetry of William Butler Yeats. Such passion, of course, was almost never associated with marriage, but rather with hot and risky adultery. And it's true that a marriage of 40 years can't be all flamenco; you obviously need some coziness too. But the attempt on the part of Western culture to situate passionate romance within the context of marriage, while in one sense was nothing but a weak compromise between the demands of the ethic of chivalry and those of church morality, in another and higher sense was a move to unite Heaven and Earth, to bring back the Golden Age, to make every home and hearth a temple of tantric worship.

As Bly says, we need to be able to rejoice in all the pairs of opposites which make up cosmic experience, but we also need, sometimes, to choose clearly one side against the other, stand, and fight (p. 174).

When dealing with polarities such as man/woman, sky/earth, inner/outer, we can understand immediately how reconciliation within polarity is true wholeness. But when confronted with fiercer polarities, such as good/evil, not to mention truth/illusion, we had better have the humility to admit that such oppositions transcend our human state. If we try to reconcile them within our psyches, or between ourselves and the outer world, on the basis of our own intelligent willfulness, then we will fall into massive hubris and turn into mad dogs; such polarities can only be reconciled within the Divine Nature itself. Only in the core of God is all true, even the illusion, and all good, even the terror.

Perhaps the wisest thing Bly says in all of *Iron John* is that our passion requires that we choose the "one precious thing," after which we will be forced to deal with the anger of the "divinities" we have rejected. I have alluded above to the story (which Bly also uses) of Paris's decision to give the beauty prize to Aphrodite, which earned him the enmity of the runners-up, Hera and Athena. If we remain on the purely psychic level, such an enforced choice between archetypes can only be unfortunate. It's something like having to answer the question, "Which eye would you rather lose?" or "Which hand do you want cut off?" If, as Blake says, "all deities reside in the human breast," if the gods and goddesses are the elemental components of the human psyche, then to choose one over the others can only be, on the psychic level, a dangerous one-sidedness, a kind of mutilation. This is why polytheists are so attached to their many gods; they are struggling to be whole, to cultivate the many sides of their nature, but they are doing so in a possessive, quantitative, self-defeating way. To quote Blake again, "More! More! is the cry of a mistaken soul, less than All cannot satisfy Man."[27] Thus it is true to say that one who lacks the courage to choose, or be chosen by, the one precious thing can never be truly balanced or whole, but the import of this is that such a choice begins to take us beyond the psychic level of things. It leads, in fact, to the discovery and establishment of the center of the psyche, the Self archetype, the heart. And the heart is the point at which, over the extreme eastern horizon of the psyche, the Spirit begins to dawn, the light of unity which holds the power to constellate and synthesize psychic multiplicity. In Bly's words, "the King wakes up."

The one precious thing is the thing we love most in life, the thing we are willing to die for. Ultimately, the one precious thing is God, and the thing we love most in life will either be our uniquely particular way of opening to God or the idol we put in God's place, whoever or whatever that may be.

To Die for Love

Intimations of the one precious thing may appear when we are in a state of psychic expansion and imaginative freedom, but we can only embrace that precious thing when we are at the end our rope, at the deepest point of our *katabasis*, at the bottom of all we know. This is why, in Shakespeare's *The Merchant of Venice*, the portrait representing Portia's soul is to be found not in the gold or silver caskets, but in the leaden one: "man's extremity is God's opportunity." In a certain sense, what takes place at the nadir of a man's psyche is the marriage with the goddess, which may take the form of physical death, and is, in any case, a psychic death. Thus the beloved we encounter at this point of deepest surrender is not the expression of our vanity and narcissism, but of our fated, and willing, submission to our destiny. That spiritual seed, which is planted at midnight in the depths of the Earth, is the one which, when it sprouts, has the power to transform our whole being, our whole world. Other seeds, planted in the shallower soils of mentality and sentiment, may sprout more quickly, but their issue also withers more quickly. The spiritual seed takes a long time to mature, but by the time it breaks surface, its roots have struck to the center of being. And in another sense, we ourselves are the spiritual seed, which "if it fall to the ground, and rot, will bring forth much fruit."

When encountering the abysmal pole of the psyche, nothing can protect us but total surrender. If we resist, we will find ourselves in the pit of hell. If we surrender only a little, then we've handed our power over to the demons living there, who will be delighted to take advantage of our weakness. Only total surrender will work, because nothing else posits the presence of the Divine, the infinite and absolute, the only reality to which total surrender is possible. This is the exact point where Kali as the horrendous projection of our desire to live, embodied as our fear of death, is transformed into Kali as pure mirrorlike receptivity. The Great Goddess we encounter in the depths of the psyche is the universal nature, the objective aspect of the Divine unity. As we come into the field of this objectivity, we are forced to let go of the last shreds of our subjective identity. In terms of our existence as knowing and acting subjects, we die. The result of this death is a complete identification with the Divine receptivity, or, to say it another way, a complete receptivity to the Divine will. Instead of acting, we are acted upon; instead of knowing, we submit to being known. Here is a poem about this particular passage:

Death & Resurrection

I walked, a corpse, through the arches of the wood;
I knelt & lay long in the wet lanes of darkness,
     moldering in a phosphorescent sanicle:

till with a low thunder there split & fell the old
     masonry of my eyes—
Raw—while I watched the herds that sprang from my
     parted rigs
spread out the Earth beneath them with their hooves;
and from their eyes and from the tips of their horns,
how the stars rose & flew like arrows & studded the
     night,
wounds of the alphabet wheeling slow in emptiness . . .

and when the print of my bone, like the lace of a
     rotten leaf was obliterated in the mould,
then the Sun broke & rose & spiked out his head
     over the brow of the woodland,
and roared down on my absence, till his accurate eye
     found the seven days of my death complete,
a tender planet green & rippling beneath his dancing
     beams—

     and I stood up then from my mother's loins
     and walked abroad upon her, satisfied.

The Tibetan Buddhists have a very rigorous and deliberate way of going through this death and resurrection. They call it the *Chöd* rite, or "The Yoga of the Mystic Sacrifice." The practitioner travels alone into a desolate wilderness, yogically dedicates himself or herself to perfect enlightenment, then invokes all the demons of the vicinity and offers them his or her body, speech, and mind to devour. In other words, each of the elemental energies of the human ego is offered to the terrifying forms which embody our fear of losing it. Pride is overcome by turning it over to the demons who live on pride; lust by offering it to the demons who live on lust; and the same is done with anger, jealousy, and stupidity. Furthermore, it is significant that the body of the practitioner in this rite is yogically identified, through visualization, with All-Performing Wisdom envisioned as a goddess.

Any man who is able to consciously meet, sacrifice himself to, and marry the feminine aspect of the Divine unity in the psychic depths will gain the power to become conscious of his anima, the feminine aspect of his own psyche. She will live for him as a conscious inner image; consequently, when he projects this image upon a woman in the outer world, he will be able to watch himself doing it. Unconscious projection in the psychological sense is here transformed into conscious projection in the tantric sense. Such a man holds the power to worship the Divine in the form of a woman, rather than simply making a woman his idol, in an attempt to avoid the encounter with his Lord.

But the road which leads, for a man, from faithfulness to his inner feminine soul image, to a fruitful relationship with a woman in the outer world can be long and hard, both before and after the outer relationship begins. The transition from an alchemical union between the inner King and Queen—the spirit image and the soul image—to a tantric union between a man and his destined beloved, is filled with dangers, not the least being that the man's introverted conscious ego must symbolize the inner King at one point, at the necessary risk of a massive inflation (see my poem "She Stepped Out" below). On the other hand, to the degree that we know that the only real being is God, and therefore live the truth that we are no more than symbols of this being, empty of self-nature, then we can, through the many deaths and resurrections which will be required of us, keep the woven pattern intact and establish the continuity of Divine love. The following poems deal with this soul transition from inner to outer eros, a process which might be called "the humanization of the anima":

THE FORGOTTEN

She sways like a willow tree
over something she has forgotten;
her head is bowed on her breast—

the wind passes her by
on the street like a stranger,
and her skirt and her sleeves and her
hair lean east—

but her eyes,
they sink into her heart
and her heart into the earth over
something she has forgotten;

and she is blind, enraged, cold as
    diamonds,
remorselessly sinking, and will not
    release
the fist of what she has forgotten—

and I pray God
I may follow her down
by some other opening
than the Darkest way.

SHE STEPPED OUT

What are you waiting for?
Here I am.
The walls are down, at last.
I step out
Under the same moonlight
We have held so long together—
Shy still,
Still uncertain of your courtesy—

But here I am:

Take me.

My waist is thin
As the stem of a wine glass
Between your hands,
I fear you will break me—

But no more the darkness under leaves,
I can't stand that;
I know the Sun will not kill me:
I swear I will live . . .

So take me, lead me out,
Robe me in that nakedness—
I have been frozen so long,
Barren and clotted as the Moon.
Cross my breast now
With your blood-heat,
Your burning Gold—

Listen, Lord:
I am your Soul—

Take me.

To My Wife

somnambulistic, I sweep the river—
—it carries the bones of the dead—
-the Roman centurion—wounded by
magic—become a serpent—his plumes
and armor roll pulled by the current
along the lucid bottom, the wave-striped
cobbles—

all that I was—broken. all that I
call myself—the shards of my name—
taken by the river. And,
nameless, my bone and my pith—

my will is a great cable—it will not
let you fall. beneath my ribs
the day is breaking—while you mourn
the passing of my shadow, confused
in the traces of the night—

for a moment you will miss me,
while the day is taking us—
my wife. my true one. the reason
I have not died. the basis
of my work—for a little while you
will not know the strength of my love—
you will see me taken by reveries—
—by battles whose field is hidden
from you—while I hide myself
in indifference, or foolishness—

but know that I have come to you
out of a distance farther than I can
remember, and not die. because I am
skilled in lamentation. because I
did not recoil from the despair I
owed to the wound I suffered to
those whom once I loved.
I have finished it. I have paid the
price. I am free. Now bind me.

Clinschor

Once love is established in the inner world—either the inner
world of the psyche, or that of the "love grotto," the deep erotic
union of a man and a woman which exiles the outer world to a
distant horizon—then the regime of collective blindness, ruled by the
unconscious social mores, will return as a formidable barrier if not
active enemy. Because This World (the *established* system of reality,
both psychic and social), officially though not explicitly, hates love.
Therefore, the Dragon or the Evil Knight or the castrated magician
who rules the loveless Wasteland—the one named Clinschor in the

Parzifal romance—will appear and do all in his power to destroy the newly formed union. (These negative masculine forces are elements of the personal and collective shadow, but on a deeper level, and behind the scenes, they are ruled by the negative anima, the Goddess of Fate.)

At this point, a man must recognize what is actually happening and fully admit that for him to make a real love match, which means putting his love for his beloved before all other earthly values, including those of social acceptance and economic security, will require him to go to war against the Dragon of this world, both within the psyche and in terms of outer circumstances. This is quite literally a life-and-death struggle and demands absolute dedication; it is not a path for everyone. Love for one's lady is a symbol of one's love for God; and since, ultimately, we are nothing other than symbols, there is a sense in which what the Sufis call *figurative love*, love on the human plane, is a full theophanic manifestation of Divine love. If all intelligible realities are figures and symbols, then the symbol of the thing, while never ceasing to be a symbol, is necessarily the thing itself.

Divine love is higher than human love; but since every higher reality includes all that is below it, it is also intimately united with human love. The recognition of this union, however, will tend to be veiled by what I will call the shadow of the absolute, which is a kind of fundamental misperception of the nature of the Divine on the part of a deeply buried stratum of the human ego, both individual and collective (what the Gnostics call an *archon*). God is love, but when our dedication to this love becomes possessive, fanatical, it ends by making us loveless. God is infinite, but when our vision of this infinity becomes abstract and reified, it casts its freezing shadow on all that is less than infinite, all that is partial and limited, like human affection or social justice. So we use the concept of infinity to cut some things out of legitimate being instead of including them, which is obviously not infinity's role. And this shadow of the absolute, which the Muslims call *Eblis*, the Buddhists, *Mara*, and the Christians, *Satan*, nowhere operates more destructively than in the field of religion, especially esoteric religion. This is why Blake, who once said that only the Catholics (among Christians) teach the true love of God, could also write:

> And priests in black gowns, were walking their rounds
> Binding with briars, my joys & desires.[28]

Spiritual values cannot reach maturity in any scene that is actively destructive to individual relatedness, as spiritual groups often are, unconsciously if not openly. The hermit, the monk, and the cloistered nun may choose to forego sexual love and human friendship, but they do so in the name of a highly individual relationship with the Beloved. Such a lover is alone with God, and the duty of his or her fellow monastics is to nurture and to protect that solitude, precisely by cultivating their own.

Love's Knights

In these times without fathers and mentors, sometimes only an adversary can initiate us, and no initiation is more dangerous and more likely to fail than one in which we encounter the powers of the darkness without sufficient human preparation. Yet we all carry within us a seed of transcendent light, which, God willing and given that we know how to listen to our dreams and intuitions, will appear to counsel us and fight by our side. To encounter the shadow successfully, then, is (potentially) to receive the sword of God from the inner world. This sword may be entrusted to us by our inner mentor, our Merlin, but if it is our destiny to fight in defense of love, then we may glimpse behind the figure of our inner sorcerer, our martial arts master, a second figure, that of the Lady who represents in her own person the transpersonal values we fight for. In the Arthurian legends, Arthur receives his sword Excalibur from the Lady of the Lake; and the Welsh "Romance of Math ap Mathonwy" contains evidence of a matriarchal culture stratum in Britain in which the Goddess, and undoubtedly her human representative, held the power not only to arm the hero, but also to name him. So we can see that not even a warrior initiation is an exclusively male affair. In both love and war, as ways of acting and of knowing, polarity is the key.

On one level, the warrior initiation has to do with gaining the power to stand alone, to defend one's own unique truth—not to triumph over the truths of others, but to secure the right to stand on one's own legitimate ground. And the Dragons who stand at the threshold of this particular initiation and deny passage to the unworthy, are named Persecution and Grandeur. When a man takes up arms in the name of his own personal vision of objective truth, a certain amount of egotism and inflation is inevitable, and there is really no way of separating obedience to one's inner King from promethean self-assertion, especially when it comes to public intellectual warfare, except through sacrifice, through conscious suffering.

So he who fights to help his own truth emerge from the isolation imposed on it by the collective unconscious mores—those established social rules which, collectively, we don't want to become conscious of, since they operate better in darkness—will be confronted by paranoia. Since he is required initially to take his stand with no authority beyond his own integrity (and what could be more potentially inflating than this?), he will attract the specific transpersonal forces, the specific allies, that correspond to and make up the lineage of the truth he serves, and only radical detachment and humility can prevent a battle alliance with transpersonal forces from degenerating into schizophrenia or delusive magic. (Such forces may appear in visions, in dreams, in synchronistic happenings, or in direct intuitive knowings.) If the warrior identifies these forces with his ego, he is already defeated. If, on the other hand, he recognizes them as energies coming from beyond his boundaries, which must be related to on the basis of vigilance, courtesy, and courage, then they will be revealed as angelic emissaries sent to his conscious personality from his archetypal identity, his Lord. Power is not to be wielded—it is to be obeyed. And *then* wielded. And then sacrificed. And then obeyed again.

The inner world analogue of social revolution is psychic revolution against the collective unconscious mores and belief systems which are, in St. Paul's words, "the rulers of the darkness of this world." And when this inner revolution takes the form of a symbolic drama, it appears as the resurrection of the dead. Thus in any viable Christian culture, the prototype of the work of the revolutionary leader or organizer will be Christ's harrowing of hell. What Jesus did for the dead, the revolutionary leader struggles to do for the living dead, the wretched of the earth.

I will end this discussion of the warrior initiation with sections 107–112 of *The Wars of Love*. The character called "Ruha" and "ghost-goddess of the SS" in these sections is the Goddess of Fate, counterfeit and veil of the Sophia, who is contemplative wisdom and who has her epiphany in another part of the poem. The character Adam is the primordial man who, after having been awakened by his brother Jesus from the sleep of death, rises from the underworld as

the power of the ancestors, the army of the human dead. He is my
own rendition of the Wild Man, my own Iron John:

107

Then Adam loosed his bloody hand
And sank through the Ocean of Eve,
Down a long, heavy sigh of grateful death
Till he came to rest on the flowering Earth.
She split the crumbling masonry of his eyes;
She unraveled his belly's chain mail
Till it rang with a throng of bees, in a cloud of pollen,
Fallen apples opening their rips to the moist earth,
Green summer grass, blasted
To a hide of tawny gold,
Sentient stars vibrating, alive
In the mulch of the great Rains.
                            The dead—
    let them die.
Let them lay down their ancestral sorrow
In the bosom of the black Earth—
Shivering out the last threads of darkness like carrion
        on the ground—
Stinking fertility teeming
With mildew, worms and seeds—

To relax the fist of the weeping, not nurse the bloody
        babe of the weeping,
But give him to earth, and heat—
To dip him in a cauldron of Power, three days in Eve's
        green cavern turning
Till the Earth groans in labor, and volcanic love . . .

108

And as Adam sank, the Darkness rose:
Black residue of self-will—the smoke of bound labor—
A muttering cloud of demon insects, the sting and itch
        of ancient battles, rising like ash—

The elementals of Satan—they who whip the human body
    ahead of them under the eye of Ruha—
Now released: Soot, snarls, yelps of anger, and the
    gnashing of teeth
Pour from the burning pit of the solar plexus, ascend
    the human spine
The black pipe of Sushumna-nadi, to the aperture of
    Brahman
Where they hit blue-black sky:
                    A squeak of bats, flittering,
        cross-hatching their own lines of flight
Till they disperse in the
All-accepting dusk . . .

Then Adam turned, gripped his hammer
And hammered down Satan, the black statue of Prometheus
    into shards of volcanic glass—
And broke the shell of Man.

"I am Adam" said the victor; "I am he who labors
Under the sign of the Red Hand.
It was my hand that first took up the red clay of
    Earth, and worked it
Kneading it to bricks to build the red walls of Erech,
And so incurred the guilt of human action. The War of
    Liberation
Has been won on the Cross, the debt of action paid.
Nothing remains for us
But to appropriate that victory now, in the streets of
    world history
Where light breaks over the bureaucracies, the markets,
    the armies,
Where blade is broken against blade forever
And all enemies are brothers. God lead me to my true
    adversary now,
So we can fight, and embrace, and let our two bloods
    mingle
In accordance with the Savior's command. Because that
    command

Has finally come: To draw the blade of purified anger
Against all that is not God. And once drawn, it encounters
    no alien flesh, it meets no enemy—
Because only God is."

109

And Satan reeled; he faltered; he lifted his eyes to the
    Northeast
And saw his Future above him, like a white, receding star,
Fata Morgana of knights, warriors, empires . . .
Grail of Ahab—Pacific Ocean leviathan gliding west to
    Vietnam—
Ghost-goddess of the SS, who sounds the knell of all the
    cultures,
Ghostly Galahad's meat: White-helmeted astronauts golfing
    on the Moon in
Black zero-air-resistent Vacuum—Madonna of all who say
    we must reach the Future
Through immense acceleration and vast Promethean
    struggle—

Forgetting that the Future streams in, every instant,
Effortlessly and perfectly given,
Rising and falling as breath
In Love's humming emptiness—

So let the pirates of self-will, Satan's gallant mercenaries—let
    them follow that Lady;
Let her make a bed for them in the black night, the hollow,
    lifeless void
Where their perfectly-realized desire will take them;
Let them enter that bed, clutching about them the rags of
    their machines,
Orphaned beyond all orphans (as was your word for them,
    Vallejo . . .
Babylon, whore and tower, will dig a grave for them in the
    bottomless sky

Whose hearts never learned to scent, and breathe
The sweet air of Earth . . .

110

The Voice of Adam: *A Call to War*

I say all will be pressed into service.
I say all will be required to fight.
The passive, the coward, the innocent will be trampled
    down,
Unless locked in single combat with God
In mountain solitude and stillness.
Invoke, therefore, the war in your marrow;
Call on the fight you were born with, that enemy
Whose lie is cut and tooled, precisely
To cover your single truth.
Pick targets. Each man is alone with all men
In this night of War. The conglomerate form of Death
Stands guard on each human door,
Solid to the bullet, or the chisel—
Like those cliffs in the Sinai
Inside which our skirmishers discovered, still living
The imprisoned forms of men.

111

And the followers of Adam, recruited from soil and wind
    and ocean
Are the Ancestors of Humanity—the Army of the Human
    Dead.
And this is their word:

"We are those
Who lie slandered under the name of death.
We have incontrovertible reason, proof to silence laughter.
From palaces of torture, from twenty terms
In the grey, damp, infinite dusk
We raise our voices and salute you, our fathers and mothers,

You who still sit laboring in your Dream—
We are the strength of your arms and your loins, the voice
    of your living memory.
You carry our blood—now remember our names; uncover
    for us
The True Names we struggled for, as you now struggle for
    your own—
Speak us, man! tell our story—we've been muttering too
    long in our ruined halls, those narrow beds,
The groves still barren of our voices—
We have lain too long in the seed-houses, the uneasy
    archives, the crucibles of sleep—
Herald us now, you living men and women, still clothed in
    the sweetness and the dignity
Of human flesh—say we rise, we return!
Because if you worship us, you will lose us; if you hold to
    us, we will only drag you down.
The dead are hungry for those who will not live . . .
The ones who die into a coward's dream, we consume;
We eat but are not satisfied.
But for those with the courage to live, who release their
    blood and their seed
Into the vessels of life, then start on their journey,
We fill the sails of that fortunate life
With a fresh wind out of the East.
So tell them we rise! Say our sleep is ended—
Tell them their ancestors
Will be their children again."

(Understand me: it is only by the authority of the heroic
    dead, of those I never knew
Martyrs who went into death willingly, in Love's tortured
    body—
SANDINO—BIKO—ROMERO—MALCOLM X—
SITTING BULL—CRAZY HORSE—QUANG DUK—
    BOBBIE SANDS—
—that I hold the right to name these dead of mine, ghosts
    pleading for the womb,

And the torn blood, and the birth-cries, and the new Sun,
    dancing on the waters. . .)

112

And the dead rose into the giant flesh of Adam till he stood
    united, radiating his sons, his children at work around
    him
In all the mountains and plains of Gaia,
Inheriting the strength of the human past forever
Under Christ's eternal sunlight—
Labor integrated in service
To the valleys of the living Earth.

Thus the Primordial Humanity was unveiled in its Southeast
    quarter—
ESHU-ELEGBA, Legba Ati-bon:
Memory of the Fathers—Tree of Justice—Payer of the Price
    of blood-guilt—
Road of new souls about to be born (they who make the
    River Danbhallah)—
Your red deeds are green now;
Your face shines clear in Erzulie's Mirror—

    "Police cordon please;
    Police cordon please;
    Make way for an important visitor
        from the Underworld."

This section of the *The Wars of Love* is specifically about the redemption of the chthonic masculine principle, the faculty of human
will. Earlier in the narrative, Jesus descends into hell after his death
on the cross, in willing *katabasis*, to instruct and redeem Adam, who is
the totality of the human ancestors. This is the traditional "harrowing
of hell," and the ancestors are those elements of our humanity which
are alienated from us under the state here called *Satan*, who is *self-
will*. In terms of the human will, this Satan is one aspect of the
Shadow of the Absolute, since our failure to submit to the absolute
Will of God makes our own wilfullness seem like an absolute to us,

with the well-known unfortunate consequences. As any aikido master will tell you, the warrior who fights on the basis of self-will, instead of submitting to the Will of God, the Tao, and letting it empower him and move him, will leave destruction in his wake till he himself is destroyed by a self-will more violent or more cunning than his own, if not directly by his own stupidity. (In the same way, the Shadow of the Absolute appears to contemplative wisdom as fate, to divine imagination as restrictive law, and to passionate feeling-energy as shallow chaos.)

In an earlier section, Adam has already submitted to the command of his own essential nature in the guise of Jesus, and been empowered to enact it; he has vowed to serve a transcendent cause in the shape of his own Inner King. And later in the poem (which is available in its entirety from the author to anyone who wants to hear the whole story), Adam can come into a tantric polarity with the humanized earth—who is also empowering emotion and vital sentient energy—because he has already submitted to the Transcendent Spirit in the inner world. But before that can occur, Adam, like the hero of *Iron John*, must complete his warrior-initiation. He must release the "dead" within him, his ancient wounds (which, in one sense, are *grievances*) in purifying sorrow; otherwise his warriorhood will be an expression not of service, but of revenge. As he does so, his satanic self-will is exorcized. His war is transformed into the greater jihad, the war against the passional soul, "that lie which is cut and tooled, precisely, to cover your single truth." And into the space left open by the release of these karmic residues rushes the power of the ancestors, the human dead. He is initiated by the Fathers, by the totality of those men of the past who labored to make human life both possible and worthy on this earth. The human past becomes present to him again, just as it was before he ate of the Tree of the Knowledge of Good and Evil, and fell into time and generation. So now he is Adam indeed. And in redeeming Adam, the ancestors are themselves redeemed; they become, in eternity, the manifestation of his organs and faculties—his sons.

In the Vedanta philosophy, two paths are open to the soul after death: the path of the Ancestors and the path of the Gods. The path of the Ancestors is taken by those who may have led virtuous lives and piously sacrificed to their forebears (i.e., carried on their work), but who never realized Divine Truth in eternity. It is essentially a path where will takes precedence over intellect; according to whether the actions of the will were predominantly good or evil, it leads to fortunate or unfortunate rebirth.

The path of the Gods leads, not to rebirth, but to final liberation via the Door of the Sun. It is taken by those in whom intellect has precedence over will; who, while in this life, came under the rule of the Spirit and realized the eternal Now. But those who take the path of the Gods do not simply leave the ancestors behind; the ones who pass through the Sun Door into *moksha* also in a sense redeem their own ancestors, their own partial and contingent past. In the words of the Old Testament, "I will restore to you the years that the locust hath eaten." For those who have returned to God, the ancestors are transformed into the very energy and stream of that return—which is why "the Buddha sees only Buddhas." It is in this sense that the resurrected individual, like Christ, also redeems the universe. In like manner, at the end of the tale of *Iron John*, the hero marries his beloved, the totality of his universe, and the Wild Man returns as a King.

7

Pearls Before Swine

IN HIS SEVENTH CHAPTER, "Riding the Red, the White, and the Black Horses," Bly deals with the episode of the story in which the hero catches the golden apples tossed by the Princess—a badge of completed initiation.

Bly begins by giving an overview of what a full initiatory sequence might be. He calls it the "Classic Initiation" and gives the stages as: bonding and separation from the mother; bonding and separation from the father; the dawning of the mentor, or "male mother"; apprenticeship to a god; and the Sacred Marriage. I am basically in agreement with this scheme of development, but I'd like to expand on it:

The first two phases, having to do with bonding and separation from our mother and our father, are physical and psychic. Our mother gives us physical birth and (hopefully) primal psychic nurturing. Our father (ideally, but now rarely) initiates us into the outer physical world of work and social adaptation and provides the psychic nurturing appropriate to this phase. But with the third phase (the dawning of the mentor) the spiritual level, the world beyond nature, psyche, and society is consciously encountered, or should be.

Often, however, this third initiation fails us. Since the first two initiations have themselves likely been incomplete, we often use our "mentor" period to try to repair the psychological damage we sustained in our relationship, or lack of relationship, with our parents.

125

Instead of going on to a mature spiritual worldview and religious commitment, we project the mentor archetype onto our therapist and confuse psychological healing with spiritual initiation. And some therapists can play at least part of the role of a real spiritual mentor for us. Nonetheless, the role of psychologist is fundamentally different from, and sometimes radically opposed to, the role of spiritual initiator. Merlin was Arthur's spiritual guide, not his shrink.

By the time we get to phase four, apprenticeship to a god, we will need to have clearly distinguished Spirit from psyche, otherwise we will become fetishists who think we can choose our own spiritual destinies on the basis of preference. Any god we choose is necessarily a fetish; the deity who is the unique face of our spiritual destiny always chooses us. And, as I have worked to make clear above, such a god is not one god among many. He or she is not my god versus yours, my ally or fetish or familiar spirit versus yours, but my own particular and incomparable path toward the One. My wife is not any less mine because other men have other wives; whatever their experience of their partners may be, she is my one and only. And the same is true of the unique and particular face which the Divine Essence turns toward my own particularity: He is my Lord.

Initiation into the service of a particular name of God is the beginning of the knowledge that God transcends all we know, and if we are faithful in this service, the fifth phase of initiation will dawn, at which point God will appear not alone as the unknowable Essence, but simultaneously as our very Beloved. The seed of Divine transcendence will have then produced the flower of Divine immanence; the knowledge that God is totally beyond our possible experience will have bloomed into the knowledge of God as the Divine substance of every item of our experience. And these two kinds of knowledge are also the two hands of love: transcendent knowledge is respect and detachment; immanent knowledge is passion and union.

Simone Weil said, "Appearance clings to Being, and pain alone can tear them apart." This is the passion of transcendence; without this sacrifice, we can never encounter the Divine as it is, only its relative and contingent image. But the contrary of this is also true: appearance is estranged from being, and only love can reunite them. This is the passion of immanence; without this recklessness, we can never encounter the Divine as it is, only its abstract and distant name. And the movement from transcendence to immanence is, in a sense, natural: as soon as Spirit is encountered in its own kingdom and our relation with it firmly established, it begins to flow into manifestation out of the invisible world. It officiates (on the psychic level) at the marriage of the King and Queen, sulfur and quicksilver, the Spirit image and the Soul image; and finally (on the material level) it embraces the entire sensual universe as the living body of God. In Sufi terminology, the Divine will then no longer be limited to the *batin*, the inner world, but will encompass the *zahir* or outer world as well. In his story "The Zahir," Jorge Luis Borges attributes to Attar the following lines:

> The Zahir is the shadow of the Rose
> And the rending of the veil.[29]

But if we have failed, at the phase of the mentor, to ascend to the level of Spirit, phases four and five will remain on the psychic level; they will produce nothing beyond emotionally moving fantasies under the rule of time, destined to decay with the ebbing of our vital energies, ultimately leading us not into a wise old age, but into one of pathetic nostalgia or numb petrification.

Acid on the Plates

Some spiritually inflated *pueri aeternae*, after they have started to come to terms with life and get their feet on the ground, may discover in themselves a deep vein of bitterness; often their words seemed filled with the acid of a wounded idealism. (The perceptive reader will immediately understand that I am including myself in this description.) But that bitter acid has the potential of maturing into something deeper; it may lead us into what Bly calls the Black stage of the Masculine Sequence and be transmuted into compassion and dark wisdom. At this point we may learn how to use this acid as Blake did, when he made his method of printing with acid-etched copper plates a symbol of "melting away apparent surfaces, and exposing the Infinite which was hid" by means of metaphysical satire. *The Marriage of Heaven and Hell*, from which this quote is taken, is just such a satire, printed from just this type of copper plate.

William Butler Yeats, in his book *A Vision* (a complex psycho-historical/eschatological system, largely channeled by his wife

Georgie, a spirit medium) assigns twenty-eight different character types to the twenty-eight phases of the moon, thus founding an entirely new branch of astrology, still in use today. According to the phase under which I was born, in terms of my basic intent, I am "the consumer" or the "pyre-builder." My mask is "rejection." My creative mind is "moral iconoclasm." And my body of fate is "enforced belief." Historical examples of this type include Spinoza, and, more pertinent to this book, Savonarola, who, many centuries before Tom Wolfe, built the real "bonfire of the vanities." And personally I would include Kierkegaard as well.

To bless is delightful and nourishing. To curse is exhausting and is only justified when to acquiesce would exhaust us even further and put us in danger of spiritual despair. And to call down God's curse is out of bounds in any case; we need to face and suffer the consequences of our own cursing and not make the childish error of expecting God to pay our debts. The ancient Celtic poets knew this, which is why they ruled that the one who composes an *aer* or poetic satire against someone who does not deserve it (and a successful satire in the culture of the Celts could so destroy a person's character in the eyes of his tribe that he was often driven into exile) will suffer the fate of having his face break out in red blotches and dying on the spot. Therefore, I am going to aim my satire well, not against individuals, who have committed all the same sins I have, but against beliefs. Specifically, I will take aim at that set of cultural mores, ancient yet always new, which identifies spirituality with *display*—the stance that Christopher Lasch called "the culture of narcissism."

After following the hero of *Iron John* through profound and agonizing spiritual struggles—the time of ashes, the cultivation of the Garden, the defeat of the soldiers of the Enemy—Bly then sets him up as little more than an aesthetic dandy. The hero's reward for all his sufferings is that he gets to put on his peacock feathers and strut in front of the ladies—or rather, in front of himself. To my value sense, this is bathos, a descent from the sublime to the ridiculous. And to the degree that the display Bly touts is really vanity and narcissism—and some of it definitely sounds that way—this is also, to my value sense, an instance of blasphemy. It outrages my sense of the sacred. But since Bly's sense of the sacred is clearly different from mine, and (as far as I can know) equally valid, it is obviously not blasphemy for him. But I believe that it is vitally important

for the reader to understand that a whole world of values exists—
one that is in no way identified with religious fundamentalism—
which can experience Bly's worship of display as an instance of cruel
oppression. In my terminology, this world of values is the realm of
the Sophia, the Holy Wisdom of God.

At the same time that Bly enthrones display, he also introduces
the concept of sacred space. Somewhere he knows that we are coming to a time—the courtship leading to the Sacred Marriage—which
requires a holy seriousness. But then he compares the hero's prom-
enade before the Princess to the "zany grace" of the mating dances
of herons and peacocks (p. 196), which he sees as "outrageous
display" (p. 198). He says, "the young man learns to modulate out of
aggression through display, form and ritual; the young men display
their beauty as they pass in procession, and 'luck' determines who
gets the apple" (p. 193–94). He sets up display as opposite to shame
and implies that we overcome shame in part through display. He
says, "The knights. . . are lovely emblems of the stage in which the
infinitive *to win* is replaced by the infinitive *to be seen*" (p. 199). But in
the world of display, to be seen *is* to win. When the Native American
warrior returned from battle decked with the scalps of slain enemies
and promenaded before the women, he was not "modulating out of
aggression"; he was being rewarded for it. (The ultimate question
is not whether we are aggressive or nonviolent, but what values our
aggression or nonviolence is serving.) "Poetry is a form of display,"
says Bly. "The poet bird repeats vowels and consonants in order to
widen his tail. Meter and counted syllables make up a peacock's
tail. The poem is a dance done for some being in the other world"
(p. 198). He explains that the ritual space he's referring to is "closer
to art than strutting" (p. 196), but if repeating vowels and syllables in
order to widen your peacock tail is not strutting, I hope someone will
tell me what is. Most art is strutting, after all; the days when cathedrals
were built by anonymous artisans and the stonework signed *Adamo me
fecit* ("Adam made me") are over. "Dionysus. . . founded the Greek
theater," says Bly. "Greek tragic theater amounts to a transfer of. . .
ritual space to a public event" (p. 194). This is certainly true, and
there is nothing more dangerous, nothing which treads closer to
the edge of profaning the Mysteries. The creation of the Greek
theater was nonetheless a real spiritual achievement, since tragic
drama may actually have replaced human sacrifice at one stage of

Greek culture. But Euripides' drama, *The Bacchae*, produced at the festival of Dionysus in Athens, proves that some Greeks at least remained ambivalent about this imported Phrygian deity, as well as about the very role of *spectator* which his theater created. The story is bone-chilling. Pompous, moralistic King Pentheus vows to stamp out the Dionysian revels as a menace to civilization. But then Dionysus himself appears to him, in disguise, and says, "Ah yes, the revels, the women's mysteries—by the way, would you like to *watch* them?" So Pentheus takes him up on his offer and is torn limb from limb by his own mother in a bacchic frenzy. Such are the ambiguities of display.

Now let me admit before I go any further that public display can be beautiful and can act as a vehicle for social, psychological, or spiritual truth, as Shakespeare and the Greek playwrights themselves abundantly prove. And without public access to true art, as opposed to artistic narcissism, the body politic falls deeper into repression and despair. (The free memorial concert for rock promoter Bill Graham in San Francisco in 1991, for example, was beautiful. Three hundred thousand people in attendance; only two arrests for drunkenness. It carried emotional truth. It was an act of community healing.) But the contemporary kingdom of display is not ruled by sincere and spontaneous moments of communal ritual, but by a deeply entrenched and vicious narcissism. How right Bly is to say that when our soldiers returned from Vietnam, they should have been met by a Golden Princess, tossing apples to her heroes. That image actually made me weep. But if we had really tried to do that, we would have run into the fact that we were, and are, very short on princesses; the one in *Star Wars* was not a princess, but a cross between an Amazon and a Puritan schoolteacher. Marilyn Monroe might have been able to fill the role of Golden Princess, but by the mid–70s, she was gone, and all the soldiers would have gotten was Elizabeth Taylor. And after years of the terror-guerilla warfare, defoliation, civilian massacres—a Golden Princess wouldn't have been enough; the vets would have needed a Dark Princess too. Formally, that is, not simply *de facto*. (The Dark Princess did finally appear, though in a totally repressed form, as the black wall of the Vietnam Memorial.) Bly says that in ritual space, "delight replaces fury" (p. 194–95), but even to begin to deal with the wound of Vietnam, a display of delight would not have been enough. We didn't need Alfred Lord Tennyson to purge the trauma of that war; we needed Euripides.

No one can deny that social and artistic display can be a valid community catharsis. Many of us are so shamed by a repressive society that to have the courage to display our wound—and, on a deeper level, our integrity—can be a real act of healing. But how many of us are aware of how important it is to be able to hide our integrity? It's a crucial survival skill in times like these. As my wife once said, "to tell the truth is not always to serve the truth." (I quoted this line once to an artistic young man in a metaphysical bookstore. He was shocked and loudly denied it.) But if it is not wise to throw our pearls to the swine, to whom and under what circumstances can we make a valid gift of them? When is display an instance of poisonous narcissism, and when is it an act of love and courage?

Clearly a separation needs to be made here, with what the Tibetan Buddhists call "the sword of Discriminating Wisdom." In the words of Blake, from *The Four Zoas*: "Evil is created into a State, that Men may be delivered. . .Learn therefore. . .to distinguish the Eternal Human. . .from those States or Worlds in which the Spirit travels. This is the only means to Forgiveness of Enemies."

Blake also said that you can't be dissipated unless you have something to dissipate. The whole question of the value or danger of manifesting emotional or spiritual energy in terms of aesthetic display hinges on this truth. If you are rich, you can afford to be generous. But if your account is overdrawn, and you are still writing checks for the goods and services (the social attention) that you need, then you are a thief. In times of high religious culture, when spiritual realities are more available to the community and a lot of fruitful spiritual labor is being done, or has been done, then there will be enough in the account to pay for such magnificent acts of generosity as the *Mathnavi* of Rumi or Dante's *Divine Comedy*. "Out of the fullness of the Heart, the mouth speaketh." But now the collective heart is empty. It is an overdrawn account, a hungry vacuum which sucks all remaining cultural and spiritual values into annihilation, like a black hole. In times like these, our account can only be replenished out of the treasuries of the Unseen. And until it is, those who continue to write grandiose paper against it are self-destructive thieves.

I am not saying that the artistic rendering of spiritual truth is impossible in these times. I am saying that it is now easier than ever—so easy as to be almost inevitable—for vanity and narcissism to produce billions in rubber checks, rubber religions and social

translation to Avalon (which is called by mortals "death"). Is this the same lake in which Iron John has lived imprisoned? Is the rust-red bearded Wild Man, in some sense, that very rusted blade?

Iron must be smelted, heated, hammered, and refined before it becomes steel; and the same is true of the human soul. It needs to be refined and tempered before it can know and defend the truth.

The Pagan Ethos: Immanence or Materialism?

We are now living in an age when many high spiritual truths, due to the decadence of those traditions whose duty it is to preserve them, are failing us, just as we have failed them. They are falling from their high estate into the lake of the collective unconscious. What were once living and redemptive spiritual powers have been transformed into whimpering ghosts in need of redemption themselves. They have "changed their throats" (in Yeats's chilling words) and have "the throats of birds." The name of this age is the *Kali Yuga*—"the Age of Iron."

Throughout this book I have talked about the reality of the Divine as being both transcendent and immanent—a doctrine which is strictly in line with traditional wisdom. I would like to take some time now to expand on this theme.

The material and psychic worlds are limited; therefore God, who is infinite, must transcend them. But by the same token, if God is infinite, there is no place where God is not, including the psychic and material worlds. Thus we can say that the transcendence of God and the immanence of God are not two aspects of the Divine reality, but essentially one.

This union of transcendence and immanence is expressed in the Mahayana Buddhist doctrines of *shunyata* and *tathata*—"void" and "suchness." The psychic and material objects we perceive are not things in themselves; they are empty of self-nature (void) and therefore not limited by their own forms. This is *shunyata*, the transcendence of God, the impossibility of limiting reality to any form whatever. But by virtue of this very voidness, things are exactly what they are, and what they are is none other than the Reality. The secret of things is not that the truth is hidden in them; the secret of things is that they *are* the truth, but not as objects of a subjective ego. This is *tathata*, the immanence of God. In the extremely subtle words of Beat Generation poet Lew Welch: "I try to write accurately from the poise of mind which lets us see that things are exactly what they seem."[37] Because things are nothing in themselves, what they seem to be is necessarily what they are.

But although transcendence and immanence are one in essence, in terms of historically conditioned human ways of seeing, they tend to alternate. The Christian aeon was a vision of the Divine transcendence which dawned upon us in reaction to a decadent vision of the Divine immanence. Thus Christianity superseded Paganism not because Paganism was untrue, but because the ability to grasp the essential truth of Paganism had decayed.

When the vision of God as immanent in all things degenerates, the result is *pantheism*, the belief that all is God in the sense that everything that can be experienced must add up to God. Pantheism sees the universe not as a manifestation of That One, but as an object which must be God, since it's all there is. The parts of the universe are the parts of God. This fallen order of perception is what René Guénon called "the reign of quantity." As soon as we limit God to our actual or possible experience of God, we turn God into an object called "the universe"; That One becomes partial, quantifiable, and therefore material. Materialism begins exactly here; and since materialism sees us as parts of the whole, the only way we can become whole in ourselves according to this view is to incorporate the whole. This is the equation between materialism and egotistical greed. In Blake's words: "More! More! is the cry of the mistaken soul, less than All cannot satisfy Man."[38] The polar opposite of this pantheistic vision is the one Blake expressed in "Auguries of Innocence": "To see a World in a Grain of Sand/And Heaven in a Wild Flower/To hold Infinity in the palm of your hand/And Eternity in an hour." The grain and the flower are not parts of the whole but mirrors of the whole. They are not quantifiable material objects, but are void of self-nature, and therefore incomparable. They are exactly what they are. The vision is holographic, not material. If we can let go of the world as an object of our own perception, then we will see the infinite in all things; as Blake wrote, "I question [in other words, consult] not my Corporeal or Vegetative Eye any more than I would Question a Window concerning Sight, I look thro it & not with it."[39] If we let go of the world as an object of our own perception, then we will know ourself as perceived. To quote Muhammad from the *ahadith* (the traditional sayings of the Prophet): "Pray to God as if you saw Him, because even if you don't see Him, He still sees you."

Christianity made it possible for us to know, again, that God transcends the visible universe. But because it limited the Divine immanence to a single and unique incarnation, it simultaneously made it less possible for us to see the universe as a *theophany*, a manifestation of God. This vision of Divine transcendence has carried us for two thousand years; but now it, too, is becoming old. The truth that God transcends the visible universe is starting to sound like a meaningless abstraction to us, based on a fear of sense experience. God is not elsewhere, we chant, but here; God is not unique, but universal. We are clearly living in a time when the vision of the Divine immanence is attempting to reassert itself.

Unfortunately we are also living in a time of unparalleled materialism, a time when electromagnetic energy or DNA or nuclear force or quantum mechanics seem to us like valid synonyms for God. And the contradiction inherent in materialism is that we take the manifestation, not the Source of the manifestation, as our center—a tendency which Matthew Fox epitomizes in his phrase, "Creation-centered spirituality." The noun *creation* can only mean "that which is made by a creator"; therefore, "Creation-centered Spirituality" can only mean "the worship of the effect, not the cause." To say "creation-centered" is like saying "circumference-centered"; it's a contradiction in terms.

Source is one; manifestation is many, which is why the worship of manifest existence will always tend toward polytheism and why the incomplete and partly materialistic reassertion of the Divine immanence now going on must take up arms against the monotheistic tradition. From the point of view of a manifest existence which takes itself as its own source, a monotheistic God will look like a monolithic God, an arbitrary imposition, a tyrant. The truth that the many, when taken quantitatively, are a fragmented and abstract manifestation of the all-embracing and concrete reality of the One will thus become veiled. But insofar as monotheism itself failed to know the One as absolutely transcendent, seeing it instead as a quasimaterial object, a polytheistic reaction was to be expected.

The age is moving away from the religions of transcendence and toward neo-Paganism; the resurgence of fundamentalism is no more than a reaction to this deeper drift. And from one point of view, this is a clear fall. According to the perennial wisdom, however, such a fall is inevitable, and every fall, from the Golden Age to the Silver, the Silver to the Bronze, the Bronze to the Iron, entails a heroic effort on the part of humanity to cut its losses, to recompose and restabilize on a lower level what has been lost on a higher. This is one reason why neo-Paganism may represent a legitimate response to the needs of the time—if, that is, it can avoid falling into literalistic materialism and succeed in unfolding a new vision of the immanence of God out of a rooted knowledge of the transcendence of God (the last being the seed of the first).

Perhaps the highest, subtlest, and most comprehensive vision of reality is that which sees the many as not other than the One, and each unique item of experience as perfectly manifesting that One by its very uniqueness. This is Blake's doctrine of "minute particulars." But only a vision of the Divine transcendence in and through phenomena—which, in Buddhist terms, is the voidness of phenomena—can prevent this vision of minute particulars from degenerating into a chaotic mass of details.

This vision of reality might be called *Transcendental Paganism* —an awkward term which I use only to express the truth that polytheism contains the seed of something higher than a simple quantitative greed to pile up psychic power and experience by making alliances with more and more deities. In Vajrayana Buddhism, for example, a multitude of Buddhas, bodhisattvas, *mahasiddhas* (sages), and peaceful and wrathful deities are invoked through mantra, *mudra* (hand gestures), and visualization. The effect of such spiritual exercises, when correctly performed, is the farthest thing from psychic fragmentation, since both the deity and the body, speech, and mind of the practitioner doing the invoking are recognized as void— without self-nature, spontaneous manifestations of the principle of enlightenment. Similarly, within the spiritual universe of Hinduism, it has always been possible (at least for the correctly instructed) to recognize the many gods and goddesses of the pantheon as modes and symbols of the one. As it says in the *Bhagavad Gita*:

> Ah, my God, I see all Gods within your body;
> Each in his degree, the multitude of creatures;
> See Lord Brahma throned on the lotus;
> See all the sages, and the holy serpents.

Universal Form, I see you without limit,
Infinite of arms, eyes, mouths and bellies—
See, and find no end, midst or beginning.[40]

Not all the polytheism of our time, however, is on this high a
level; and some forms of polytheism are in danger of capitulating
to what is worst in the time (though the same could be said for
some forms of Christianity). It's true that no responsible neo-Pagan
supports Satanism and that white magicians and shamanic healers
are fighting daily against the tide of psychic evil which threatens to
engulf us. But if magic means that we have forgotten the higher
spiritual worlds and see nothing beyond the human ego and the
subtle natural forces that ego attempts to wield, in the name of either
personal aggrandizement (black magic) or the ego's idea of the good
(white magic) then we are in deep trouble. Because magic is all
too common. Anyone exerting self-will to create one effect or avoid
another is doing magic, and that includes about all of us. It's the
moment when we stop doing magic that is the gateway to miracle.

It's conventional to oppose Earth-nurturing neo-Paganism to
Earth-destroying technology, and this perspective is not without its
truth. But in a deeper sense, both share the same magical ethos,
as indicated in the title of Jerome Rothenberg's famous anthology
of aboriginal and shamanic poetry, *Technicians of the Sacred*, and by
magazines like *Omni*, which come out of the interface of magic and
technology. Just as the blind technocrat looks at the Earth as a
resource to be exploited, so the spiritually darkened sorcerer sees
the subtle energy of the Earth as something to be dominated and
exploited by his or her ego; such a person strip-mines the world soul
just as modern technology strip-mines the mountains. To him, the
totem Spirit is not the particular Divine archetype he serves, and
out of which he springs into existence, but merely a psychic slave to
the human self-will. Such a person may use the forces of the subtle
material plane, but he or she does not respect them.

The essence of Paganism is nature worship, and nature worship
is either the ability to see the forms of the natural world as living
symbols of higher realities, or the idolatrous belief that nothing
beyond these forms exists, which entails the sacrilegious denial that
phenomenal existence springs from, and therefore can act as a path
of return to, an invisible and absolute Source. This is how I've used

the term in most of this book. The former (the symbolic union
of nature) is what I've called *Trancendental Paganism*; it includes
a contemplative reverence for the Earth as a manifestation of the
Divine. The latter (the belief that nothing exists beyond natural
forms) is no more than glamorized materialism which, by turning
the Earth and her subtle energies into objects for manipulation by
the human ego, directly participates in her destruction.

Bly versus Yeats, Bly versus Blake, Bly versus Gurdjieff

The materialistic nature worship of our time has its roots in the
Deism or Natural Religion of the Enlightenment. Natural Religion
is the doctrine that humanity is "naturally" good, that without the
sacrifice of our passional tendencies, and without any saving reve-
lation emanating from the higher spiritual worlds, we can unfold
our potentials in a healthy and balanced way. Naturally it includes
the exaltation of the "noble savage" and the denial of original sin.
Rousseau loved it; it allowed him to get away with murder. And it was
Rousseau who compressed it into a single tremendous line: "Man was
born free, and is everywhere in chains!" Unfortunately for the union
of melodrama and accuracy, this is not true. The truth is, we are born
in chains—the chains of contingency; of matter, energy, space, and
time; of "the darkness of the world" which Gurdjieff defined as "the
realm of forty-eight laws"; of genetics; of the unresolved conflicts
of our parents and ancestors; of repressive political and economic
systems; of collective blindness and hypocrisy. This is "original sin."
But by the power of Divine grace and through conscious labor, we
can become free of this sin.

The foremost critic of Natural Religion in his time and in our
own is William Blake. In his prophetic book *Milton*, Blake declared
himself commissioned "to display Nature's cruel holiness, the deceits
of Natural Religion." In his Song of Experience entitled "Infant
Sorrow"—to take only one example out of dozens possible—Blake
takes aim at one of the central myths of Natural Religion, the belief
that infancy is the ideal human state:

> My mother groand! my father wept.
> Into the dangerous world I leapt:
> Helpless, naked, piping loud;
> Like a fiend hid in a cloud.

Struggling in my father's hands:
Striving against my swaddling bands—
Bound and weary I thought best
To sulk upon my mother's breast.

It is my conscious intent to follow in the footsteps of Blake in his mental war against Natural Religion, in whatever guise it may appear. Just as he carried on a metaphysical critique and satire of the dominant myths of his time—those of Hume, Locke, Gibbon, Voltaire, Rousseau—so I have chosen to do the same thing for my time, using (in this case) Bly's *Iron John* as a convenient target. My "bow of burning Gold," to quote Blake again, is bent not against Bly as an individual, nor against the Men's Movement, but precisely against the dangerous and seldom-criticized modern myths bursting from the seams of *Iron John*.

Unless Bly is defining the "Wild Man Path" as something infinitely greater than simply getting in touch with one's chthonic masculinity, his statement that "Blake and Yeats are for readers of poetry the masters of the Wild Man Path. Blake takes his imagined God, Orc, as his image; Yeats takes Cuchulain as his image of the Wild Man" (p. 227) betrays at best an extremely limited understanding of Yeats and a treatment of Blake I can only call a complete error. Blake's Orc is a symbol not of natural wildness, but of a revolt against tyranny which is ultimately transformed into tyranny, just as many of the myths of, say, the French Revolution have become the basis for the repressive technocracy of today. S. Foster Damon writes, in *A Blake Dictionary*, "Orc is only a stage, and no immediate answer to the problem: revolution in the material world degenerates, till in its fury it loses all of its original meaning. The illustrations to *America* show this progressive descent, ending in the agony of Nature herself."[41] And as for Yeats, he is, after all, the poet who said, "Once out of nature I shall never take/My bodily form from any natural thing."[42] I pray that Bly's Wild Man is restored to his true kingship, like Iron John, and doesn't end up like Cuchulain did in the following poem entitled "Cuchulain Comforted," written by Yeats on his deathbed:

A man that had six mortal wounds, a man
Violent and famous, strode among the dead;
Eyes stared out of the branches and were gone.

Then certain Shrouds that muttered head to head
Came and were gone. He leant upon a tree
As though to meditate on wounds and blood.

A Shroud that seemed to have authority
Among those bird-like things came, and let fall
A bundle of linen. Shrouds by two and three

Came creeping up because the man was still.
And thereupon that linen-carrier said:
'Your life can grow much sweeter if you will

'Obey our ancient rule and make a shroud;
Mainly because of what we only know
The rattle of those arms makes us afraid.

'We thread the needles' eyes, and all we do
All must together do.' That done, the man
Took up the nearest and began to sew.

'Now must we sing and sing the best we can,
But first you must be told our character:
Convicted cowards all, by kindred slain

Or driven from home and left to die in fear.'
They sang, but had nor human tunes nor words,
Though all was done in common as before;

They had changed their throats and had the
    throats of birds.[43]

In *Iron John*, Bly tends to support the Pagan/materialist con-
ception of things as against the transcendent high religions, otherwise he wouldn't risk portraying Blake, our greatest critic of nature
worship, as a worshiper of nature. And insofar as he sides with
the Pagan/materialist view, Bly must at least pay lip service to the
psychic polytheism of James Hillman, as when he says that "A whole
community of beings is what is called a grown man" (p. 227).

From my point of view, a whole community of beings is what is called a schizophrenic. Once we get to the point of saying "fragmentation is wholeness," how far are we from saying "war is peace; freedom is slavery; ignorance is strength"?

G. I. Gurdjieff also looked at the average adult personality as a collection of subpersonalities and complexes, but he didn't idealize it. On the contrary, he made it terrifyingly clear that whoever remains in this "natural" state, with no real ability to act because he or she lacks any real "I" to act with, is destined to "perish like a dog." Maurice Nicoll, a student of Jung and Gurdjieff, gives the following picture of the psychic disintegration of the "natural man" in his book *Living Time:*

> This multiple man is described thus by Plutarch: " . . . each one of us is made up of ten thousand different and successive states, a scrap heap of units, a mob of individuals." (See "Concerning the E at Delphi" in A. O. Prickard's *Selected Essays of Plutarch.* Oxford University Press, 1918.) Having no unity, Plutarch remarks that we never really *are.* Nor can we feel *now.* "*Now* is squeezed into the future, or into the past, as though we should try to see a point which of necessity passes away to right or left."
>
> It is well described in a recent article: "A person is an assembly. This assembly exists of many *dramatis personae* who have come from different directions, animated by different inclinations and tending to different ends. Sometimes one of them gets up, gives a discourse or accomplishes an act, then reseats himself and remains silent, motionless, while another in his turn speaks and acts. At other times several of these personages get up together, support each other in their discourses and combine activities. But often too, those who get up are not in agreement one with the other, they dispute fiercely, quarrel, and anathemize each other. Occasionally the assembly grows very tumultuous, all the members rise together and fight frenziedly. That is a person, and such is each one of us."
>
> Since we are an assembly, inner development and the reaching of unity cannot be taken separately. The one necessarily implies the other. "Unless he attains inner unity man

can have no 'I,' can have no will. The concept of 'will' in relation to a man who has not attained inner unity is entirely artificial. . . . " (Ouspensky, *A New Model of the Universe*)[44]

Contra Hillman

The most brilliant and influential contemporary apologist for psychic fragmentation is post-Jungian analyst James Hillman, whom Bly greatly respects and often quotes. Many of the ideas I have criticized in this book have Hillman as their source.

Hillman is a deconstructionist of both Christianity and classical Jungianism and an advocate of "psychological polytheism." He also has, to my taste, a strong nihilistic streak, a desire to destroy meaning. He speaks half the time in veiled contradictions and half-truths; his intellect is infectious rather than enlightening. And almost every page he writes contains some glaring intellectual falsehood, which might show itself as a real emotional truth, if only he could reveal the personal core he is at pains to protect with his contradictory dialectic.

For example, Hillman compares the central sacred act of the Christian tradition, the crucifixion and resurrection of Christ, to a depressive episode flipping over into mania. In this, he seems to be attempting to measure the Sea of Truth with the teaspoon of analysis:

> Because Christ resurrects, moments of despair, darkness and desertion cannot be valid in themselves. . . the individual's consciousness is already allegorized by the Christian myth and so he knows what depression is and experiences it according to form. It must be necessary (for it appears in the crucifixion), and it must be suffering; but *staying* depressed must be negative, since in the Christian allegory Friday is never valid per se, for Sunday—as an integral part of the myth—is pre-existent in Friday from the start. The counterpart of every crucifixion fantasy is a resurrection fantasy. . .
>
> In Christian theology the heavy sloth of depression, the drying despair of melancholy was the *sin* of *acedia* . . . our culture on the New Testament model has only one paradigm for meeting this syndrome. Even though the Christ myth is supposedly no longer operative, tenacious residues remain in our attitudes toward depression.

Depression is still the Great Enemy. More personal energy is expended in manic defense against, diversions from,
and denials of it than goes into other supposed psychopatho-
logical threats to society: psychopathic criminality, schizoid
breakdown, addictions.

. . . Depression is essential to the tragic sense of life. It
moistens the dry soul, and dries the wet. It brings refuge,
limitation, focus, gravity, weight, and humble powerlessness.
It reminds of death. *The true revolution begins in the individual
who can remain true to his or her depression.*[45]

The amount of error and contradiction in this passage is staggering, but I believe I can counter it. "*Staying* depressed" is "necessary,"
"suffering," and "negative" only because we come from a Christian
cultural background? This is obviously absurd, and not very funny.
Anyone who has fallen into a depression knows just how "necessary"
it is. It is, of course, *suffering*, a word which comes from the Latin
verb *ferre*, "to carry." When we are depressed, we have a lot to
carry, and it's hard to bear. It hurts. When an Egyptian poet of
the Twelfth Dynasty wrote: "Behold, my name stinks/more than the
odor of carrion birds/On summer days when the heaven is hot,"[46]
he was suffering depression. And he didn't have Jesus to blame for
it, because Jesus hadn't been born yet. Furthermore, I am unable
to see how psychopathic criminality and addictions can be termed
"supposed" threats to society. In my view, they are very real problems.

Hillman's ignorance of Christianity is surprising. He treats the
crucifixion drama as if Jesus went through it in the smug expectation
of a *deus ex machina*—as if, after praying "let this cup pass from me"
during the agony in the garden, the Father had said: "That's alright,
Son, you're off the hook. I'll take care of it." When Jesus on the cross
cried, "My God, my God, why have you forsaken me?" he really meant
it. Moreover, when Hillman says that the sin of *acedia* represents the
Christian view of depression, he is only half right. *Acedia* is specifically
the depression which comes from meditating too much and doing
too little physical labor. It is a "sin" because it is a form of self-
indulgence which can and should be remedied. But what about "the
dark night of the soul" of San Juan de la Cruz? This is not considered
a sin, but a visitation from God, a mortification of the natural faculties
through the power of the dark side of Divine grace. Hillman writes

as if to stay with pain and depression, for years if necessary, and even
on many occasions to seek them out, were not part of the Christian
tradition. Let him read the story of St. John Chrysostom from *The
King and The Corpse.* Let him read almost anything written by or about
the medieval saints. The image of crucifixion and resurrection as
manic-depressive psychosis is a pure, mocking shadow, accurate to
the way Christianity can degenerate, but profoundly inaccurate as a
statement about what Christianity is in itself. The quick manic fix for
depression through Christian faith is not Catholic. It is not Puritan.
It's probably no older than Norman Vincent Peale. To knock down
a straw man is easy, but Dr. Hillman should be careful that his fist
doesn't connect with the stone wall hidden behind it. The "residues"
of the Christian myth are "tenacious" indeed, precisely because they
have more truth to them than anything which claims to replace them.
One of the central truths of the Christian tradition is Divine mercy
and human compassion. But if Hillman is going to imply that staying
depressed may be a valid way to live, he had better not glibly deny
that depression is suffering, but admit that he is talking about the
possibility of serious pain over a long period of time. Anything less
is a failure of compassion.

It looks to me as if Hillman, for all his willingness to criticize
our tendency to think in simple antitheses, when confronted with
depression can see no third alternative beyond either sinking into it,
possibly forever, or going into a manic reaction. This stance bespeaks
a soul wound, not unlike my own. Mania misses it. Despair misses
it. Verbal intelligence dances over the top of it. But the wound itself
is frozen—a void bristling with thorns. Such a wounding is central
to our collective soul in these times. Profoundly denied, brilliantly
rationalized, it spreads like a hedge of thorns from Grail Castle. What
ails thee, uncle?

When Hillman describes depression as that which moistens the
dry soul and dries the wet one, bringing humility and refuge, and
reminding us of death, he is profoundly accurate. But if there is
no such thing as Divine mercy, humility is useless, and thoughts of
death, something we should logically do all in our power to avoid.
Without mercy, only the pretense of salvation remains, and mania *is*
that pretense. The third alternative, the path which breaks the cycle
of depression and mania, is that of crucifixion and resurrection,
which are, precisely, mercy at the core of agony. Hillman complains

that Good Friday is allowed no validity in itself, because Easter Sunday is pre-existent within it. But that drying, that moistening, that refuge, that humility are themselves the beginning of Sunday—the pre-dawn hours.

The danger in Hillman's argument is that he resurrects traditional esoteric concepts without sufficient understanding, and so turns them into parasites—"negations" in Blake's terminology—which act to destroy the truths on which they feed. The central mystery on which he bases his worldview is the concept of the *alam al-mithal*, the "imaginal realm" brought to light by Henry Corbin. Hillman says:

> Our distinctions are Cartesian: between outer tangible reality and inner states of mind, or between the body and fuzzy conglomerate of mind, psyche and spirit. We have lost the third, middle position which earlier in our tradition, and in others too, was the place of soul: a world of imagination, passion, fantasy, reflection, that is neither physical and material on the one hand, nor spiritual and abstract on the other, yet bound to them both.[47]

This is strictly accurate. It's a restatement of the classic Neoplatonic triad of *pneuma* (or *nous*), *psyche,* and *hyle* which I've been using throughout this book. But when he comes to the point of clarifying the distinction between Spirit and psyche—one of the most crucial distinctions we can ever make—Hillman, like Bly, betrays an essential lack of understanding. Nor is he alone; in fact he's in very good company. He quotes from a letter written by the present Dalai Lama:

> . . . I call the high and light aspects of my being *spirit*
> and the dark and heavy aspect *soul.*
> Soul is at home in deep, shaded valleys. Heavy torpid flowers saturated with black grow there. The rivers flow like warm syrup. They empty into huge oceans of soul.
> Spirit is a land of high, white peaks and glittering jewel-like lakes and flowers. Life is sparse and sounds travel great distances.[48]

I have to disagree with this and explain my disagreement by assuming that the Dalai Lama is not completely conversant with the terms *Spirit* and *soul* as used in the West. According to the Tibetan mandala of the Five Transcendent Wisdoms, the Wisdoms which occupy the four cardinal directions on the mandala are *Vajra*, intellectual clarity, which is transformed at enlightenment into Mirrorlike Wisdom; *Padma*, fascinating erotic beauty, transformed into Discriminating Awareness Wisdom; *Karma*, labor and struggle, transformed into All-Accomplishing Wisdom; and *Ratna*, emotional richness and nostalgia, transformed into Equanimity Wisdom. In terms of their separate qualities, these four are aspects of psyche, or soul.

But the fifth and central—or quintessential—Wisdom on the mandala is Buddha, which in the unenlightened state is ignorance, but which is transformed at enlightenment into the Wisdom of All-Encompassing Space. This is the simple quality of being awake, or, in my terms, Spirit. When we say, "things are exactly what they are because they are nothing in themselves," we are speaking out of Buddha energy, a quality which has no quality, the tasteless taste of enlightenment. And precisely because enlightenment has no quality of its own, the four psychic qualities that surround it in the mandala are also empty of self-nature, and so can function as doorways to enlightenment, paths from psyche to Spirit. Thus when the Dalai Lama identifies "high, white peaks and glittering jewel-like lakes" with Spirit, he is talking not about what *I* call Spirit (Buddha) but rather about one of the four psychic qualities which are the particular flavors exhibited by the soul when it aspires towards, or identifies with, the Spirit. For me, the "high, white peaks" have a Vajra flavor, just as Ratna (with some Padma thrown in) is the flavor identified with the "heavy torpid flowers" of the maternal Earth. Vajra may reflect Buddha, but only when we can use its psychic qualities as well as those of Padma, Karma, and Ratna in the service of enlightenment, can we say we have actually realized Buddha. As the Six-fold Wheel of Existence proves, every psychic quality is equidistant from the truth.[49]

Hillman hammers out his distinction between *soul* and *spirit* in these terms:

> . . . the soul [is connected] with the night world, the realm of the dead, and the moon. We still catch our soul's most essential nature in death experiences, in dreams of the night, in *lunacy*.

The world of spirit is different indeed. Its images blaze with light, there is fire, wind, sperm. Spirit is fast, and it quickens what it touches. Its direction is vertical and ascending; it is arrow straight, knife sharp, powder dry, and phallic. It is masculine, the active principle, making forms, order, and clear distinctions . . . higher and abstract disciplines, the intellectual mind, refinements, and purifications.[50]

This distinction between lunar and solar realities—especially when identified, as it is here, with the feminine/masculine polarity—is not too hard to understand. What is hard to understand, apparently, is that this distinction is not between soul and Spirit, but between two polarized qualities of the soul itself. In alchemy, quicksilver is usually identified with soul, and sulfur—that which is windy, fiery, and powder-dry—with Spirit. But since alchemy is in essence a psychic art, a soul-craft, the sulfur it speaks of is not Spirit per se, but that higher and lighter aspect of the soul (in the Dalai Lama's words) which identifies with Spirit. And as sulfur is psyche's image of Spirit, so quicksilver is psyche's image of its own essential nature. Once again, Spirit is not zenith, but center.

The imaginal realm, the *alam al-mithal*, which in Sufi terms is the *barzakh* (isthmus) between the two seas (the world of Spirit and the world of matter), is the soul, the psyche; and this realm, according to Corbin, is a world of multiple centers. He writes: " . . . spiritual circles . . . differ from material circles in that their *centre* possesses the property of being simultaneously the *circumference* . . . In the world of spiritual forms there are as many of these *centres* embracing, or totalling, a universe, as there are spiritual individualities."[51] And again, following the Sufi writer Abu'l Barakat: "He envisages . . . neither the separate Active Intelligence, one for all, nor an active Intelligence immanent in each individual, but a plurality of separate and transcendent active Intelligences, corresponding to the specific diversity among the multitude of souls."[52]

It's fairly easy to see how a literal mind could take such formulations as the basis for a polytheistic belief system, since Corbin is saying here that each of us has a unique relationship with the Deity via our own particular archetypal counterpart in the spiritual realm, which, using the Zoroastrian term, he calls our *fravashi*. That he does not intend by this to posit a multitude of gods is proved by the following passage:

What a human being attains in mystic experience is the "celestial pole" of his being, that is, his person as the person in whom and by whom the Divine Being manifested Himself to Himself in the origin of origins, in the World of Mystery, and through whom He made Himself known in the Form which is also the Form in which He knew Himself in that person. . . . A self-determination of the Divine Being was then the theophany constitutive of this human being's eternal individuality; in this theophany the Divine Being is totally *God*, but God as He is in and for this microcosm, *singulatim.*[53]

This is the very point Hillman misses; he therefore fails in his stated intent to discriminate between soul and Spirit. And as a logical consequence, he is forced to defend the position that, since the unconscious psyche is polyvalent, the conscious ego needs a polytheistic worldview in order to maintain its flexibility in the face of the powerful, transpersonal archetypes. If the ego holds on to a monotheistic belief system, he says, it will petrify; and a petrified ego, when it encounters the forces of the unconscious, is in danger of breaking up. He quotes Jung:

The individual ego is much too small, its brain much too feeble, to incorporate all the projections withdrawn from the world. Ego and brain burst asunder in the effort; the psychiatrist calls it 'schizophrenia.' (*Collected Works* 11, sec. 145)

Hillman continues:

Without a conscious polytheistic psychology are we not more susceptible to an unconscious fragmentation called schizophrenia?[54]

Given Hillman's view that human consciousness contains nothing higher than the psyche (the ego plus the unconscious), he can't be accused of intellectual dishonesty in this case; his conclusions follow from his premise. And since what he calls *Spirit* is merely the higher or subtler fraction of the psyche, a kind of superego ideal, he is justified in despairing of whatever unity seems to emanate from that quarter. Because if there were nothing in us ontologically higher and more inclusive than the conscious ego and the forces of the unconscious, then it would be entirely true to say that polytheism is the road to psychic health. Any traditionalist would agree with Hillman that no human ego can hope to maintain its own self-willed unity in the face of transpersonal forces. The only real unity is the unity of God, but Hillman, looking at this unity from the point of personal ego, can see it only as a kind of arbitrary tyranny: "[Polytheistic psychology] will more likely reflect the illusions and entanglements of the soul," he says, "even if it satisfies less the popular vision of individuation from chaos to order, from multiplicity to unity, and where the health of wholeness has come to mean the one dominating the many."[55]

But the one cannot dominate the many unless it is one among the many, and it can never be that, because it is the *one.* Does the ocean dominate the fish? Does space dominate the stars? Why this terror of unity, which would rather take refuge in the "illusions and entanglements of the soul" than face the thing it fears? Only the part which takes itself for the whole experiences unity as oppression. The only way the human form can attain unity is by transcending itself, dying to itself, at which point the energy forms of the unconscious become not fragments of the soul which the ego must always despair of being able to synthesize, but symbolic renditions of the Divine unity, refracted through the planes of cosmic manifestation. Hillman is right when he says that the ego can never be one, but he is wrong to assert that a consciously multiple ego is a safeguard against schizophrenia. In reality, it *is* schizophrenia. Only the unity of God can save us from attempting to build a spurious unity on the basis of ego, an attempt which is doomed to failure, as the three-headed Satan frozen in the ninth circle of Dante's hell symbolically demonstrates. But Hillman, sadly, would rather embrace the failure:

> The polytheistic perspective is grounded in the chthonic depths of the soul. A psychotherapy which reflects these depths can therefore make no attempt at achieving undivided individuality or encouraging a personal identity as a unified wholeness. Instead, psychotherapeutic emphasis will be upon the disintegrative effects of the dream, which also confronts us with our moral disintegrity, our psychopathic lack of a central hold upon ourselves . . . only by falling apart into multiple figures do we extend consciousness to embrace and contain its psychopathic potentials.[56]

I take Hillman at his word here. To embrace the psychopathic potentials of the soul, to court disintegration, is exactly what he's after. How right Maurice Nicoll is in *Living Time*, when he quotes Emile Brunner (*The Word and the World*, 1932) to the effect that ". . . man is no more a unity; the inward unity or harmony of his existence is disintegrated into a diversity of autonomous functions . . . the will is separate from knowledge, feeling from intellect. . . . Empirical psychology has to do with this disintegrated man, never with the integral."[57] Only God knows us in our integrity; and that knowledge, particular in terms of the known, universal in terms of the Knower, is the Self archetype, the heart. "Heaven and earth cannot contain Me," says God in the *hadith* of Muhammad, "but the heart of my loving slave can contain Me." But Hillman seems to have more or less dispensed with the archetype of the Self. He seems eager to forget that Carl Jung ever mentioned it, as when he claims that "Jung used a polycentric description for the objective psyche"[58]—a strategic half-truth. What Jung actually did was to plumb the multiplicity of the psychic depths in search of the center, the One. Jung writes:

> Wholeness is . . . an objective factor that confronts the subject independently of him, like anima or animus; and just as the latter have a higher position in the hierarchy than the shadow, so wholeness lays claim to a position and a value superior to those of the syzygy. The syzygy seems to be at least an essential part of it, or like the two halves of the totality represented by the royal brother-sister pair, and hence the tension of opposites from which the divine child is born as the symbol of unity.
>
> Unity and totality stand at the highest point on the scale of objective values because their symbols can no longer be distinguished from the *imago Dei*.[59]

Hillman may be a fascinating writer, but I for one would not choose him as my physician; he doesn't seem to believe in health.

Tearing and Being Torn

By the end of *Iron John*, it's pretty clear that Bly has largely chosen to identify not only with Paganism as against Christianity, but with the darker Dionysian forms of Paganism as against the lighter, more civilized Apollonian forms. And to the degree that his theme is the Wild Man, this seems fitting. But what are the consequences of this choice?

In the final chapters of the book, Bly deals with the theme of castration. In Chapter Eight he tells the story of the castration and death of Adonis from a boar wound, which was apparently connected with human sacrifice as practiced in the Adonis cult of the Near East. Of this, he says a very interesting thing: "This sacrifice is shocking only to those who have not read the extensive literature" (p. 213). It's true, of course, that any atrocity is more shocking the first time you hear of it; nonetheless, I detect in Bly's attitude an implication that such things are only shocking to those of us with a naively ethical worldview, that anyone who is really sophisticated will smile at such crimes as castration and human sacrifice. The feminist writer Simone de Beauvoir revealed a similar attitude when she wrote in defense of the Marquis de Sade as a serious intellectual. De Sade, it may be recalled, did not limit himself to merely writing about sexual torture, but actually practiced it. Of course Madame de Beauvoir presented the necessary disclaimers, but it remains unclear how she could reconcile her treatment of de Sade as more or less a colleague with her feminism.

As I see it, the real reason why the practices of the Adonis cult do not shock us is that they happened thousands of years ago. But the contemporary rash of psychopathic sex crimes and murders, some of which have a ritual element, should caution us against becoming too blasé in these matters. I detect an uneasy drift in this way of facing—or not facing—the reality of evil. Early in the book, Bly talks about the importance of "learning to shudder" as a defense against the "domination system" which allows boys to become "Titans," who can torture animals without compunction (p. 84). But by the time he describes the Adonis-cult sacrifices, Bly himself seems to have forgotten how to shudder.

The most passionate and responsible Pagan I know, Sharon Devlin, once said to me: "If the crucifixion meant anything, it meant that human sacrifice was finished as a religious dispensation."

"That's because it was Jesus' mission to institute the sacrifice of ego in place of the sacrifice of victims," I replied. But is such ego sacrifice still collectively possible to us? Which is to say, can we still tell the difference between humility and self-hatred? Or are the darker powers of the psychic universe moving abysmally to compensate for our vanity by demanding payment in blood?

Bly writes: "Ethical philosophy wants Apollo, morality and perfection. The pagans want tearing and ecstasy" (p. 218). He then goes on to quote the following stanza from Yeats's poem "Crazy Jane Talks with the Bishop":

> A woman can be proud and stiff
> When on love intent:
> But love has pitched his mansion in
> The place of excrement;
> For nothing can be sole or whole
> That has not been rent.[60]

"That expresses beautifully the pagan and Dionysian praise of tearing and being torn," says Bly; "the tiny explosion that happens in the head during the last four lines is a testimony to Yeats's greatness, but also to the power of this old pagan idea."

Something is wrong here—actually, a number of things. To begin with, it's garbled to say that ethical philosophy wants Apollo and the Pagans want tearing and ecstasy. Why? Because Apollo himself is a Pagan god, of course. And I wonder how many present-day Pagans would appreciate this view of their intents and practices, especially those who are trying to distance themselves from any imputation of the practice of blood sacrifice.

Moreover, a poet like Bly should remember that Orpheus, the archetypal Greek lyric poet, was dismembered by the Maenads, the female followers of Dionysus, it being their practice to rend animals (and sometimes human beings) to pieces in their ecstasy, possibly, as Robert Graves thinks, given the necessary muscular strength by the use of *amanita muscaria.* Look down, look down that long lonesome road, men of the Men's Movement, before you travel there. Look to see exactly how much of the Men's Movement is based on a radical and deeply denied fear of women, or on both the fear of castration and the attraction to it.

Clearly this old Pagan idea *is* powerful, rising up on the tide of collective psychic darkness, both in the sense of evil and in that of blindness. Obviously Bly does not condone such practices as human sacrifice; he is a good and caring man. Yet his argument here can be read as an apology for such extremes.

Freudian psychology talks about castration anxiety; Jungianism deals with the symbolic meaning of human sacrifice, when Esther Harding in her *Women's Mysteries* interprets the goddess Cybele's sacrifice of her son Attis as representing a mother's need to overcome possessiveness over her offspring. Ever since Frazer's *The Golden Bough*, it has been a commonplace among cultural anthropologists to trace the roots of many major religions, especially Christianity, to the archaic practice of human sacrifice, though in Frazer's nineteenth-century England, such practices could comfortably be viewed (rightly or wrongly) as long ago and/or far away. And the degree of violence one must live through vicariously during any day of watching American television, or experience firsthand during any month of living in one of America's inner cities, would also seem to be telling us that we had better learn not to be shocked by such realities. So isn't it unfair that I should criticize Bly's ethically responsible work of being a bit bloodthirsty?

My answer is that Bly has taken on a vital cultural task. And my fear is that his ideas will be used to swell a rising tide from the collective unconsious that tends to lead men—and all of us—in a direction unworthy of his higher purpose.

One of the common collective responses to the repeated shocks we must process in these grim times is what is called *psychic numbing*. And one of the most widespread reactions to such numbing is our tendency to think and feel in terms of numinous, emotionally charged images rather than human relationships (a trend which is obviously intensified by the visual media, as well as by drug use). If the Victorian era was *all too human*, meaning shallow, petty, and personalistic, in our own times the reality of the human person is becoming lost in a flood of autonomous "deities," or subconscious complexes, pouring through our unprotected mass psyche. To the degree that our finer feelings are numbed, we require more and more intense experiences to keep us from feeling the raw, frigid, flayed condition that our psyche is in. And the more such experiences we process, the more stripped and vulnerable we feel. This is the root condition behind most forms of addiction. Insofar as the human matrix is wounded, both individually and collectively, only an ever-increasing dosage of inhuman experience can make us feel human again for a while. The personality of a crack addict, for example, may be so wounded that without a hit of crack he doesn't even have the self-confidence, the pure ego-charge it takes to walk across the street. His ego is so fragile that the only way open to him to respond to a passing insult without being totally destroyed may be to draw his Uzi and fire. And in the punk ethos, an individual must publically impersonate a mythological monster just to retain any sense of identity at all. Such fetishism, from my point of view, is becoming increasingly common in the remnant of the counterculture, if not in society as a whole.

The human form is greater than the gods and goddesses by virtue of the fact that only from the human vantage point can we attain any degree of humility, either through service to transpersonal values or through conscious submission to the Source which creates us. In Blake's words, "these . . . Gods ought to be made to sacrifice to Man, not man compelled to sacrifice to them," because "all deities reside in the human breast."[61] But insofar as contact with the human form is lost, we are forced to serve collective subhuman powers, whether we view them mythopoeically as deities, or scientistically as the forces of nature. Such service seems to bring real benefits, except that in performing it, we have already lost our human soul, and so none of these benefits really matter. If we can no longer feel, the psychic deities respond by bringing us ready-made and automatic emotional responses. If we no longer have any true inner direction to our lives, any authentic destiny, they answer by providing us with prerecorded fates which we are allowed or forced to live out. And if we no longer possess any real self-knowledge or individual integrity, they fill that vacuum by letting us impersonate them. Instead of human beings, we become transhuman personae, magical power masks through which we look down in scorn on those who are still weak and stupid enough to be human. (The practice of mask making which is common in the Men's Movement may allow men to purify and transmute these tendencies instead of being unconsciously possessed by them.) A vacuum in our integral humanity always fills with magic. I will never forget Marie-Louise von Franz's observation that many schizophrenics don't really want to become normal, because they know that if they do, they'll lose their very real psychic powers. The same is true of anyone who courts ego-inflation through identification with the archetypes instead of carrying on the hard and often humbling work of relating to them, integrating them, and ultimately transcending them.

This being the state of things just under the social skin, I can hardly blame Robert Bly for stumbling once or twice. Just as it used to be common practice for a warrior returning from battle in which he had taken life to go through a period of purification before being reunited with his tribe, so those of us who, like Bly, are called to descend into the underworld of the collective unconscious to gather treasures of psychological insight for the good of society need to return to fully human form before they make these treasures available. And this is something that no one can do without help.

In the following poem I attempt to de-glamorize the myth of the castration and sacrifice of the young god Attis or Adonis by connecting it with the theme of teen suicide and to show the quality and the consequences of an undeveloped psychic life, driven by mythological fate:

A PURE VICTIM

And then, the grief.

The beautiful young man
Decorated like a god of fertility
With a garland of roses—

Castrated. Disemboweled.
Shot through the head.
The bedroom rug
Stained with his young blood
Like a field in Springtime
Shot through with a
        riot of red flowers...
Anemones!

His mother didn't kill him;
No mother is capable of such
        act;
She bears no guilt.

It was her brutal boyfriend who
    did him in,
The dark hunter—

But no: No stepfather is
    capable of such an act—
He was killed by a wild boar,
His belly torn
With the moons of his tusks.
The stepfather bears no guilt.

Deny it, and speak the truth:
The boar didn't kill him;
No mythological beast is capable
    of such an act—
It was the young man himself
    who did it:
He took his own life.
Innocent nature
Bears no guilt.

Nor does the young man himself—
No child of promise
With life and the world before him
Is capable of such an act—

It was Fate who killed him,
His very Mother—killed him
Before breath was drawn,
Before the first protest
Of life against Life.

And we watch—numbed—frozen—
Our hearts,
Chunks of ice
In porcelain bowls

Filled with warm blood—
Our hands dangling, helpless,
From our wrists—

We watch the dance of the
Mythological beasts.

The fascination with human sacrifice is a reflection of the far from uncommon collective belief that we are liberated from our cramped and frozen ego through chaos and fragmentation. This belief is an inversion and counterfeit of the primordial truth that, in transcending ourselves, we are annihilated in a Divine unity which is higher than the ego, not lower. Human sacrifice is now and always has been a literalist misreading of the esoteric imperative to "live like a dead man" (as Zen would say), or to "die before you die" (in the words of Muhammad).

And what particular character type might be especially vulnerable to this inversion of the truth, this contamination with transpersonal darkness? Let's go back to the story of Orpheus. The underworld had claimed Euridice, his beloved, in death. So Orpheus traveled there and charmed Pluto and Persephone so completely with his singing that they released Euridice, with the caveat that he must not look at her on their way back to the upper Earth, or she would be lost forever. But looking at her was the one thing he could not resist. Orpheus here is the *aesthetic* personality, the one who can only love a woman as an image, most likely a youthful one. So Orpheus loses Euridice through his inability to sacrifice his shallow artistic sensibilities. It's only after he's betrayed his soul through aestheticism in this way that the Maenads arrive and finish him.

There is nothing more literal than evil. So, when it comes to the choice between Apollonian ethical philosophy and literal Dionysian rending (which Bly clearly opposes), then, at the terrible risk of being thought bourgeois, I will choose Apollo.

But, in truth, we are rent anyway. The Dionysian energies are really there; they cannot be dispelled by a few platitudes, a few chords on the lyre, which is what Yeats is really saying in "Crazy Jane Talks with the Bishop." One form this rending takes is schizophrenia; another, as Bly points out, is grief. We are torn not because we are foolish or unlucky enough to fall in with the revels of the Maenads;

it's life itself that rends us, marks each of us with our unique and destined wound. "Character is fate," said Heraclitus. That wound is the point at which our primal identification with the body and the natural psyche is broken, and it therefore functions as the seed of our character development. It is the signature of our spiritual vocation, our only way back to the house of our Lord. And when the Lord of the Dance (an epithet of both Dionysus and Shiva) calls us to enter the dance, he is also calling us to meditate on the uniqueness of our own rending. Bly says, ". . . where a man's wound is, there his genius will be" (p. 42). A wise thing, but it has a shadow to it, because a man's wound is also the place where his ego will be, his mass of defense mechanisms and numbing addictions. And those who are caught in this whirlpool are in danger of being attracted to the literalism of tearing and being torn (like the character in the motion picture *The Deer Hunter*, who became addicted to Russian roulette in Vietnam). Whoever gets caught on this literal level is in flight from his own real wound, and thus from his own destined healing.

In another part of Yeats's poem, Crazy Jane describes herself as

> Learned in bodily lowliness
> And in the heart's pride.

So exactly what is rent, according to Crazy Jane? If the body is rent, we are killed or deformed; if the soul is rent, we become psychotic. What is the particular kind of rending that leads to soleness and wholeness?

It is the rending of the ego (not the ego in the psychological sense—the conscious personality—but the ego in the spiritual sense—our addiction to a particular set of self-images). One of my teachers in Catholic high school, Father Lacy, said something that I've never forgotten: "True pride and true humility are the same thing." (The synthetic term, I think, is *self-respect.*) Sometimes soul and even body must be torn to break down the satanic pride of the ego and call up that deeper pride which is the pride of the heart. Without this self-respect, which is in no way our own pride but rather the pride of Divine love within us, there can be no such thing as spiritual chivalry. The Muslims say that humanity is both '*abd*, "the slave of God," and *khalifa*, "the vice-regent of God." Infinitely humbled before our Lord, we are also infinitely exalted in God's service. Because, in reality, there is no you or I; there is only that One, and we are the secret form of that One. Those who are learned in bodily lowliness and in the heart's pride have mortified "the natural man" and made their hearts the throne of the King or Queen.

Hatred of Christianity, Concluded

Bly ends *Iron John* with a further criticism of Christianity. He tells the story of a traveler to Mt. Athos who was greeted by an old monk with the statement that "women are evil." I sympathize with Bly's outrage at such a statement, particularly since it was made within the walls of a spiritual fortress that is under the protection of the Mother of God. (In view of this story, it must have taken a degree of moral stamina on Bly's part for him to admit, on p. 249, that "asceticism . . . has its own dignity.") Next, however, Bly goes on to complain about the practice of self-castration among early Christian monks and theologians, the most famous case being that of Origen, and proceeds to oppose to this the ethos of Paganism—the wild energy of Pan, or the willingness of the Hindu religious imagination to honor sexual energy in the form of Shiva. There's no question that Christianity has not been able to deal with the world of *eros* in a balanced way, but there's still something wrong with this picture.

What's wrong is that the pagan devotees of the goddess Cybele also castrated themselves; and Shiva himself, in one of his guises, is the Castrated God. When his wife died, he went into a frenzy of grief and sexual frustration; he had to be castrated to prevent the destruction of the universe. The main ritual object of the Shiva cult, the shivalingam (which takes the form of polished, elongated egg-shaped stones and phallic shrines), is actually a representation of his severed penis. Why is castration "not shocking" in the Pagan world and a crime to be deplored in the Christian one? Perhaps it is because we expect a higher ethical response from Christianity than we do from Paganism, but am I alone in detecting an anti-Christian bias in Bly's treatment of the castration theme?

Or is his treatment simply denial, a way of saying, "the castration energies which both terrify and attract me are all in the opposition's camp, not in mine"? Because it is an unbreakable cosmic law that, to the degree that the feminine principle is excluded, she will return in a seductive and terrifying form. She may even come up through the darkness of the personal and collective unconscious and suggest that we might castrate ourselves in the service of Cybele, or let ourselves be torn apart by Maenads. It would do for the leaders and followers of the Men's Movement to be very clear on this law. Men can get together and build the male spirit, up to a point. But after that point the truth must dawn that the sexes, in isolation from each other, don't really exist. They are a polar reality. It's no wonder, then, that the adolescent, homoerotic, male-oriented society of classical Greece invoked the Maenads. They were there to prove that to isolate one's maleness from female energies is ultimately to lose one's masculinity. And to be pressured by social forces to define oneself primarily in terms of gender or sexual preference, as women and homosexuals have been, is both a necessary response to oppression and a form of oppression in itself; it can never be a valid ideal.

Bly opposes the energy of the Wild Man to that of the Christian religion. But things aren't quite that simple. For example, there are two saints of the Eastern Orthodox Church—St. Cyril of Rome and St. John Chrysostom—who actually appear iconographically *as* the Wild Man. (For the story of Chrysostom, I refer the reader to *The King and The Corpse*,[62] an exquisite selection of myths and romances by Heinrich Zimmer, one of Joseph Campbell's mentors.)

For the second time in this book, I ask the question: Why do we hate Christianity? Is it because of the Inquisition? For some reason, I hear a lot more complaints about the Inquisition than about, say, the Pagan Druid practice of burning human beings inside of giant wicker figures. Is our hatred due to the resurgence of right-wing fundamentalism? All in all, that's a much better reason. But another reason, I think, is that we are taught to believe that the Christian denial of the value (or more accurately, the ultimate value) of earthly life is at the root of the environmental crisis.[63] But this is not historically accurate. The roots of the environmental crisis are not in the transcendent spirituality of the Christian Middle Ages, but in the pantheism tending to materialism which came back into Western society via the revival of Pagan values during the Renaissance. Deism in the eighteenth century and Social Darwinism in the nineteenth were the continued fruits of this revival, and both played decisive roles in the desacralization of the material universe. Nor did the Nature romanticism of Rousseau and Robespierre before and during the French Revolution in any fundamental way stand against the materialism of the French encyclopedists; in reality they were the soft/sentimental and hard/rationalistic sides of the same coin. Greek science, not monks and nuns praying in their cells and cultivating their gardens of medicinal herbs, was the seed of our environmental destruction.

If we simply open our eyes and look around us, we will see that it is worldly people who destroy the environment, not otherworldly ones. Industrialists do a lot more damage than contemplatives; they always have. Those who believe that this world is all there is must attempt to satisfy their innate desire for the Divine infinity within a finite environment; they must squeeze the Earth dry in a desperate attempt to turn it into paradise. But those who have "laid up their treasure in Heaven" will walk in balance, take from the Earth only what they need, and give back even more than they've taken. If we worship the visible Earth as God, we cut her off from the transcendent Source of her own life; consequently she sickens. But if we make that invisible Source the conscious center of our own lives, then we will radiate the vital spirit of that Source into the total environment. In terms of our egotism, we are the destroyers of the Earth; but in terms of our inner reality, we are the preservers of the Earth, the channel through which God creates the material universe as defined by our senses, instant by instant. If we are united with God, then the Earth will see God in us, turn toward that Source of infinite vitality, and live. As Blake wrote:

> O Earth, O Earth, return!
> Why wilt thou turn away?
> The starry floor, the watery shore
> Are given thee till the break of day.[64]

9

 What Then?

P ERHAPS WE CAN NOW RISK ASKING the following questions: What values might stand against the rising barbarism we see around us? What particular character traits might incarnate and serve these values? Before answering such questions, however, a clear distinction needs to be made between what are perhaps the two main divisions of the individual psyche: the *character* and the *personality*.

When the Jungians and other psychologists use the word *personality*, they are usually referring to the totality of the individual psyche; they tend to speak of "personality development" rather than "character development." And while much of the Jungian "personality development" is actually development of character, the fact that the term *personality* has expanded to cover more and more psychic territory is symptomatic of the natural bias of psychology toward the psychic plane at the expense of the Spirit.

Personality develops from the set of tendencies we are born with; it is our "nature." The growth of personality has to do with the unfolding of our natural talents. Character, on the other hand— though it, too, is posited at birth as a potential—is built in relation to transpersonal values, and its development is inseparable from the willingness to subordinate the values of personality, which are primarily psychic, to transcendent norms, which are essentially of the Spirit. Both character and personality unfold in relation to inner

189

and outer circumstances, the difference being that circumstances stimulate the personality to develop its potential, while challenging us to build character by learning how to take a stand on principle. Those who develop personality at the expense of character become vain and irresponsible; in alchemical terms, they have too much quicksilver. Those who develop character at the expense of personality become humorless and dogmatic; they have too much sulfur. Yet in a certain sense, character will always have precedence over personality, since character development is what allows the personality to unfold without dissipating itself. The one with character but little personality has kept his or her integrity intact; the one with personality but little character has betrayed it.

To the Jungians, the *persona*—the way we relate to others in terms of how we appear to them—is (paradoxically) a transpersonal archetype. And though it is related to what I am here calling *personality*, it isn't quite the same thing. Those with fascinating personalities, or even profound ones, do not necessarily have well-developed personas; persona development requires strength of character as well as power of personality. The individual with a healthy persona will neither blindly manifest his personality without noticing its effect on others—like a Dostoyevsky character, say, or a raving artistic genius— nor will he become so dependent on other people's views of him, or his view of that view (like many performers, also many shy persons), that he becomes a puppet of other people's projections, without whose attention he hardly feels that he exists. A healthy persona allows us to attract and nourish ourselves on the attention of others without being controlled by it and also to repel the attention of others without starving for it—two skills which obviously require a great deal of character. (And the Sufis mention a third and even harder to develop skill: the ability to attract negative attention deliberately for a specific purpose, without being wounded by it.)

Since perhaps the Civil War, American society has been moving away from respect for character and toward fascination with personality. If you read letters written by nineteenth-century Americans, you will (perhaps) be struck by the fact that people in those days had the habit of asking themselves, when meeting someone new: "What sort of character does this person have? Is he or she trustworthy? Noble? Ignoble? Generous? Of 'low character'? How does the essential character of this person manifest?" But nowadays, when we meet someone new, the questions will more likely be "Is this person interesting? Boring? Does he or she have a sense of humor? Would he or she impress my friends? Is he or she my 'type'?" In other words, we tend to ask about a person's personality, not his or her character and make our decisions accordingly.

This trend in American society started to become dominant after the Civil War, in the Gilded Age of predatory capitalism and all the medicine-show hucksterism that went with it. One need only compare *Moby Dick* or *The Scarlet Letter* with *Huckleberry Finn* to sense the change: we are no longer so interested in character; now we are after personality. And as the Gilded Age followed the War Between the States, so the Roaring 20s followed World War I, and the Beat Generation, World War II. In each case, the admired social traits were traits of personality, not character. This is why we exalted Hollywood into a kind of fifth estate, and finally elected a Hollywood president— Mr. Reagan—who was, literally, a "personality": he had no character at all.

The worship of personality took a quantum leap during the 60s, when every neighborhood had its culture hero, and the archetype of this era of personality expansion was John Kennedy. In the 1963 *Encyclopedia Britannica* you can see the radical discontinuity (though Franklin Roosevelt possibly foreshadowed it): every portrait or photograph of an American president before Kennedy is calculated to express statesmanship, strength of character, personal seriousness, and gravity. But as soon as we get to JFK, there's that big, gleaming, Hollywood smile. Kennedy was the master salesman. And if we sometimes ask whether he was perhaps America's greatest president, it's because he was a genius at selling us to ourselves, at selling us on the greatness of America. But that era of national glamour didn't last, and Dallas wasn't the only thing that tarnished it.

Now that the United States has lost its position of global, cultural, and economic dominance, while enjoying its political dominance by sheer military might (in a certain sense by default, due to the collapse of the Soviet Empire), we may become capable of remembering that while the values of personality are comparatively ephemeral, the values of character are more lasting, more what we need to survive in times like these. It is the strong character, not the interesting personality, that can stand against barbarism. Furthermore, it is the overemphasis on personality at the expense of character that opens the door to barbarism in the first place, since the individual who has sold his soul to vanity has exposed that soul to the forces of psychic corruption. And this is equally true of Hollywood burnouts like Judy Garland, artistic self-destroyers like Jack Kerouac, revolutionary sellouts like Eldridge Cleaver, New Age hucksters like Werner Erhardt, and fundamentalist mountebanks like Jim Bakker. The house founded on personality—no matter how sincere it may be—is founded on sand. But as of the Reagan years, when John Wayne was posthumously awarded the Congressional Medal of Honor for *playing* heroes, while all the others who had ever gotten it did so for *being* heroes, we had not yet learned this lesson.

I would now like to define four character traits which I believe can help us arm ourselves against vanity and resist the barbarism that necessarily follows in its wake. In times when character development was respected, they were widely understood as integral parts of the mature masculine character (which doesn't mean that they can't be, or don't need to be, developed by women as well). I will define these traits, but can I really recommend them? Character traits, after all, are not merchandise; we don't acquire them simply by buying them. The first step in developing positive characteristics is to understand them well enough to admire them; but no amount of admiration for a given trait—physical courage, for example—can make it ours if we don't already contain the seeds of its future development. With that disclaimer, I am willing to name *Dedication to Principle, Objectivity, Dignity,* and *Courtesy* as four qualities which, if we are willing and able to develop them, will purify and strengthen our character, and act as a healthy balance to the more chthonic Wild Man virtues, such as zaniness, physical courage, and erotic passion. If we want to be men, let us not simply be men from the waist down, or up.

Dedication to Principle

If it is a virtue to act on the basis of principles, first we need to know what principles actually are. Are they moral rules? And if so, how do we encounter these rules? Through education? Through moral introspection? Through experience of life? And how can we determine whether or not a particular ethical standard is valid?

One way that principles manifest is in terms of moral standards, but that's not what they essentially are. Principles are fundamentally metaphysical in nature; they are objective spiritual laws. The Ten Commandments, for example, are eternal truths first and moral laws second; they are metaphysical statements about the way things really are. To say, "I am the Lord thy God; thou shalt not have strange gods before me" is to state the objective truth that Spirit is higher than psyche. To say, "Remember thou, keep holy the Lord's Day" is to declare that we can only become conscious of, and therefore able to respond to, the spiritual reality from which we spring by attending to the present moment, the "Lord's Day." Prohibition of idolatry and the command to keep the Sabbath represent effective spiritual practices—what the Buddhists call *upaya*—which help us to conform our lower natures to these higher truths. Principles, in other words, are not rules imposed upon us from without; they are the eternal realities through which God creates us, which is why willing conformation to them has the power to redeem us. All we know ourselves to be in terms of our own subjectivity is a subset, a son or daughter of these eternal laws. Far from being limitations on our existence, they are the very roots of our existence, which doesn't mean, of course, that they can't become sources of darkness and oppression if they are incorrectly understood or unjustly applied. Nothing, in fact, is more tyrannical and destructive than a metaphysical principle perverted into the service of spiritual blindness and addiction to power. On the other hand, willing dedication to principles which are both clearly understood and objectively true is the root of the upright character. He who is "upright" knows what is hierarchically above him; he knows his Father, his Origin, and he conforms himself in obedience to that Origin, which is no less than his own true nature. And he who is able to subordinate himself to that which is above him will be protected against falling into the power of that which is below him: addictions, violence, destructive self-indulgence, and the temptation to sell his soul for power.

Respect for principles—along with the second of the four in-traits, objectivity—is traditionally recognized as being related to the Masculine Principle (which, since it is a transpersonal archetype, both sexes have access to, though in different ways). So dedication to principle is one of the things that makes a man a man. But nowadays we tend to view such dedication as a kind of emotional insensitivity, if not ruthless fanaticism. This is not surprising, since the ranks of those who do most of the talking about obedience to principle in these times, the Christian and Muslim fundamentalists, are not without their ruthless fanatics. But even someone like Gandhi was vulnerable to the shadow side of the principled man. When his son was seriously ill and the doctor prescribed goat's milk, Gandhi refused to allow it: "I have made a vow for my son that he will never drink goat's milk." At this point his wife Kasturbai intervened and prevailed: "Vow or no vow, my son will have goat's milk!" Such stories are often recounted to show how empathy and emotional wisdom, traditionally identified with the Feminine Principle, are more valid guides to action than abstract principles. But apart from the fact that to make a vow for someone else is not necessarily a principled thing to do, we could also say that in this case Kasturbai was invoking a higher principle than Gandhi was. And we need also to remember that just as emotional wisdom and empathy can help us refine our understanding of objective principles, so these principles can help us form and clarify our emotional wisdom and so deepen our empathy.

Talk about obedience to principles calls up for some of us the specter of the Puritans, who burned women alive as witches, supposedly in the name of objective spiritual laws. But this dark view of our Puritan ancestors, while entirely valid, is also one-sided. We tend to forget, for example, that the Puritans were also the ancestors of the abolitionist movement, which was preached from pulpits all across the North as a holy crusade in the name of Christian principles, much as Martin Luther King was to do over a century later. And John Brown, a true militant slave-liberationist and American revolutionary, was nothing if not Puritan in character (and a fanatic as well). It's enlightening to remember that, in the years before the Civil War, liberal politics called both for political liberation for the oppressed and for an end to vice. Abolition and women's rights made common cause with prohibition; slavery was seen as an evil not only because it oppressed the slaves, but because it was a source of moral corruption to both slaves and masters. What could be more logical? How could political freedom mean anything to those who were slaves to alcohol and sexual immorality?

Even as late as Adlai Stevenson, the image of a morally upright liberal didn't seem so far-fetched. But after JFK, whose well-documented sexual exploits apparently had a power motive, the traditional identification of liberalism with high moral character was clearly breaking down; and the substitution of hipness for morality during the 60s, which entailed dedication to hip fashions in thought or art or dress as if they were moral principles, spelled the end of liberalism's moral ascendancy. It only remained for the cultural revolution of that time to identify freedom with self-indulgence for the value of dedication to principles (what, after all, could be less hip?) to be buried under the triumph of essentially bohemian values in society at large. We are living today amid the ruins of, and the reaction against, that triumph. But you can't stand against the mores of an oppressive and self-indulgent society on the basis of an alternate form of self-indulgence. Those who have not cleaned up their act can in no way work to bring peace, social justice, or cultural renewal.

Objectivity

Dedication to principle directs our attention to the inner world, where we encounter intimations of the higher planes of being. Objectivity is the fruit of this dedication, manifesting in our relations with the outer world. He who knows his subjectivity as absolutely contingent upon a Divine principle which transcends it will not overvalue it; instead of identifying with his subjective experience of himself and the world, he will view this experience objectively. From the standpoint of principle he will see his own experience as an objective factor in the situation at hand and view other people's experience in the same way, rather than in terms of his own projections upon it, as determined by fear and desire. To find one's center in the realm of principles is to view the world objectively. To view the world objectively is to relate to it with detachment. He who sees his own partiality as it is—as a part of the whole—will thereby become impartial. Fear and desire continue, but only as objects of perception, not as determinants of our basic mode of perception; therefore they do not ultimately control our relationships with things, persons, and situations in the outer world. As soon as we really see them, we have already seen beyond them.

Objectivity based on dedication to principle lets us interact strategically with people and situations without giving them more than they deserve, less than they deserve, or something other than they deserve. And so objectivity is the root of justice.

According to the present social mores, at least certain sectors of liberal/counterculture mores, someone who speaks in the name of objectivity is in danger of being seen as too rational and insensitive, too left-brained, too narrowly and one-sidedly male. But objectivity is not primarily a rational quality; it is first and foremost a contemplative one. And speaking now on the level of the archetypes, when the Masculine Principle in us contemplates objective truth, it contemplates it in feminine form, as the Prajnaparamita of the Buddhists, the Sophia of the Gnostics and Orthodox Christians, the Torah of the Jews, the Layla of the Sufis. That One *is* the truth that transcends and encompasses our contingent subjectivity. In unmanifest mode, the Feminine Principle of truth is the dark essence of God, beyond both knowing and being. As manifest, she is the Divine substance of every item of our experience, the immanent Divinity which redeems that experience from all subjective limitations and carries it back forever into the matrix of objective truth. It is she who overcomes the subjective bias of our perception and allows us to witness all things as they are: as the lines and contours of her form, in which beauty and truth are one.

When objectivity fails on a collective level, we tend to evaluate all statements only in terms of their effects, as in advertising. We use *buy* as a synonym for *believe*: "I'll buy that"; "I don't buy that." Whether a particular statement *works* or not becomes the only criterion for its so-called truth. (I remember that at the climax of the Watergate scandal, President Nixon published a statement to the effect that his former statements were "no longer operative," by which he probably meant that he had discovered that they no longer worked.) We evaluate statements by public officials in terms not of their truth but of their credibility. We even conduct polls on the credibility of public statements, instead of trying to find out whether or not they are actually true. In such a climate, unsubstantiated rumor or government disinformation, if they are believed, become strategically and even historically "true." The truth which has the power to prevail is established as objectively valid, and so all statements become politicized. Thus certain feminists will fantasize about earlier Goddess cultures and justify their fantasies as true because they provide women with inspiring role models and historical hope. Some Blacks will do the same thing with African history. And the government will lie in a big way about global conditions, because such lies justify what are perceived as necessary actions. Of course political and social propaganda of this kind is nothing new, but such interested pragmatism has probably never before spread so far into the collective psyche. The attitude which replaces "the truth shall make you free" with "the good story shall get you what you want" is closer to being the moral status quo than at any time in our history.

One of the psychological consequences of this interested pragmatism is the inability to see situations as they are, since those who employ lies often end up believing them. To take one example, reassuring but untrue government statements about the state of the environment or the economy often act to feed the government's own denial of the seriousness of these conditions; consequently everyone suffers, including our leaders themselves. Just as spending money we don't have increases the deficit, so lying, which could be defined as spending truth we don't have, creates karmic debt.

So the very concept of objective truth is being eroded. We are capable now of holding two or more absolutely opposed beliefs with little or no anxiety—a condition which George Orwell called "doublethink." Belief One is useful for some purposes, and Belief Two for others; who cares if they contradict each other? After all, didn't Walt Whitman say, in "Song of Myself": "Do I contradict myself?/Very well, then, I contradict myself;/ (I am large—I contain multitudes.)"? Whitman was the kind of natural mystic who could contemplate the One in terms of the minute particulars of the many, but according to the contemporary mindset, it would be truer to say: "On the contrary: your mind is so narrow that you can't see more than one fragment of it at a time, which is why you are filled with hundreds of mutually exclusive beliefs." Whitman was writing in a time when his particular way of expanding into experience could bring a real enhancement of being, because we had the psychological space for it: democracy; the future; the Golden West. But now this space has shrunk. Confronted with excruciating trade-offs, struggling to find reliable criteria for decision making in a world filled with chaos, the contradictions inherent in the earlier years of American expansion are coming home to roost in our collective unconscious and tearing us apart, stunning us into paralysis and despair. Many of us have so many contradictory beliefs at war with each other in our unconscious psyches that we avoid encountering any new idea for fear that the contradictions in question will go into the internal equivalent of a feeding frenzy. This fairly common mental state is one reason for the progressive breakdown of our society into mutually exclusive cults:

we want to live our lives surrounded only by people who identify with the same ideas we do—or even better, with people who do their best to have no ideas. After all, why risk inciting violence?

In a democracy we all have a right to our opinion. But if we train ourselves never to ask whether our own or another's opinion is true or not, but instead treat opinions as if they were no more than a matter of personal taste, like a favorite food or a style of dress, then democracy dies. And this is precisely why I am willing not only to assert that my own ideas are true (while remaining willing to be prove wrong), but that some of Robert Bly's ideas are false. Only if two opposing belief systems are able to rise above the level where their main function is to provide the security of having something to believe in, and to meet on a common field, is the existence of objective truth posited, and then remembered.

Dignity

Bly writes: ". . . funny little motions of the shoulders and weird cries are waiting inside us. When we are in a boring conversation, we could, instead of saying something boring, give a cry. We can never predict what will come out, and when it is out, we leave it to others to interpret, no apologies or explanations. Little dances are helpful in the middle of an argument as are completely incomprehensible haikus spoken loudly while in church or while buying furniture. Rudeness and sarcasm may be savage, but the unexpected is not savage" (pp. 222–223). Ah, well . . . though there is something delightful about this passage, and though I could quibble about whether deliberate rudeness or inappropriate spontaneity is more likely to hurt people's feelings (as if acting out in church isn't just as rude as purposely insulting someone, and possibly just as hurtful), I would rather concentrate on Bly's apparent belief that acting out in unexpected ways, which may in fact be incomprehensible or disturbing to others, is liberating, which is a very common belief.

Now I will admit that to make funny little motions of the shoulders and weird cries may be liberating to someone who thinks he will be struck by lightning if he does so. But in the larger picture, I can't escape the feeling that this kind of wacky spontaneity is in danger of descending into simple vulgarity, though clearly this is not what Bly intends. (After all, the spontaneity of the Zen Master is the furthest thing from that of, say, a vulgar stand-up comedian, and is essentially dignified.) But American culture as a whole is now pressuring us from all sides to become as vulgar as possible, since people who have lost their self-respect can be more easily controlled than those who have retained it. What we desperately need, and what we are losing, is our dignity. Now if by dignity we mean simple fastidiousness, then let us by all means make quacking sounds while waiting in line at the bank; the elimination of fastidiousness will in most cases move us closer to true self-respect instead of further away. But speaking as someone with a definite zany and/or vulgar streak, which is to a certain degree an obsessive defense mechanism, I believe that the cultivation of a more dignified behavior is both a manly thing and a way of supporting the survival of human dignity itself, without which we ourselves will probably not survive, nor will we want to.

Some years ago, in a series of audiotapes entitled "Fairytales for Men," Bly did a wonderful presentation of various male character traits, or types, in terms of the corresponding Greek gods. I remember that he made the point that the hippies had in many ways overdeveloped their Hermes energy, their mercurial, trickster-like quality, at the expense of Zeus energy, the vigorous leadership and sexual fertility of the mature male, and Saturn energy, the power of the sage or elder to bear the burden of authority, of the administration of a complex religious or cultural system developed over centuries and millennia, of painstaking foresight and faithfulness to long-range plans. (If the Golden Age of innocent bliss ever was as it was, it was because old men filled with Saturn energy bore the burden of things, leaving the young free to grow.) In the face of repressive social mores, trickster energy (as in Bly's quote above) can serve freedom, up to a point. But I'm convinced that our society as a whole has now moved beyond this point. The future that seems to loom before us as all but inevitable will clearly require manly heroism more than zany immaturity or aesthetic grace. (Yet the clown also incarnates a particular set of survival skills; and given conditions of barbarism, aesthetic grace may be the one thing which saves us from despair. The poems of Hafez, for example, the ultimate in Persian spiritual and erotic romanticism, were composed in the horrendous, looming shadow of Timur the Lame.)

When confronting the idea of dignity, we are often totally at a loss. What could it be but a kind of vanity? How is it possible to go around trying to be dignified without becoming a pompous ass? And the truth is, we can't simply will to be dignified, because dignity is not an individual possession. The only source of individual dignity is universal human dignity; and the source of this transpersonal dignity is the spark of the Divine nature within us. When the Declaration of Independence says, "We hold these truths to be self-evident, that all men are created equal, that they are endowed by their Creator with certain inalienable rights," it is referring to the Divine center of our being, the *imago dei* we bear stamped on our essential humanity. Only in this sense are we created equal: because we are all "sons and daughters of the Most High." In terms of intelligence, of vitality, of moral capacity, we are anything but equal; but the Divine spark within us makes each of us equal to all others in terms of human dignity. Everyone, that is, has an equal right not be starved; not to be robbed; not to be brainwashed; not to be tortured, because these things, considered as human actions, desecrate the *imago dei* within both victim and tormentor.

Considered as God's actions, on the other hand, these things are the operation of Divine justice, and I know of no better solution to this apparent paradox than the words of Jesus: "There needs be evil, but woe to him through evil comes." God exalts some and humbles others, but even on the level of God's acts, our essential equality in terms of human dignity is not violated. In other words, each of us is worthy to be a locus of manifestation for this or that name of God. Some of us manifest God's mercy, some God's wrath, some God's outwardness, some God's hiddenness, but all of us, equally, are masks in the play of universal manifestation, in which the One is the only player.

But, returning to the human level, this does not mean that we can take the human dignity within us for granted; we are required to develop it, first by recognizing it as a living potential and then by refining our behavior accordingly. Those who serve their own dignity are blessed by it; those who betray it earn its curse.

One of the most powerful contemporary stories of the realization of our essential human dignity is that of Malcolm X. This great Black leader rose from the level of a zoot-suited, Lindy-hopping Harlem thief and drug dealer to become an internationally respected representative of America's Black liberation struggle to parliaments and heads of state throughout Africa and the Near East. And it was his conversion to Islam, first in the form of the Nation of Islam (the Black Muslims) and then by a second conversion to orthodox Sunni Islam, which put him in touch with a transpersonal norm by which humanity is known both as God's slave and as God's vice-regent on earth. Through his experience of radical humiliation before circumstances, progressively revealed to be a humbling in the face of God, he became empowered (in the words of a *hadith* of Muhammad) to "speak truth before tyrants," which the Prophet defined as the highest outer aspect of holy war, the corresponding inner aspect being the war against the passional soul, the soul of the pimp.

Dignity is not always heroic in this public sense, but it is always based on radical submission to the principle of Divine truth. Insofar as we say to this principle, "not my will but Thine be done," it fills us to the soles of our feet and the tips of our hair, simply because we are no longer standing in its way. In Blake's words: "Annihilate the Selfhood in me; be Thou all my life!"

This is what it means to live faithful to the privilege of human birth, which Buddhists say is so rare that the chances of attaining it are like those that a great sea turtle will rise from the depths and put his head through a yoke floating aimlessly on the surface of all the oceans of the world. Self-respect is respect for the Self within us; human dignity is faithfulness to the "Human Form Divine," the only mirror in the created universe which reflects not only the totality of the archetypes within the nature of God, but the unknowable essence of God as well. (Note that the Human Form Divine—a term of Blake's—need not be restricted to earth-based humanity alone. Any form of incarnate consciousness which is potentially aware of both the material and the higher spiritual worlds, and which is capable both of reflection on its own nature and willing subordination to the Divine Source of all life, is "Human" in this sense.)

When Bly says "rudeness and sarcasm may be savage, but the unexpected is not savage," he is expressing one of the essential dogmas of nature worship: that, since humanity is basically good by virtue of our simple biological identity (there being no such thing as original sin), spontaneity is therefore the essence of human morality. But if we rephrase this dogma and assert that "unconsidered action is never destructive," we will immediately see that it's simply not true.

(If there is anyone on this planet who has never had the experience of creating a problem by acting out an unexpected impulse, I would like to meet him or her.) In the Preface to *Iron John*, Bly makes a distinction between the "Wild Man" and the "Savage Man" (p. x), the two polarized aspects of the archetype of chthonic masculinity, which are represented in the Christian universe by Adam and Satan. Bly has repeatedly tried to make it clear that bloody violence and healthy wildness are not the same thing. But when the archetype of the underworld male comes up, it doesn't arrive neatly divided into positive qualities to be adopted and negative ones to be avoided. The things we need to integrate and those we had better get rid of dawn upon us as a single complex; and only through a long course of shadow integration can they be clearly separated. Thus when Bly calls us to worship the spontaneous, the unexpected, he is invoking appropriate wildness and destructive savagery at the same time.

Marie-Louise von Franz, in her *Interpretation of Fairy Tales*, makes it clear that not everything that arises unexpectedly from the unconscious is necessarily good:

> One alchemist observed that in the *prima materia* there is a certain intractable amount of *terra damnata* (accursed earth) that defies all efforts at transformation and must be rejected. Not all dark impulses lend themselves to redemption; certain ones, soaked in evil, must not be allowed to break loose and must be severely repressed. What is against nature, against the instincts, has to be stopped by main force and eradicated. The expression "assimilation of the shadow" is meant to apply to childish, primitive, undeveloped sides of one's nature, depicted in the image of the child or the dog or the stranger. But there are deadly germs that can destroy the human being and must be resisted, and their presence means that one must be hard from time to time and not accept everything that comes up from the unconscious.[65]

(Here von Franz uses the words *nature* and *instinct* to mean that which is natural in the sense of healthy, which ultimately means "in line with the Primordial or Adamic Human Nature"—the part of us which remains complete in the eternity of Eden, which never fell into time: our *fravashi*. On the other hand, I am using the word

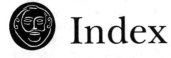# Index

'*abd*, 184. *See also* slave of God
abolitionism, 194
Abraham, 83–84. *See also* religion,
  Abrahamic
Absolute, the, 4, 38, 60, 72, 77, 205,
  209
abstraction, x, 28, 65, 78
Abu Bakr, 64
Abu'l Barakat, 173
abusive relationships, 20, 27, 147
acedia, 168–169
Active Imagination, ix, xi
Active Intelligence, 173
Adam, 37, 39, 116–123, 129, 158,
  202; Kadmon, 104; "nothing"
  (Arabic), 135; Old, 36; pre-
  incarnate, 143; Primordial, 104;
  as prophet, 6
Adonis, 20, 36, 157, 177, 181
African Genesis, 134
ahadith, 161, 176, 201
aikido, 123, 204
alam al-mithal, ix, xi, 75, 171, 173
alchemy, 69, 88, 95, 104–106,
  110, 151–154, 190; psychic art,
  173; Shakespeare, 152–153;
  sublimation, 41; von Franz,
  202. *See also* alchemical vessels;
  athenor; copper; gold; lead;

prima materia; quicksilver; salt;
  silver; sulfur
Alchemical Sequence, 151–152
alchemical vessel, 88
al-Ghazzali, 206–207
amanita muncaria, 25, 178
America, 165
Amfortas wound, 155
ancestors: path of, 123–124
androgyny, 148
anima, 19, 53, 74; projection of,
  88, 89; negative, 93, 114; man's
  soul-figure, 50, 86, 110
animals, 129, 132–137, 140; helpful,
  132–133. *See also* specific animals
animus, 89, 149
Ant King, 33, 36
Aphrodite, 77, 107
Apollo, 40, 177, 178, 183, 217
Apollonius of Tyana, 216–217
Apuleius, Lucius, 64
archetypes, 28, 74, 78, 89, 181,
  190, 196; animals as symbols
  of, 140; as material, 76; as
  spiritual, 34; human form
  mirroring, 201. *See also* anima;
  animus; persona; *puella aeterna*;
  puer aeternus; puer/senex; Self;
  shadow; syzygy

QUEST BOOKS
are published by
The Theosophical Society in America,
Wheaton, Illinois 60189-0270,
a branch of a world organization
dedicated to the promotion of the unity of
humanity and the encouragement of the study of
religion, philosophy, and science, to the end that
we may better understand ourselves and our place in
the universe. The Society stands for complete
freedom of individual search and belief.
In the Classics Series well-known
theosophical works are made
available in popular editions.